THE CONGREGATION OF SACRED RITES

The Catholic University of America
Canon Law Studies
No. 352

The Congregation of Sacred Rites

A DISSERTATION

Submitted to the Faculty of the School of Canon Law
of the Catholic University of America in Partial
Fulfillment of the Requirements for the
Degree of Doctor of Canon Law

BY

Frederick Richard McManus, A.B., J.C.L.
Priest of the Archdiocese of Boston

THE CATHOLIC UNIVERSITY OF AMERICA PRESS
WASHINGTON, D. C.
1954

Nihil Obstat

Eduardus G. Roelker, S.T.D., J.C.D.

Censor Deputatus

Imprimatur

✠ Ricardus J. Cushing, D.D.

Archiepiscopus Bostoniensis

Copyright 1954

The Catholic University of America Press, Inc.

FOREWORD

The first of the duties of religion is the worship of Almighty God. This worship must be public as well as private, and social as well as individual; thus it becomes the object of ecclesiastical law. The celebration of the sacred mysteries and of the public offices of the Church is the principal source of the Christian spirit, and the regulation of Catholic worship holds a place of corresponding importance in the Church's law.

In the government of the universal Church the Roman Pontiffs make regular use of the several Congregations of Cardinals. These serve as the advisers and consultants of the Pontiffs and, in ordinary matters, they act in the name and by the authority of the Pontiffs. Among their number the Congregation of Sacred Rites is charged with matters affecting the worship of the Latin Church, and for nearly four centuries it has regulated and watched over the liturgical services and rites.

The purpose of the present study is to examine in particular the nature of the authority possessed by the Congregation of Sacred Rites and the limits of the competence attributed to it by the Popes, together with the legal force of its decrees and declarations. In addition, a description of the Congregation's history, constitution, and procedure is offered.

An important phase of the competence and activity of the Congregation of Sacred Rites is its power over the causes of beatification and canonization of the Servants of God, whose veneration is clearly a part of the Church's public worship. Questions concerning these causes are primarily theological and, so far as the law is involved, procedural. This study purposely omits, as beyond its immediate scope, the norms of procedure followed in the processes of the Servants of God. These processes have therefore been considered here only in summary fashion.

The first half of the present century has been a period of liturgical revival, initiated by Pope Pius X and extended even more widely by the present Holy Father. In this a principal part belongs to the Congregation of Sacred Rites, and it may be expected that the Congregation, largely because of its control of the emendation of the liturgical books, will have an increasing importance in the future. This treatment of the Congregation may serve to indicate its nature and workings and the significance of the matters which, as an organ of the Apostolic See, it regulates.

It is a pleasure to express my sincere gratitude to His Excellency, the Most Reverend Richard J. Cushing, Archbishop of Boston, for the opportunity of graduate studies and for his constant kindness; and to offer my thanks to the Faculty of the School of Canon Law, the Catholic University of America, for their generous and valuable assistance.

TABLE OF CONTENTS

CHAPTER I. LITURGICAL LAW 1

A. Introduction 1

B. Power of the Church over Sacred Worship 5

C. Power of the Holy See over Sacred Worship 9

D. Practice of the Holy See 14

CHAPTER II. HISTORY OF THE CONGREGATION
OF SACRED RITES 23

A. Background 23

B. Establishment of the Congregation 24

C. Subsequent Development of the Congregation 28

D. Allied Congregations and Commissions 32

    1. *Ceremonial Congregation* 32

    2. *Congregation of Indulgences and Relics* 35

    3. *Commissions of the Congregation of Rites* 36

E. Apostolic Constitution 'Sapienti Consilio' 39

F. Changes in the Congregation after 1908 42

CHAPTER III. AUTHORITY OF THE CONGREGATION 45

A. Nature of the Power 45

B. Legislative Power 49

C. Judicial Power 58

D. Executive Power 61

E. Sede Vacante 62

CHAPTER IV. COMPETENCE OF THE
CONGREGATION 67

A. Competence before the Code of Canon Law 67

B. Present Competence of the Congregation 71

    Canon 253 § 1 72

    Canon 253 § 2 85

    Canon 253 § 3 87

C. Relation to the Other Congregations — 91
   1. *Congregation of the Holy Office* — 91
   2. *Congregation for the Oriental Church* — 92
   3. *Congregation for the Discipline of the Sacraments* 95
   4. *Congregation of the Council* — 98
   5. *Congregation for Religious* — 99
   6. *Congregation for the Propagation of the Faith* — 100
   7. *Ceremonial Congregation* — 101
D. Faculties of the Congregation — 102
   1. *Extraordinary Faculties — Cases of the Servants of God* — 103
   2. *Other Extraordinary Faculties* — 105
   3. *Ordinary Faculties* — 109

CHAPTER V. CONSTITUTION AND PROCEDURE OF THE CONGREGATION — 117
A. Personnel of the Congregation — 117
B. Procedure of the Congregation — 122
C. Processes of the Servants of God — 125

CHAPTER VI. DECREES OF THE CONGREGATION — 131
A. Kinds of Decrees — 131
B. Obligation of the Decrees — 134
C. Customs Contrary to the Decrees — 141
D. Collections of Decrees — 145
E. Forms of the Responses — 149
F. Archives of the Congregation — 152

CONCLUSIONS — 155
APPENDIX — 156
BIBLIOGRAPHY — 160
ABBREVIATIONS — 171
INDEX — 172
BIOGRAPHICAL NOTE — 180

CHAPTER I

LITURGICAL LAW

A. Introduction

The Sacred Liturgy is the worship of God by His Church. Fundamentally, it is the Catholic "public service" offered to Almighty God by the Christian people, the common practice of the virtue of religion.

The Liturgy has been variously defined, sometimes with deep realization and appreciation, at other times from a limited viewpoint. For example, it has been called "the ecclesiastical ordering of the exercise of public worship,"[1] or "the manner of worshipping God by external rites, publicly exercised by ministers and lawfully instituted by Christ and the Church."[2]
Defined in greater detail,

> Liturgy is the exterior and collective exercise of the virtue of religion, practiced by the members of the ecclesiastical society, with a representative of the Church presiding, who acts in virtue of a priestly mission, according to the norms established by the Church.[3]

On the other hand, a narrower expression of the meaning of Catholic worship is often found, of which the following is an instance: "Liturgy is the system of things, words, and actions through which worship is offered to God by the ministers of the Church."[4]
Such a description fails to take fully into account the essentially

---

[1] Callewaert, *Liturgicae Institutiones* (2. ed., Vols. I-II, Brugis: Beyaert, 1925-1939), I, 5.

[2] Pastè, "Quid liturgia?" *Ephemerides Liturgicae* (Romae, 1887-   ), XLI (1927), 412.

[3] Coelho, *Corso di Liturgia Romana* (5 vols., Torino, Roma: Marietti, 1935-1940), I, 9.

[4] Dal Sasso, *Liturgiae Sacerdotalis Compendariae Institutiones* (2. ed., Patavii: Domus Libraria Gregoriana, 1939), p. 7.

sacramental character of rites and ceremonies—as external signs indicative of internal worship, the latter being the principal element of the Liturgy.[5] Nor does it embrace a proper understanding of the Church—the whole Church, Christ and His members—as the offerer of divine cult.[6] A similar identification of the offerer exclusively with the deputed ministers is common but imperfect: "Liturgy is the form of divine worship, exercised in the name of the Church, by lawful ministers, under the guardianship of legitimate authority."[7] Here the phrase, "form of divine worship," is well chosen to express not the superficial aspects of ceremonial but the *essence* of sacred rites—the words, things, actions, joined to the inward movement of the mind and will, and directed to God.[8]

A very profound and satisfactory definition of the Catholic Liturgy, given recently, is that of Pope Pius XII:

> The Sacred Liturgy is the public worship which our Redeemer, the Head of the Church, offers to the heavenly Father and which the community of Christ's faithful pays to its Founder, and through Him to the eternal Father; briefly, it is the whole public worship of the Mystical Body of Christ, Head and members.[9]

These words indicate clearly that Christ is the principal offerer of Catholic worship and that the entire Christian people are associated with Him in that offering. The definition also suggests the importance of that liturgy which is the sacred action of public worship.

The essential elements of Catholic liturgy, those of divine origin, are unchangeable. For example, the matter and form of the sacraments were, at the very least, generically determined by their

[5] Pius XII, ep. encycl. *Mediator Dei et hominum*, 30 nov. 1947 (hereafter cited as *Mediator Dei*)—*Acta Apostolicae Sedis, Commentarium Officiale* (Romae, 1909-1929; Civitate Vaticana, 1929-   ), XXXIX (1947), 531 (hereafter cited as *AAS*).

[6] Pius XII, ep. encycl. *Mystici Corporis Christi*, 29 iun. 1943—*AAS*, XXXV (1943), 202-203, 232-233; *Mediator Dei*—*AAS*, XXXIX (1947), 554-555.

[7] Menghini, *Elementa Iuris Liturgici* (2. ed., Romae, 1906), p. 11.

[8] *Loc. cit.*

[9] *Mediator Dei*—*AAS*, XXXIX, (1947), 528-529.

Founder.[10] Yet the liturgy is by no means static. The rites and ceremonies, words and actions, are subject to change and to development, so long as the substance of the Sacrifice and the sacraments is preserved. Additions and subtractions are quite possible. They result from varying human needs and desires; they have as their object the greater honor of God, together with the devotion and instruction of the faithful.[11] And it is in the striving for perfection in the worship of God that the holy liturgy becomes the object of canonical legislation[12] and, in particular, falls within the scope of the Congregation of Sacred Rites.[13]

Since the sixteenth century, the possibility of change and development in liturgical worship has not been so apparent in the Western Church. At that time a unique reform of the Roman Rite was effected—as an aftermath of the Council of Trent,[14] and principally on account of the new Breviary and Missal of Pope St. Pius V.[15] The unification thus achieved brought to an end the centuries of ritual formation; it seemed to forestall further development. For the most part this has been the result and subsequent development in the forms of public worship has been in fact comparatively slight.

Even in our own century, however, great changes in the Roman liturgy have occurred. A complete redistribution of the Psalter of the Divine Office was made in 1911;[16] in 1945 a new version of the Psalter itself was introduced into liturgical use, in place of a text

[10] Piolanti, *De Sacramentis,* Collectio Theologica Romana, VI (2 vols., Romae, Taurini: Marietti, 1944-1945), I, 128-132; cf. Pius XII, const. *Sacramentum Ordinis,* 30 nov. 1947—*AAS,* XL (1948), 5-6.

[11] *Mediator Dei—AAS,* XXXIX (1947), 554; Pius XII, const. *Sacramentum Ordinis,* 30 nov. 1947—*AAS,* XL (1948), 5.

[12] Pius XI, const. *Divini cultus,* 20 dec. 1928—*AAS,* XXI (1929), 33.

[13] Can. 253; *Mediator Dei—AAS,* XXXIX (1947), 543.

[14] Sess. XXV, Continuatio Sessionis, decr. *De indice Librorum et Catechismo, Breviario et Missali*—Schroeder, *Canons and Decrees of the Council of Trent* (St. Louis: Herder, 1941), pp. 519-520.

[15] Pius V, litt. ap. *Quo primum tempore,* 14 iul. 1570—*Bullarum Diplomatum et Privilegiorum Romanorum Pontificum Taurinensis Editio* (24 vols. and Appendix, Augustae Taurinorum, 1857-1872), VII, 839 841 (hereafter cited as *BRT*); Pius V, litt. ap. *Quod a nobis,* 9 iul. 1568—*BRT,* VII, 685-688.

[16] Pius X, const. *Divino afflatu,* 1 nov. 1911—*AAS,* III (1911), 633-638.

that had been recited for fifteen hundred years.[17] Sometimes these
changes affect matters of lesser import, such as ecclesiastical
vesture[18] or the omission of the saliva in the administration of Baptism.[19] At other times rites of the most venerable and sacred character may be changed, as in the case of the experimental restoration, in 1951, of the Paschal Vigil.[20] The very fact of such changes,
taking place during a period of ritual uniformity, shows both the
need and the purpose of law governing the liturgy.

The formation and regulation of Catholic worship belongs properly to *liturgical law,* namely, "the system of divine and ecclesiastical laws by which the liturgy of the Church, in the broad sense,
is ordered."[21] This system includes not only positive written law
but also legitimate custom; the history of Catholic liturgy demonstrates the large part played by the latter, especially during the
first centuries of the Christian era when the sacred rites were in
the process of formation.

Without any anticipation of the discussion concerning the identity of the legislator from whom such law issues, it may be indicated that liturgical law is found, in general, in the directions or
rubrics of the ritual books and in the laws and decrees published
by ecclesiastical authority. Unlike the non-liturgical private law
of the Church, the laws of liturgy have never been analytically
codified in any form other than that of the liturgical books. When
the Code of Canon Law excludes from its legislation the mass of

[17] Pius XII, motu propr. *In cotidianis precibus,* 24 mart. 1945—*AAS,* XXXVII
(1945), 65-67.

[18] Pius XII, motu propr. *Valde solliciti,* 30 nov. 1952—*AAS,* XLIV (1952), 849-
850; S.R.C., *Dubia,* 4 dec. 1952—*AAS,* XLIV (1952), 888; decr. *Iuxta Caeremoniale Episcoporum,* 4 dec. 1952—*AAS,* XLIV (1952), 887.

[19] S.R.C., decr. *Quanta cura ac vigilantia,* 14 ian. 1944—*AAS,* XXXVI
(1944), 28.

[20] S.R.C., decr. *Dominicae Resurrectionis vigiliam,* 9 febr. 1951—*AAS,* XLIII
(1951), 128-140; decr. *Instaurata vigilia paschalis,* 11 ian. 1952—*AAS,* XLIV
(1952), 48-63.

[21] Wernz-Vidal, *Ius Canonicum ad Codicis Normam Exactum* (7 vols. in 8,
Romae: Apud Aedes Universitatis Gregorianae, 1923-1938; Vol. II, 3. ed., 1943),
IV, n. 318.

liturgical law, there is perhaps a suggestion that such a codification of the law of worship is not necessary or feasible.[22]

Again, before any consideration of the position of the Congregation of Sacred Rites, it may be well to mention the meaning of the terms, "sacred rites and ceremonies." Some make a sharp division between the two, describing the texts or words of the liturgy as rites, and the various gestures, actions, and attitudes as ceremonies.[23] It is more satisfactory, however, to admit the common meaning of ceremonies as outward acts and to consider sacred rites as embracing both words and actions. Then a sacred rite is the complexus and order of ceremonies, an entire function of worship.[24] This agrees with the usage of ecclesiastical law, in which the phrase "sacred rites and ceremonies" is taken in a broad sense and made equivalent, in general, to the liturgy itself. Thus sacred rites and ceremonies embrace the interior and exterior acts of worship offered to God by the Church, through designated ministers with the participation of the faithful.[25] It is in this sense that Pius XII speaks of the "lawful rites of the Church" and the sacred liturgy itself.[26]

B. Power of the Church over Sacred Worship

The ordering and regulation of the sacred liturgy make up liturgical law. The making of such law would seem to be the clear and exclusive right of the Church, since the worship of God is necessarily and intimately bound up with the Church's unique end. For this reason writers on the public law of the Church often dismiss the matter briefly: The Church's right to legislate for divine worship is so evident that it need not be proved.[27] That its power in

[22] Can. 2; Menghini, "De legibus liturgicis in peculiarem codicem redigendis," *Ephemerides Liturgicae*, XXXV (1921), 217-222.

[23] Monin, *De Curia Romana* (Lovanii, 1912), p. 300.

[24] Menghini, *Elementa Iuris Liturgici*, p. 27.

[25] Oppenheim, *Institutiones Systematico-Historicae in Sacram Liturgiam*, Series I (6 vols., Taurini, Romae: Marietti, 1938-1941; Vol. I, 2. ed., 1945), VI, 40.

[26] *Mediator Dei—AAS*, XXXIX (1947), 543.

[27] Sotillo, *Compendium Iuris Publici Ecclesiastici* (Santander: Sal Terrae, 1947), p. 112.

this connection is of the widest scope is in fact apparent from the very mission of the Church.[28]

However obvious this power may be, there have been many instances in which civil powers have usurped the regulation of Catholic worship, as they have usurped other ecclesiastical functions. One example is to be found in the liturgical reforms of Charlemagne, where happily reform meant the extended influence of the Roman usage.[29] In this case at least, the purposes of ecclesiastical authority were served and the liturgy strengthened. The same cannot be said of the less friendly attempt in modern times of the Emperor Joseph II, who intervened directly in matters of liturgical law "for the public safety and the purity of religion."[30] This was a bold and autocratic assertion of civil authority over the least details of ritual, the celebration of processions, the observance of feast days.[31]

Liturgical law of divine origin is small in content under the New Dispensation. There is little beyond the "Do this in commemoration of me" of the Last Supper,[32] or the substantial requirements for the sacrament of Baptism.[33] Over and above this, outside of the substance of the Mass and the sacraments, the ordering of divine worship belongs to the Church alone. Such law comes within the scope of the Church's power to rule, a power which includes the legislative, judicial, and executive functions of the ecclesiastical society. It is based on these and other words of Christ:

> All authority in heaven and on earth, he said, has been
> given to me; you, therefore, must go out, making
> disciples of all nations, and baptizing them in the name

[28] Cappello, *Summa Iuris Publici Ecclesiastici* (2. ed., Romae, 1928), p. 531.

[29] Capitulare Aquisgranense, LXXX—Hardouin, *Acta Conciliorum et Epistolae Decretales ac Constitutiones Summorum Pontificum* (12 vols., Parisiis, 1714-1715), IV, 843; *Monumenta Germaniae Historica, Legum* Tomus I (ed. Georgius Pertz, Hanoverae, 1835), 66 (hereafter cited as *MGH*).

[30] Ottaviani, *Institutiones Iuris Publici Ecclesiastici* (3. ed., 2 vols., Romae: Typis Polyglottis Vaticanis, 1947-1948), I, 228.

[31] Geier, *Die Durchführung der kirchlichen Reformen Josephs II* (Stuttgart, 1905), pp. 188-189.

[32] Luke 22, 19; I Cor. 11, 23.

[33] Matthew 28, 19; John 3, 5.

of the Father, and of the Son, and of the Holy Ghost,
teaching them to observe all the commandments which
I have given to you.[34]

The power of the Church over the Mass, the sacraments, other
sacred functions, and divine cult in general, is the *potestas ministerii*.[35] From the aspect of performance of the liturgy, the
Church's power is part of the *potestas ordinis;* from the aspect of
governing the liturgy, the power is part of the *potestas iurisdictionis*. It is the latter in which a share has been claimed for civil
authority. The problem is, of course, only one side of the larger
question of the relation of the two societies, religious and civil.[36]

The first reason for excluding secular interference in the regulation of the liturgy is the intimate connection between sacred worship and the doctrines of faith. To subject the expressions of
Christian doctrine found as an essential part of the liturgy to the
legislation of the state would be to expose such truths to error and
would give the state the right to impose its own religion upon the
faithful.[37] This is to deny the truth of the one religion founded by
Christ. The Church must rather remain free to profess the faith
in the liturgical forms, according to the maxim, *Lex supplicandi
statuat legem credendi*.

With reference to the rights alleged for the lay power, namely,
to intervene in liturgical matters in order to prevent abuses and to
defend the ecclesiastical law, both are based on misconceptions.
So far as the doctrines of the liturgy are concerned, it is heretical
to suggest that abuses can arise by authority of the Church; so
far as liturgical discipline is concerned, it is a denial of the Church's
infallibility to suggest that there is evil in the common and universal law imposed for the glorification of God and the sanctifica-
tion of men.[38] Moreover, the position of the civil power as de-

---

[34] Matthew 28, 18-20; Parente, *Theologia Fundamentalis*, Collectio Theologica
Romana, I (Romae, Taurini: Marietti, 1946), pp. 155-157; Ottaviani, *Institutiones Iuris Publici Ecclesiastici*, I, 201; 224-225.

[35] Cappello, *Summa Iuris Publici Ecclesiastici*, p. 188.

[36] Bouix, *Tractatus de Jure Liturgico* (Parisiis, 1853), p. 80.

[37] Menghini, *Elementa Iuris Liturgici*, p. 49; Oppenheim, *Institutiones in Sacram
Liturgiam*, II, 49-50.

[38] Oppenheim, *op. cit.*, II, 52.

fender of the Church requires not opposition to ecclesiastical law but co-operation and protection for it.[39]

Finally, any insistence on civil authority's rights over the liturgy ignores the true relation of the two societies, according to which each is supreme in its own order. The worship of God falls within the province of the Church's end and mission; its regulation belongs exclusively to the Church. Where things touching the liturgy are in fact mixed matters, the law of the Church must prevail from the principle of indirect subordination of the society which has the less excellent end—all the while preserving the independence and the rights of the state.[40] Moreover, in the profession and practice of religion, the latter being sacred worship, the rulers of the state are themselves obliged to observe the ecclesiastical laws. This was firmly expressed by Innocent X in 1653 when the senate and governor of Milan attempted to legislate concerning feast days: "In the things of the Church lay princes have the need to obey rather than the authority to command."[41]

All of this has been repeatedly declared in the positive law of the Church, as well as in the practice of liturgical legislation. The Council of Trent, for example, insisted that the Church as steward of the mysteries of God[42] may change and determine whatever she wishes in the dispensation of the sacraments, *salva illorum substantia.*[43]

In the nineteenth century Leo XIII, in defining the limits of ecclesiastical and civil power, taught clearly concerning the holy liturgy:

> Whatever in human affairs is in any way sacred, whatever pertains to the salvation of souls or *the worship of God,* whether it be such by its nature or so considered on account of the cause to which it is referred, all this is in the power and judgment of the Church; but it is

[39] Menghini, *op cit.,* p. 51-52.
[40] Ottaviani, *Institutiones Iuris Publici Ecclesiastici,* II, 140-141, 144-146.
[41] Const. *Cum nuper,* 6 oct. 1653—*BRT,* XV, 739.
[42] I Cor. 4, 1.
[43] Sess. XXI, *de communione,* c. 2—Schroeder, *Canons and Decrees of the Council of Trent,* pp. 133-134; 407-408.

proper that other matters which are civil and political
in nature should be subject to the civil authority . . . . ."[44]
More recently the same point was made by Pius XI, although
his teaching was not directly concerned with the intervention of
the state or of any other body external to the Church in the government of the liturgy. The Church's authority in this matter, he
explained, comes from Christ; it is a right to prescribe ceremonies,
rites, formulas, prayers, chant, which make up the public service
of God.[45]

C. Power of the Holy See over Sacred Worship

The ordering of the sacred liturgy belongs exclusively to the
Church. Next there must be discussed: Where in the Church does
the authority over the liturgy repose? Again, the question of this
jurisdiction is part of the larger matter of the Church's constitution. To give a brief answer, the Roman Pontiff possesses a power
over the liturgy that is supreme and, in modern times, exclusive.[46]
To phrase it differently, the jurisdiction of the Pontiff is complete
and absolute, but the exercise of that power may or may not be
exclusive; since the sixteenth century it has been exclusive in all
liturgical matters of importance.

This doctrine has been challenged, and that even in the modern
period. Among the errors of the Synod of Pistoia, for example,
there were ritual aberrations that had to be condemned by Pius
VI.[47] And in the nineteenth century, nearly three hundred years
after the unification of the Roman liturgy, a group of confusing
neo-Gallican rites existed in France. These, initiated under the
authority of local Ordinaries, formed a theoretical and a practical
opposition to papal rights over sacred worship.[48]

[44] Ep. encycl. *Immortale Dei*, 1 nov. 1885—*Acta Sanctae Sedis* (41 vols., Romae,
1865-1908), XVIII (1885), 166-167 (hereafter cited as *ASS*).

[45] Const. *Divini cultus*, 20 dec. 1928—*AAS*, XXI (1929), 33.

[46] Callewaert, *Liturgicae Institutiones*, I, 101-102.

[47] Const. *Auctorem fidei*, 28 aug. 1794—Mansi, *Sacrorum Conciliorum Nova et
Amplissima Collectio* (53 vols. in 60, Parisiis, 1901-1927), XXXVIII, 1269.

[48] Rousseau, *The Progress of the Liturgy* (Westminster, Maryland: Newman,
1951), pp. 23-24; Guéranger, *Institutions Liturgiques* (2. ed., 4 vols., Paris, Brussels, 1878-1885), II, 605-606.

The matter of liturgical law based on custom may be put aside in discussing the identity of the ecclesiastical legislator. In the Church custom derives its force as law from the consent of the competent superior, whoever that may be.[49] Theoretically, then, the liturgical law might come from the Roman Pontiff (or from an Ecumenical Council approved by him), from the Bishop ruling his diocese, or from the other members of the Church, clerical or lay.

The last alternative has barely to be mentioned. It is a Protestant theory of ritual law, contrary to the hierarchical constitution of the Church. The words of Christ are clear enough: "All that you bind on earth shall be bound in heaven, and all that you loose on earth shall be loosed in heaven."[50] In the case of the liturgy as with other ecclesiastical law the Church is a sheepfold ruled by shepherds whose authority is from God.[51]

Again, the Bishop in his diocese or any body of bishops acting independently of the Roman Pontiff have no power over the law of liturgy. In other words, their jurisdiction is exercised subject to the successor of Peter. To suggest that the local Bishop has power limited only by the territory of his diocese is, in fact, to limit the supreme power of the Sovereign Pontiff.[52] Moreover, because of the necessary connection between doctrine and worship, the independent exercise of liturgical authority by inferior prelates infringes upon the teaching office of the chief pastor.[53]

The supreme authority of the Roman Pontiffs in matters liturgical is included in their power to rule the Church, defined by the Council of Florence as a "full power of feeding, ruling, and governing the Church universal."[54] The doctrine is amplified in the teaching of the Vatican Council:

[49] Can. 25.

[50] Matthew 18, 18; Ottaviani, *Institutiones Iuris Publici Ecclesiastici*, I, 392-395.

[51] John 21, 15-17; I Peter 5, 1-4; Menghini, *Elementa Iuris Liturgici*, p. 52.

[52] Menghini, *op. cit.*, p. 52.

[53] Bouix, *Tractatus de Jure Liturgico*, p. 149; Oppenheim, *Institutiones in Sacram Liturgiam*, II, 57.

[54] Eugene IV, const. *Laetentur caeli*, 6 iul. 1439, n. 8—*Codicis Iuris Canonici Fontes, cura* E.mi Petri Card. Gasparri ed. (9 vols., Romae: Typis Polyglottis Vaticanis, 1923-1939; Vols. VII-IX, ed. cura E.mi Iustiniani Card. Serédi), n. 51 (hereafter cited as *Fontes*).

. . . . This power of jurisdiction of the Roman Pontiff, which is truly episcopal, is immediate: pastors and faithful of whatever rite and dignity, taken individually and all together, are bound by the duty of hierarchical subordination and true obedience to it, not only in matters of faith and morals, but also in what pertains to the discipline and rule of the Church spread through the whole world.[55]

This general authority of the Apostolic See has been repeatedly referred to the regulation of the sacred liturgy. So Clement VI asserted the fullest power of jurisdiction in this matter,[56] and Benedict XIV explained that changes of ritual belong not to private, but to public authority, namely, to the head of the Church universal.[57] Similarly, Pius VII required of Ordinaries that they should enforce liturgical law rather than make it.[58] And Pius IX declared that it is insufficient to be united to the Holy See in faith and dogma, but that Catholics must be subject to the Roman Pontiff with regard to "rites and discipline."[59]

In 1947 Pope Pius XII insisted upon papal authority over liturgical worship in his encyclical letter on the Catholic liturgy. He argued especially that the *potestas ordinis* requires the hierarchical government of the worship of God by His Church, to the exclusion of private authority, clerical or lay.[60] And his teaching agreed exactly with the fundamental norm of present law: "To the Apostolic See alone belongs the right to order the sacred liturgy and to approve the liturgical books."[61]

[55] Sess. IV, const. *de Ecclesia Christi*, cap. 3—*Acta et Decreta Sacrorum Conciliorum Recentiorum, Collectio Lacensis* (7 vols., Friburgi Brisgoviae, 1870-1892), VII, 484; cf. can. 218.

[56] Ep. *Super quibusdam*, 29 sept. 1351—*Fontes*, n. 42.

[57] Ep. encycl. *Allatae sunt*, 26 iul. 1755, § 27—*Fontes*, n. 434; ep. encycl. *Inter omnigenas*, 2 febr. 1744, § 18—*Fontes*, n. 339.

[58] S.R.C., *Dubiorum*, 17 sept. 1822—*Decreta Authentica Congregationis Sacrorum Rituum* (5 vols., Romae, 1898-1901; Vol. VI, 1912; Vol. VII, 1927), n. 2621, ad 1 (hereafter cited as D).

[59] Ep. *Non sine gravissimo*, 24 febr. 1870—*Fontes*, n. 555.

[60] *Mediator Dei*—*AAS*, XXXIX (1947), 538-541; 544.

[61] Can. 1257.

Yet it must not be supposed that the authority of the Roman Pontiff over the liturgy need exclude absolutely any authority of the subordinate hierarchy. To a greater or less extent, depending upon the will of the supreme legislator, the bishops may exercise power of jurisdiction in sacred rites. Their right to regulate divine worship requires the express or tacit consent of the Holy See, and from time to time the reservation of liturgical authority to that See may vary.[62]

As has already been suggested, in modern times and according to the present dispositions of law, the exercise of supreme authority over the liturgy by the Roman Pontiff is exclusive in things of importance.[63] There are exceptions to this in favor of the Bishop's authority, but these are of a limited character. The local Ordinary may command the celebration of extraordinary processions,[64] and he may require the recitation of one or two Collects at Mass, in addition to those prescribed by the rubrics.[65] He may also require, under certain conditions, the celebration of votive Masses at the time of a papal election[66] and upon his own anniversaries.[67] And he may determine a day for the celebration of the anniversary of the consecration of the churches of the diocese, other than the Cathedral.[68]

Moreover, the law leaves to the Bishop the granting of many permissions in connection with the liturgy, as well as the right to delegate certain blessings.[69] For example, he may permit a solemn votive Mass for a grave and public cause,[70] and allow the nuptial blessing within the *tempus clausum* for a just cause.[71] He has cer-

---

[62] Bouix, *Tractatus de Jure Liturgico*, pp. 149-150.

[63] Callewaert, *Liturgicae Institutiones*, I, 101-102; Oppenheim, *Institutiones in Sacram Liturgiam*, II, 58.

[64] For this he must hear the chapter or the board of consultors, according to Canon 1292. Cf. S.R.C., *Elboren.*, 14 ian. 1617—D. 346, ad 1.

[65] *Missale Romanum*, Additiones et Variationes in Rubricis Missalis, VI, 4.

[66] S.R.C., *Bergomen.*, 8 mart. 1879—D. 3487, ad 2.

[67] *Missale Romanum*, Additiones et Variationes in Rubricis Missalis, II, 5.

[68] S.R.C., decr. gen. 28 oct. 1913—D. 4308, I, 1, f.

[69] Can. 1156; 1304, 4°.

[70] *Missale Romanum*, Additiones et Variationes in Rubricis Missalis, II, 3.

[71] *Ibid.*, II, 2.

tain powers in connection with the rites of Baptism,[72] the veneration of sacred relics,[73] and the exposition of the Blessed Sacrament, both for Benediction and for the regulation of the Forty Hours' Devotion.[74] In a more general way, the local Ordinary has authority over prayers and exercises of piety in churches and oratories. These he has power to approve, except for more difficult cases and for new litanies intended for public recitation. This right to approve prayers that are not contained in the liturgical books is an instance where the Bishop acts with the consent of the Holy See in a matter not reserved by the Holy See.[75]

Over and above these examples of the exercise of subordinate jurisdiction in sacred worship, the Bishop's right and duty is limited to the correction of abuses and the vigilant enforcement of the common liturgical law of the Church. His negative right to legislate against the introduction of superstitious practices into divine cult, as well as anything foreign to the faith, tradition or the purity of worship, is extensive; even exempt religious are bound to obey.[76] The conduct of processions and the cult of relics are especially mentioned as falling within the province of the Ordinary's concern.[77]

The right to enforce the existing liturgical law is the first of the Bishop's powers over sacred worship. There are repeated instances which uphold the Bishop's right to compel the observance of the rubrics and of decrees issued by the Holy See.[78] Pius XII, paraphrasing the two principal canons determining this matter,[79] sums up the doctrine on the relation of the bishops to the Roman Pontiff in the regulation of the holy liturgy:

[72] Can. 755, § 2; 759, § 2.

[73] Can. 1282-1286.

[74] Can. 1274, § 1; 1275.

[75] Bouix, *Tractatus de Jure Liturgico*, p. 150; Wernz, *Ius Decretalium* (6 vols., Romae, 1898-1914), III, 349.

[76] Can. 1261.

[77] Can. 1284; 1295.

[78] S.R.C. *Oscen.*, 16 mart. 1591—D. 9, ad 19; *Egitanien.*, 4 apr. 1626— D. 399, ad 2; *Dubiorum*, 17 sept. 1822—D. 2621, ad 1.

[79] Can. 1257; 1261.

It follows that the Sovereign Pontiff alone has the right to permit or establish any liturgical practice, to introduce or approve new rites, or to make any changes in them he considers necessary. It is the right and duty of bishops, in their turn, to enforce vigilantly the observance of the canonical rules on divine worship.[80]

D.   Practice of the Holy See

The practice of the Holy See during the past four hundred years, together with current liturgical law, reflects the strong assertions of pontifical authority over the liturgy. Yet the practice of the Holy See may vary, the reservation of powers may increase or decrease, and local usage or authority may be allowed more or less liberty. In point of fact the strict regulation of nearly every aspect of public worship which we know is not paralleled in the first fifteen centuries of the Church's history—as the diversities of rite and the differences within rites testify.

On the other hand, it must not be thought that the Bishops of Rome failed to exercise their universal authority in matters of liturgy prior to the sixteenth century reform and unification of the Roman Rite. An examination of some of their legislative acts shows rather that the Roman Pontiffs have always been jealously concerned with the development and the purity of Catholic worship.

First of all the allowance of diverse rites is to be noted. This is true of the Oriental rites in every age, including our own;[81] with few exceptions it is also true of the lesser rites of the Latin Church, the Ambrosian and Mozarabic in particular.[82] Even in times of firm exercise of supreme papal authority there was great generosity on the part of the Popes toward the Eastern usages, not only in dealing with schismatics, but also for the Greeks living in and

[80] *Mediator Dei—AAS*, XXXIX (1947), 544.

[81] Benedictus XIV, ep. encycl. *Allatae sunt*, 26 iul. 1755—*Fontes*, n. 434; Leo XIII, const. *Orientalium*, 30 nov. 1894—*Fontes*, n. 627.

[82] Righetti, *Manuale di Storia Liturgica*, Vol. I, *Introduzione Generale* (Milano: Editrice Ancora, 1945), I, 128; King, *Notes on the Catholic Liturgies* (London, 1930), pp. 262-263.

about Rome.[83] Thus in 1215 at the Fourth Lateran Council, held under Innocent III, careful provision was made for the celebration of the liturgy according to the different rites within a single city or diocese;[84] and Eugene IV at the Council of Florence showed the constant willingness of the Roman Pontiffs to embrace the varying rites of the East, provided these are lawful and in keeping with true doctrine.[85]

From the earliest periods of ecclesiastical history little legislation has been preserved on the ritual details of the liturgy. Information must be sought elsewhere than in papal documents, for example, in the *First Apology* of Saint Justin, written in the middle of the second century.[86] This contains a lengthy description of the Eucharistic service and of the baptismal liturgy,[87] as does the *Apostolic Tradition* of Hippolytus from a somewhat later date.[88] These writings show only the usages existing in the city of Rome during the period mentioned; they do not name the authority from which these usages issued. Both refer to the liberty exercised by the celebrant of the liturgy with regard to the form of prayers, as permitted at the time.[89]

There also exist, for the early centuries of the Church's history, the many attributions of ritual matters made by the *Liber Pontifi-*

---

[83] Salaville, *An Introduction to the Study of Eastern Liturgies* (London: Sands, 1938), pp. 52-53.

[84] Schroeder, *Disciplinary Decrees of the General Councils* (St. Louis: Herder, 1937), pp. 250-251; 566.

[85] Eugene IV, const. *Laetentur caeli*, 6 iul. 1439—*Fontes*, n. 51; const. *Exultate Deo*, 22 nov. 1439—*Fontes*, n. 52.

[86] Quasten, *Patrology*, Vol. I, *The Beginnings of Patristic Literature* (Westminster, Maryland: Newman—Utrecht, Brussels: Spectrum, 1951), p. 199.

[87] C. 61, 65-67; Migne, *Patrologiae Cursus Completus, Series Graeca* (161 vols., Parisiis, 1857-1866), VI, 421-422; 427-432; *Florilegium Patristicum*, ed. Bernhardus Geyer et Johannes Zellinger, Fasciculus VII, Pars I, *Monumenta Eucharistica et Liturgica Vetustissima*, ed. Johannes Quasten (Bonn: Hanstein, 1935), p. 13-21.

[88] Dix, *The Treatise on the Apostolic Tradition of Saint Hippolytus of Rome* (London: Society for Promoting Christian Knowledge—New York: Macmillan, 1937), pp. 33-39; 40-43; 50-52; Quasten, *Monumenta Eucharistica*, pp. 27-33.

[89] Fortescue, *The Mass: A Study of the Roman Liturgy* (2. ed., London: Longmans, 1913), p. 52.

calis or Book of the Popes. According to this record, various aspects of liturgical rite were introduced by authority of one or other early Pontiff. However, since the writing of the *Liber Pontficalis* dates only from the early sixth century (in the parts referring to the preceding period), its testimony cannot be readily accepted for the first four centuries, unless otherwise corroborated. This is the case when there appears to be an arbitrary distribution of the authorship of various rites to different Popes.[90]

The accumulation of these statements concerning the ritual legislation made by the early Bishops of Rome demonstrates in any event the decisions which were attributed to them in the fifth and sixth centuries. If there are few instances of legislation which have survived, it is clear that the effects of papal liturgical activity are to be found in the descriptions of early rites.

To the years following the fourth century liberation of the Church belong the many Popes who shaped the external forms of the Roman rite—Leo, Gelasius, and Gregory, the chief among them. It is a time characterized as the formation period of the Roman liturgy, after which no substantial developments would alter the pattern already set down.[91]

Saint Leo the Great (440-461) left definite monuments of liturgical law, gave his name to one of the earliest Roman liturgical books, and is thought to have had a great part in the development of the Canon of the Roman Mass. It was Leo who added the phrase *sanctum sacrificium, immaculatam hostiam* to the prayer *Supra quae,*[92] and his hand has been discovered in other texts of the Canon, particularly in the *Communicantes.*[93] The Sacra-

---

[90] Leclercq, "Liber Pontificalis," *Dictionnaire d'Archéologie Chrétienne et de Liturgie* (Paris: Letouzey et Ané, 1907-   ), IX, 403, 433; Loomis, *The Book of the Popes,* Records of Civilization: Sources and Studies (New York, 1916), p. xvi.

[91] Coelho, *Corso di Liturgia Romana,* I, 246.

[92] Duchesne, *Le Liber Pontificalis* (2 vols., Paris, 1886-1892), I, 239, 241, footnote n. 12; Fortescue, *The Mass,* p. 350.

[93] Borella, "S. Leone Magno et il 'Communicantes,'" *Ephemerides Liturgicae,* LX (1946), 96-101; Jungmann, *Missarum Sollemnia, Eine genetische Erklärung der römischen Messe* (2 ed., 2 vols., Wein: Herder, 1949), I, 71, footnote n. 22.

mentary which bears Leo's name is thought to belong to the following century,[94] but he had a part in the composition of the collects and prefaces later incorporated in it.[95]

Pope Saint Gelasius (492-496) has a Sacramentary named after him and this attribution is now considered not improbable.[96] He is thought, moreover, to be responsible for the introduction of the *Kyrie* in its present place at Mass and for an enlargement of the prayers of commemoration in the Canon.[97] Similarly, the name of Gregory the Great (590-604) has long been associated with an important reform of the liturgy. The third of the celebrated sacramentaries was attributed to him, and it has recently been proposed that this Mass book was in fact produced by Gregory himself.[98] In addition, the name "Gregorian chant" commemorates the reform of church music under Gregory, although its exact features are not certain.[99]

A different kind of record of papal concern in the regulation of sacred rites and especially in the grant of privileges and permissions is found in the *Liber Diurnus*, a collection of formulas for use in the Papal Chancery.[100] Although the date has been disputed and variously assigned (and even the precise use of the collection questioned), its first two sections belong to the seventh century.[101]

The series of forms given in the *Liber Diurnus* include many which have to do directly with requests and responses for various

[94] Jungmann, *Missarum Sollemnia*, I, 78.

[95] Cabrol, "Leonien," *Dictionnaire d'Archéologie Chrétienne*, VIII, 2552.

[96] Kennedy, *The Saints of the Canon of the Mass*, Studi di Antichità Cristiana, XIV (Vatican City: Pontificio Istituto di Archeologia Cristiana, 1938), pp. 32-33; Jungmann, *op. cit.*, I, 71, 79.

[97] Capelle, "Le Pape Gélase et la messe romaine," *Revue d'Histoire Ecclésiastique* (Louvain, 1900–   ), XXXV (1939), 34; Kennedy, *op. cit.*, pp. 33, 38, 58.

[98] Capelle, "Le Main de S. Grégoire dans le Sacramentaire Grégorien," *Revue Bénédictine* (Maredsous, 1884–   ), XLIX (1937), 27-28.

[99] Romita, *Ius Musicae Liturgicae* (Taurini: Marietti, 1936), p. 30; Oppenheim, *Institutiones in Sacram Liturgiam*, II, 75. Cf. c. 1, D. XCII.

[100] Rozière, *Liber Diurnus ou Recueil des Formules usitées par la Chancellerie Pontificale du Ve au Xe Siècle* (Paris, 1869).

[101] Van Hove, *Commentarium Lovaniense in Codicem Iuris Canonici*, Vol. I, Tom. I, *Prolegomena* (2. ed., Mechliniae, Romae: Dessain, 1945), pp. 190-192.

rites, especially those for the dedication of churches and oratories, the consecration of altars, and the ceremonies for the transfer of relics. There are texts concerned with ordinations, the ritual profession of faith by bishops, the dedication of baptisteries, and the like. The mere listing of these suggests the extent to which the Roman Pontiffs exercised their authority over liturgical privileges at the time.

Unlike the actual forming of liturgical rites, the use of the *Liber Diurnus* had to do with private responses and individual grants by the Holy See. The same can be said of the many examples, in every period of liturgical history, in which the Popes answered difficulties in letters to the various churches. In the late fourth century, for example, Pope Siricius wrote to Hymerius of Tarragona about the proper time for the administration of general baptism.[102] All priests, wrote the pontiff, must observe his law "who do not wish to be separated from the solidity of the apostolic rock." [103]

When Innocent I (401-417) wrote to Decentius of Gubbio about various details of ritual, the place of the Kiss of Peace, the commemoration of the living at Mass, and the like, he began with a strong statement insisting on conformity with apostolic tradition and usage:

> If the priests of the Lord wish to preserve in their entirety
> the ecclesiastical institutes, as they were handed down
> by the blessed Apostles, let there be no diversity, no va-
> riety in orders and consecrations. Who cannot know,
> who would not notice that what was handed down to
> the Roman Church by Peter, the Prince of the Apostles,
> and preserved up to now, must be observed by all![104]

This is a particular assertion of papal authority and the need

---

[102] C. 11, D. IV, *de cons.;* Jaffé, *Regesta Pontificum Romanorum ab condita ecclesia ad annum post Christum natum MCXCVIII* (2. ed., quam curaverunt S. Loewenfeld, F. Kaltenbrunner, P. Ewald, 2 vols., Lipsiae, 1885-1888), n. 72 (hereafter cited as JK, JE, and JL).

[103] Migne, *Patrologiae Cursus Completus, Series Latina* (221 vols., Parisiis, 1844-1855), XIII, 1154-1156 (hereafter cited as *MPL*).

[104] *MPL*, XX, 551-552; JK 311.

for conformity to the Roman tradition. From the latter point of view it may not be carried too far; at the very time the letter was written, in 416, there existed diverse rites even in the West.[105] Cardinal Bona (1609-1674) saw in it rather a curb to excessive liberty in sacred worship, to the neglect of apostolic usage.[106]

The examples might be multiplied indefinitely, instances in which the Popes gave minute directions concerning rites and ceremonies. So Leo the Great wrote to Dioscorus of Alexandria about the date for holding ordinations,[107] and Pope Vigilius (537-555) gave directions to Profuturus, the Archbishop of Braga, about the use of blessed water in the dedication of churches.[108]

Just as important for the papal control of the liturgy of the Roman rite was the diffusion of Roman liturgical books. Again the instances recorded are numerous. Pope Vigilius transmitted the text of the Easter Mass to Profuturus for the latter's use, in connection with the letter mentioned above;[109] Zachary (741-752) sent a copy of the Roman canon to Saint Boniface;[110] and Paul I (757-767) sent books of antiphons and responsories to Pepin.[111] The most famous incident was the sending of a sacramentary to Charlemagne by Pope Hadrian (772-795).[112] This was, of course, the practical way in which the rite of Rome was diffused through the Merovingian and Carolingian empire. It led to the supplanting, although partly by compromise, of the Gallican rite and the triumph of the Roman traditional usages.[113]

---

[105] Duchesne, *Christian Worship: Its Origin and Evolution* (5. ed., trans. M. L. McClure, London: Society for Promoting Christian Knowledge, 1920), pp. 64, 88.

[106] Bona, *Rerum Liturgicarum Libri Duo* (Romae, 1671), Lib. I, cap. 6.

[107] *MPL*, LIV, 625-626; JK 406. Cf. De Puniet, *The Roman Pontifical, A History and Commentary* (New York: Longmans, 1932), p. 95.

[108] *MPL*, LXIX, 15-18; JK 907. Cf. Duchesne, *Le Liber Pontificalis,* I, 127; D. I, *de cons.*

[109] King, *Notes on the Catholic Liturgies*, p. 254.

[110] *MPL*, LXXXIX, 953; *MGH, Epistolarum* Tomus I, Pars I (ed. Paulus Ewald, Berolini, 1891), pp. 197, 200; JE 2291.

[111] *MPL*, LXXXIX, 1155-1157; JE 2359. Batiffol (*History of the Roman Breviary* [3. ed., New York, 1912], p. 66) gives other examples.

[112] Oppenheim, *Institutiones in Sacram Liturgiam,* IV, 26-29; Jungmann, *Missarum Sollemnia,* I, 80.

[113] Righetti, *Manuale di Storia Liturgica,* I, 78-79.

Another factor, extending from the late seventh century throughout the middle ages, was the diffusion of the *Ordines Romani*. These correspond to the sacramentaries, giving ceremonial directions to accompany the prayer text of the various ecclesiastical functions.[114] While it would be too much to suggest that the Roman Pontiffs imposed the use of these ceremonial books—only some of which originated in Rome—yet, second to the sacramentaries, they were the most important aspect of what may be called the indirect papal influence over liturgical development.[115] Their general use and adaptation, in the instances where the services described were peculiar to papal usage, had a unifying effect on sacred worship similar to that of authentic liturgical books.

In the twelfth century an important development in liturgical law took place with the reservation to the Apostolic See of cases of canonization. Alexander III (1159-1181) is generally credited with taking this action;[116] previously the Holy See had intervened frequently enough in the case of the universal cult of saints, but the rights of local bishops remained strong.[117] With Innocent III the papal legislation was definite, that no one should presume to venerate the relics of saints, unless they were first approved by the authority of the Holy See.[118]

The fourteenth and fifteenth centuries were a period of grave liturgical decline;[119] there was a multiplication of variant books of ritual, an excessive development of series of votive Masses and the like, all indicating a trend that would be curbed only in the six-

---

[114] *MPL*, LXXVIII, 937-1368; Andrieu, *Les Ordines Romani du Haut Moyen Age* (3 vols., Louvain: Spicilegium Sacrum Lovaniense, 1931-1951).

[115] Andrieu, *op. cit.*, I, 467; Jungmann, *Missarum Sollemnia*, I, 83.

[116] C. 1, X, *de reliquiis et veneratione sanctorum*, III, 45; JL 13456. Cf. Coronata, *Institutiones Iuris Canonici* (2. ed., 5 vols., Taurini: Marietti, 1939-1947), III, 446.

[117] Naz, "Causes de Beatification et de Canonisation," *Dictionnaire de Droit Canonique* (Paris: Letouzey et Anè, 1924-   ), III, 11-12; c. 37, D. I, *de cons.*

[118] C. 2, X, *de reliquiis et veneratione sanctorum*, III, 45; Kuttner, "La Réserve Papale du Droit de Canonisation," *Revue Historique de Droit Français et Étranger* (Paris, 1855-   ), 4 sér., XVII (1938), 208, 211-212.

[119] Coelho, *Corso di Liturgia Romana*, I, 287-293.

teenth century.[120] Yet even in these centuries the Roman Pontiffs issued specific legislation on the celebration of feasts, as the church calendar developed.[121] Repeated efforts were made to purify and regularize the celebration of the liturgy,[122] and there was a foreshadowing of the uniform liturgical books when an adaptation of the Pontifical of Durandus was issued by command of Innocent VIII in the late fifteenth century.[123]

This brief enumeration of papal liturgical legislation indicates that the Roman Pontiffs constantly intervened in the regulation of divine worship, even before the modern period and the exercise of the supreme authority to the exclusion of any important diversity in the Roman rite. Allowing great liberty to lawful particular usage, acknowledging local customs and episcopal regulation as a source of rites, the Popes nevertheless asserted their full authority in liturgical matters many times.

The law of the sacred liturgy thus belongs to the Church alone. Within the Church the supreme power over liturgical law belongs to the Bishops of Rome whose principal organ in the exercise of that power is the Congregation of Sacred Rites.

[120] Jungmann, *Missarum Sollemnia*, I, 165, 169.

[121] E. g., c. un., *de reliquiis et veneratione sanctorum*, III, 21, in VI°, enumerates the feasts of double rank.

[122] E. g., Concilium Viennense, c. 10—Schroeder, *Disciplinary Decrees of the General Councils*, pp. 395, 615; c. 1, *de celebratione missarum*, III, 14 in Clem.

[123] De Puniet, *The Roman Pontifical*, pp. 44, 56.

CHAPTER II

HISTORY OF THE CONGREGATION OF SACRED RITES

A. Background

The last centuries of the Middle Ages formed a period of deterioration in liturgical observances, characterized by an excessive multiplication of rites and feasts and a weakening of the venerable principles of sacred worship.[1] Even the dogmatic decrees of the Council of Trent, which were not primarily concerned with these matters, suggest the great need for liturgical reform in the sixteenth century. This is especially apparent in the canons on erroneous views regarding external rites[2] and on the veneration of saints.[3] But the gravest need of the Latin Church in connection with sacred worship was for new and authentic editions of the liturgical books. This matter the Council considered and ultimately left to the Roman Pontiffs to accomplish. On the very last day of the Council, the Pope was requested to see to the actual preparation of the necessary books, especially the Breviary and the Missal.[4]

Pope Pius IV (1559-1565) entrusted the work to a commission of bishops, the same ones who were preparing the Roman Catechism.[5] They completed the Breviary in 1568, and it was published by authority of Pope St. Pius V (1566-1572), who imposed its use

---

[1] Jedin, "Das Konzil von Trient und die Reform der liturgischen Bücher," *Ephemerides Liturgicae*, LIX (1945), 5-38.

[2] Sess. XXII, *de sacrificio missae*, c. 4, 5, 7, can. 6, 7, 9—Schroeder, *Canons and Decrees of the Council of Trent*, pp. 146-150; 419-422.

[3] Sess. XXV, *de invocatione, veneratione et reliquiis Sanctorum et sacris imaginibus*—Schroeder, *op. cit.*, pp. 215-217; 483-485.

[4] Continuatio sess. XXV, *de indice Librorum et Catechismo, Breviario et Missali*—Schroeder, *op. cit.*, pp. 254-255; 519-520. Pastor, *The History of the Popes* (40 vols., St. Louis: Herder, 1891-1953), XV, 362, 364.

[5] Pastor, *op. cit.*, XVI, 28, 30.

upon the entire Western Church, excepting only those whose rite was at least two hundred years old.[6] By this action the other breviaries then in use were suppressed and the *Breviarium Romanum* made mandatory. Two years later the Missal was published and imposed in much the same terms, the Pope indicating clearly that no further changes were to be introduced into the Mass rite.[7]

Since the Congregation of Sacred Rites would be given, among other matters, the precise duty of approving liturgical books, the commission which prepared the Breviary and the Missal may be considered the predecessor of the Congregation.[8] Moreover, the many questions and doubts to be settled by the Congregation would arise in great part from the modern uniformity of the Roman Rite, as determined by the Council of Trent and by the new liturgical books of Pius V. Thus the Congregation of Rites may be considered the remote offspring of the Council and the liturgical reform begun by it.

B. Establishment of the Congregation

In January of the year 1588, with the promulgation of the bull *Immensa aeterni Dei*, Pope Sixtus V introduced the first systematic arrangement of the Congregations of Cardinals in the Roman Curia.[9] In the late fifteenth century and during the course of the sixteenth century, the Consistory or assembly of Cardinals residing in Rome[10] had gradually been replaced in importance by the new commissions or congregations of Cardinals. The meeting of the whole body of Cardinals had grown unwieldy in the administra-

<hr>

[6] Litt. ap. *Quod a Nobis*, 9 iul. 1568—*BRT*, VII, 685-688.

[7] Pius V, litt. ap. *Quo primum tempore*, 14 iul. 1570—*BRT*, VII, 839-841.

[8] "Des Congrégations Romaines et de leur Pratique," *Analecta Iuris Pontificii* (Romae, 1855-1868; Parisiis, 1869-1890; *Analecta Ecclesiastica*, 1893-1911), II (1857), 2262 (hereafter cited as *AIP*).

[9] 22 ian. 1588—*BRT*, VIII, 985-999.

[10] Wernz, *Ius Decretalium*, II, 740-741; Cappello, *De Curia Romana iuxta Reformationem a Pio X Sapientissime Inductam* (2 vols., Romae, 1911-1912), I, 109-110.

tion of the affairs of the universal Church, as the business of the Apostolic See increased in volume. Some of the new, smaller groups were temporary; these were established by the Sovereign Pontiffs to meet particular needs, like the many reform congregations.[11] Others were of a more stable and permanent character, of which the first was the Roman Inquisition. This was created by Paul III in 1542[12] and is now called the Congregation of the Holy Office.

When Sixtus V was elected Pope in 1585 there were several of these permanent Congregations already in existence, in addition to the Inquisition: the Congregation of the Council,[13] the Index,[14] and the Congregation for the Consultations of Bishops;[15] he himself added a corresponding Congregation for the Consultations of Regulars.[16] In 1588, determined to define clearly the position of these groups, the Pontiff personally drew up the plan for a complete system of cardinalitial congregations and announced it to the Consistory.[17]

It was the purpose of Sixtus V, as the introduction to the bull *Immensa aeterni Dei* explains, so to arrange the various Congregations that they could deal more easily with the business of the Holy See, as the pressures of the times and the multiplication of

[11] Pastor, *The History of the Popes*, III, 269; IV, 408; V, 500-501; VI, 449; X, 378.

[12] Const. *Licet ab initio*, 21 iul. 1542—*BRT*, VI, 344-346.

[13] Pius IV, motu propr. *Alias nos*, 2 aug. 1564—*BRT*, VII, 300-301.

[14] Founded by Pius V in 1571—Pastor, *op. cit.*, XVII, 203; Hilling, *Procedure at the Roman Curia* (New York, 1907), p. 58; Cappello, *De Curia Romana*, I, 260; Simier, *La Curie Romaine* (Paris, 1909), p. 60, footnote n. 3; Phillips, *Kirchenrecht* (7 vols., Ratisbon, 1845-1889), VI, 608. The faculties of the Congregation of the Index were defined by Gregory XIII in his constitution *Ut pestiferarum*, 13 sept. 1572—*AIP*, II (1857), 2256-2257. The Congregation itself was suppressed by the Code of Canon Law, and its competence attributed to the Holy Office in Canon 247, §4.

[15] Founded by Pius V in 1572—Pastor, *op. cit.*, XVII, 204; Monin, *De Curia Romana*, pp. 50-51; "Des Congrégations Romaines et de leur Pratique," *AIP*, II (1857), 2257; *Collectanea in Usum Secretariae Sacrae Congregationis Episcoporum et Regularium* (Romae, 1863), p. xxiii.

[16] Const. *Romanus Pontifex*, 17 maii 1586—*AIP*, I (1855), 1371-1373.

[17] Pastor, *The History of the Popes*, XXI, 246-247.

affairs demanded. He described the work of the Congregations in general terms as that of expediting the cases of "those who come in great numbers to this Apostolic See, mother, mistress, and refuge of the faithful—for the sake of devotion, zeal for salvation, the prosecution of rights, the seeking of favors, and various other causes."[18]

Fifteen Congregations were enumerated by Pope Sixtus. Of this number, those already established needed only to have their position and scope more carefully defined. Six of the others were chiefly concerned with the temporal affairs of the papal territory,[19] while three new Congregations were of broader importance. These were ones charged with the Erection of Churches and Consistorial Provisions, the Roman University, and Sacred Rites and Ceremonies. The contribution of Sixtus V to the Roman Curia was thus twofold: the establishment of new Congregations and the definite pattern of the congregational system, into which all subsequent Congregations would be fitted. After his time there was no major reorganization of the Roman Curia until the twentieth century and the reforms of Pius X.

The *Congregatio Quinta* newly created in 1588 was named *"pro Sacris Ritibus et Caeremoniis."* In a preliminary paragraph Pope Sixtus gave the reasons for the foundation of this Congregation:

> The Church, taught by the Holy Spirit and by Apostolic tradition and discipline, uses sacred rites and ceremonies in the administration of the sacraments, the divine offices, and the whole worship of God and the Saints. These sacred rites and ceremonies contain valuable instruction for the Christian people and for the profession of the true faith; they recommend the majesty of the sacred mysteries, lift up the minds of the faithful to the contemplation of the highest things, and inflame them with the fire of devotion. Since this is so, we desire to increase the piety of the Church's sons and of divine wor-

---

[18] *BRT*, VIII, 986.
[19] Annona, Fleet, Roads, etc., Press, Taxation, Consulta.

ship by the maintenance and restoration of sacred rites and ceremonies.[20]

Five Cardinals were named to the *Congregatio Quinta* of the Curia, although this number, set by Sixtus V, varied greatly in later times, according to the will of the different Popes.[21] The original members were Alfonso Gesualdo (who was the first Prefect of the Congregation), Niccolò Sfondrato (later Gregory XIV), Agostino Valiero, Vincenzo Laureo, and Federico Borromeo.[22]

It is not necessary to give a detailed account of the original competence of the Congregation at this point. Its scope may be briefly summarized as follows:

1. Vigilance for the observance of sacred rites.
2. Restoration and reformation of ceremonies.
3. Reform and correction of the liturgical books.
4. Regulation of the offices of patron saints.
5. Canonization of saints.
6. Celebration of feast days.
7. Reception of princes and other visitors to the city of Rome.
8. Solution of controversies over precedence and other liturgical matters.[23]

The competence of the Congregation of Sacred Rites, as determined by Sixtus V, remained substantially unchanged for more

[20] *Iam vero, cum sacri ritus et caeremoniae, quibus Ecclesia a Spiritu Sancto edocta ex apostolica traditione, et disciplina utitur, in sacramentorum administratione, divinis officiis omnique Dei et Sanctorum veneratione magnam Christiani populi eruditionem veraeque fidei protestationem contineant, rerum sacrarum maiestatem commendant, fidelium mentes ad rerum altissimarum meditationem sustollant, et devotionis eas igne inflamment, cupientes filiorum Ecclesiae pietatem et divinum cultum sacris ritibus et caeremoniis conservandis instaurandisque magis augere—BRT,* VIII, 989.

[21] Cohellius, *Notitia Cardinalatus* (Romae, 1653), c. XV, p. 54.

[22] Pastor, *The History of the Popes,* XXI, 254. An enumeration of the members of the Congregation of Rites during its early years is given together with the decrees published in *AIP,* VII (1864), 13-14.

[23] *BRT,* VIII, 989-990.

than three centuries. Only with the complete curial reorganization effected by Pius X in 1908 was there to be any important alteration of the Congregation's function.

C. Subsequent Development of the Congregation

The activity of the Congregation of Sacred Rites may be seen in its various works, as shown by the beatifications and canonizations which it proposed to the Roman Pontiffs, by the collections of its decrees, and by the liturgical books published under its authority. The last matter was a principal concern of the Congregation in its early years. In the spring of 1588 Cardinal Gesualdo, the Prefect, was seeking information for the revision of the Breviary and Missal of Pius V, and sessions of the Cardinals for that purpose were held during the summer and fall of that year.[24]

The Roman Martyrology had already been issued, in 1584, before the establishment of the Congregation.[25] During the reign of Clement VIII (1592-1605) two additional ritual books were published. The *Pontificale Romanum* appeared in 1596; it was made of universal obligation, like the Breviary and Missal, and was imposed most strictly, all other Pontificals being suppressed.[26] It was followed, four years later, by the edition of the *Caeremoniale Episcoporum*. This was likewise imposed upon all churches, and intended particularly for the use of Metropolitan, Cathedral, and Collegiate Churches.[27] Finally, during the same pontificate, the Breviary and Missal were newly edited and published, in 1602[28] and 1604,[29] respectively.

Of the several liturgical books entrusted to the care of the Congregation of Rites by Sixtus V, only the Ritual remained. It was not published until 1614, by authority of Pope Paul V. Unlike the books which preceded it, the new Roman Ritual was not made of

---

[24] Pastor, *The History of the Popes*, XXI, 256.

[25] Gregory XIII, const. *Emendato iam Kalendario*, 14 ian. 1584.

[26] Clement VIII, const. *Ex quo in Ecclesia*, 10 febr. 1596 — *BRT*, X, 246-248.

[27] Clement VIII, const. *Cum novissime*, 14 iul. 1600 — *BRT*, X, 597-598.

[28] Clement VIII, const. *Cum in Ecclesia*, 10 maii 1602 — *BRT*, X, 788-790.

[29] Clement VIII, const. *Cum sanctissimum*, 7 iul. 1604 — *BRT*, XI, 88-90.

strict obligation; instead, the Pontiff merely exhorted bishops and pastors to follow the usage of the Roman Church as contained in it.[30]

In the history of the Congregation of Sacred Rites prior to the twentieth century reform of the Roman Curia, there are several developments of a general nature to be noted. One, concerning its relation to the Sacred Ceremonial Congregation, will be considered later.[31] Besides this, mention should be made of the twofold division of the Congregation and also of its relation to the Roman Rota.

In the second half of the seventeenth century Cardinal DeLuca (1614-1683) described the functioning of the Congregation of Rites and indicated that there were two divisions, which he called the ordinary congregation and the extraordinary congregation.[32] The former handled matters of cult and ceremonies, and the conferral of favors, as well as contentious cases of precedence and the like, while the extraordinary congregation concerned itself with beatification and canonization. He further observed that the functions were so distinct as to require the labors of two groups of personnel.[33]

The distinction or division arose logically. Even in the enumeration by Sixtus V of the Congregation's field of competence, it is clear that consideration of the causes of the Servants of God is distinct from the restoration of rites, elimination of abuses, and solution of ceremonial controversies. Moreover, the division is made sharper by the judicial character of the beatification and canonization causes. DeLuca observed that the Congregation of Rites had more the nature of a tribunal than any of the other congregations, and that the resemblance to a tribunal was to be found

[30] Paul V, const. *Apostolicae Sedis*, 17 iun. 1614 — *BRT*, XII, 266-267. Pastor, *The History of the Popes*, XXV, 227.

[31] Cf. *infra*, "Allied Congregations and Commissions," pp. 32-35.

[32] This should not be confused with the use of the same terms in reference to ordinary and extraordinary sessions or meetings of the Cardinals. Cf. *infra*, pp. 125-126.

[33] DeLuca, *Theatrum Veritatis et Justitiae sive Decisivi Discursus* (16 vols. in 9, Coloniae, 1706), Relatio Romanae Curiae Forensis, Disc. XVIII, n. 1, 3, 4, 6; Schmalzgrüber, *Ius Ecclesiasticum Universum* (5 vols. in 12, Romae, 1843-1845), Proemium, n. 380.

in the processes of beatification and canonization.[34] Schmalzgrüber (1663-1735) made a similar observation, namely, that the Congregation proceeded extra-judicially,[35] with the exception of these particular processes.[36] This twofold division was regularly noted by subsequent writers and was characteristic of the Congregation.[37]

A second development is in the relation of the Congregation of Sacred Rites to the Roman Rota, in connection with the processes of the Servants of God. Cardinal DeLuca stated that matters of dispute were sometimes submitted by the Congregation to the Rota for decision, although there was no specific rule governing the relation.[38] Pope Benedict XIV (1740-1758) gave a lengthy explanation, to the effect that the Congregation had only gradually exercised complete competence over cases of beatification and canonization, and that the Auditors of the Rota continued the traditional practice of hearing such cases, probably until the time of Innocent X (1644-1655).[39] Moreover, he explained the employment of the three senior Rotal Auditors as Consultors of the Congregation of Rites as an outgrowth of the earlier jurisdiction of the Rotal tribunal in these processes.

While this last deduction is doubtless correct, it should be added that the early decrees of the Congregation indicate that it assumed complete authority in the causes of the Servants of God.[40] In par-

[34] DeLuca, *op. cit.*, Disc. XVIII, n. 9-10.

[35] The Roman Congregations were intended to be administrative and legislative bodies, leaving judicial matters to the Tribunals of the Holy See. At a later period the distinction was somewhat obscured.

[36] *Schmalzgrüber, Ius Ecclesiasticum Universum*, Proemium, n. 380.

[37] Moroni, *Dizionario di Erudizione Storico-Ecclesiastica* (109 vols., Venezia, 1840-1879), XVI, 265; Phillips, *Kirchenrecht*, VI, 654; Bouix, *Tractatus de Curia Romana* (Parisiis, 1859), p. 186; Grimaldi, *Les Congrégations Romaines* (Siena, 1890), pp. 293-294; Cappello, *De Curia Romana*, I, 313.

[38] DeLuca, *Theatrum Veritatis et Justitiae*, Relatio Romanae Curiae Forensis, Disc. XVIII, n. 9-10.

[39] Benedictus XIV, *Opera Omnia* (12 vols., Romae, 1747), *De Servorum Dei Beatificatione*, Lib. I, c. XVII, n. 7-9, 12-13; Pastor, *The History of the Popes*, XXV, 264.

[40] S.R.C., *Canonizationum*, 3 ian. 1622 — *AIP*, VII (1864), 164; S.R.C., decr. gen. 18 mart. 1623 — *AIP*, VII (1864), 166; S.R.C., *Urbis*, 23 dec. 1624 — *AIP*, VII (1864), 169.

ticular, a decree of 1628 shows that the examination of the validity of processes of this kind was done either in the Congregation or in the Rota, *de mandato S.R.C.*[41] Other decrees give further details: the three senior Auditors of the Rota made a report of their findings to the Congregation in the presence of the Sovereign Pontiff, whereupon the members of the Congregation voted on the action to be recommended to the Pope.[42] The conclusion may be drawn that the Rota assisted the Congregation of Rites in cases of beatification and canonization, but that its power was purely consultative. In the course of time the senior Auditors of the Rota were joined to the Congregation in the capacity of Consultors.

As the Roman Congregations, and especially the Congregation of the Council, assumed wide judicial powers, the Rota was more and more reduced in authority. In 1870, with the loss of papal territory, the Tribunal even lost its power over civil cases in the Papal States and practically ceased to function. In 1878, Leo XIII restored to the Rota something of its former jurisdiction in connection with the cases of the servants of God. He gave the Rotal Auditors the duty of judging the legality of the processes on the virtues and miracles of the candidates for beatification and canonization, as well as the right to decide the validity of these processes. The same Pontiff increased this in 1895, to include doubts *de non cultu* and *de fama in genere.*[43]

This development, the relation of the Congregation of Rites and the Rota, prevailed until the pontificate of Pope Pius X. The only other change in the Congregation initiated by Leo XIII was the addition of certain extrinsic commissions. These will be discussed in the next section, after a consideration of the Congregations somewhat related to that of Sacred Rites.

[41] S.R.C., *Urbis,* 29 ian. 1628 — *AIP,* VII (1864), 200-201.

[42] S.R.C., *Urbis,* 18 ian. 1631 — *AIP,* VII (1864), 226-227; S.R.C., *Considerationes,* 27 maii 1631 — *AIP,* VII (1864), 229-238.

[43] Monin, *De Curia Romana,* p. 110; Ojetti, *De Romana Curia, Commentarium in Constitutionem Apostolicam "Sapienti Consilio"* (Romae, 1910), p. 178.

D. Allied Congregations and Commissions

1. Ceremonial Congregation

Many authors speak of the Ceremonial Congregation of the
Roman Curia as an annex or auxiliary of the Congregation of
Sacred Rites.[44] Such a view follows from a consideration of the
Ceremonial Congregation's competence, namely, over the ceremonies of the Papal Chapel and Court. It is, however, incorrect
juridically. There is every indication that the two Congregations
have been autonomous since the seventeenth century, if not from
their very institution.[45]

The independence of the Ceremonial Congregation has been
demonstrated in various ways. Its early decrees were collected by
authority of Pope Clement XI (1700-1721),[46] and later privately.[47]
These decrees, which date from the year 1627, together with other
decrees published in various places,[48] show the activity of the Congregation in matters of court ceremonial. Its autonomous position
in the Curia is also clear from the lists of members and officials
regularly given in the catalogues of the Holy See.[49] They were generally headed by the Dean of the College of Cardinals, who was

[44] Phillips, *Kirchenrecht*, VI, 676; Grimaldi, *Les Congrégations Romaines*, p.
511; Lega, *Praelectiones in Textum Iuris Canonici de Iudiciis Ecclesiasticis* (4
vols., Romae, 1896-1901), II, 234-235; Wernz, *Ius Decretalium*, II, 763; Monin,
De Curia Romana, p. 29; Simier, *La Curie Romaine*, p. 79; Lalmant, "Cérémoniale (Sacrée Congrégation de la)," *Dictionnaire de Droit Canonique*, III, 258-260;
Martin, *Les Congrégations Romaines* (Paris, 1930), p. 152.

[45] Hilling, *Procedure at the Roman Curia*, p. 93; Cappello, *De Curia Romana*,
I, 343.

[46] *Edictum generale circa caeremonias profanas in Curia Romana, secundum
decreta S. C. Caeremoniali*, 14 maii 1706 — Platus, *De Cardinalis Dignitati et
Officiis Tractatus* (6. ed., Romae, 1836), pp. 65-67; Haine, *De la Cour Romaine*
(2 vols. in 1, Louvain, 1859-1861), I, 107-116.

[47] Gattico, *Acta Selecta Caeremonialia Sanctae Romae Ecclesiae ex variis
manuscriptis, codicibus, et diariis saeculorum XV, XVI, et XVII* (Romae, 1753).
— Van Hove, *Prolegomena*, p. 400.

[48] S. C. Caer., decr. 23 nov. 1742, 16 dec. 1837 — Haine, *De la Cour Romaine*,
I, 117-120; Platus, *De Cardinalis Dignitati*, pp. 69-70. S. C. Caer., decr. 21 maii
1890 — *ASS*, XXIV (1890), 379.

[49] *Annuario Pontificio* (Roma, *Notizie*, 1716-1861; *Annuario Pontificio*, 1862-
1871; *La Gerarchia Cattolica*, 1872-1911; *Annuario Pontificio*, 1912-   ).

Prefect of the Congregation; the Apostolic Master of Ceremonies was Secretary, and the other Masters of Ceremonies were Consultors.[50] Finally, the independence of the Ceremonial Congregation is attested to by Pius X. His reform left it unaltered and, as unaltered, certainly distinct from any other Congregation.[51]

A certain confusion as to the status of the Ceremonial Congregation, which was not clearly explained by seventeenth century authors,[52] perhaps arose from the lack of any document establishing it. It has been stated very often that Sixtus V created the Congregation in 1588 in the bull *Immensa aeterni Dei*.[53] Such an assertion, however, is misleading, since Sixtus V clearly attributed to the Congregation of Rites those matters that traditionally belong to the Ceremonial Congregation:

> They [Cardinals of the Congregation *pro Sacris Ritibus et Caeremoniis*] are to consider and provide carefully that Kings, Princes, their Ambassadors, and other persons, even ecclesiastics, who come to the City and the Roman Curia, be ceremoniously received in accordance

[50] Lega, *Praelectiones de Iudiciis Ecclesiasticis*, II, 235; Hilling, *Procedure at the Roman Curia*, p. 93; Grimaldi, *Les Congrégations Romaines*, p. 513.

[51] "*Congregatio haec, suapte natura, constitutionem suam ac disciplinae rationem stabilem retinet nullique mutationi obnoxiam.*" Ordo servandus in S. Congregationibus, Tribunalibus, Officiis Romanae Curiae, 29 sept. 1908, Pars II, Normae peculiares, cap. VII, art. IX — *Fontes*, n. 6460.

[52] De Luca (*Relatio Romanae Curiae Forensis*, Disc. XXIII, n. 12) lists a Congregation *super caeremoniali* among the "spiritual" congregations, but gives no further information. Lunadoro (*Relatione della Corte di Roma* [Venezia, 1664], p. 8) refers to it in connection with the papal masters of ceremonies, but does not include it in his listing of the other congregations. Cohellius (*Notitia Cardinalatus*, c. XV) does not mention it at all, but seems to assume that its field of competence belongs to the Congregation of Rites; in fact, he only repeats the terms of the bull *Immensa aeterni Dei* of Sixtus V. Even a nineteenth century edition of Platus (*De Cardinalis Dignitate*, pp. 288-289) fails to list it with the Congregations, although elsewhere in the same work (pp. 65-67) its decrees are quoted.

[53] Moroni, *Dizionario di Erudizione Storico-Ecclesiastica*, XVI, 168; Wernz, *Ius Decretalium*, II, 763; *Annuario Pontificio* for 1940, p. 731 (repeated in subsequent years); Abbo-Hannan, *The Sacred Canons* (2 vols., St. Louis, London: Herder, 1952), I, 310.

with the dignity and kindness of the Apostolic See, in the manner of the past.[54]

Because of the fact that the Ceremonial Congregation as such is not mentioned in the bull *Immensa*, authors have more often stated that it was founded subsequently by Pope Sixtus, or that it gradually assumed a separate existence, distinct from the Congregation of Sacred Rites.[55] A final alternative, and perhaps the most reasonable, is based on the assertion of Haine (1815-1900) that the Sacred Ceremonial Congregation antedated the Congregation of Rites, and was in fact founded by Gregory XIII in 1572. This claim was proved, according to Haine, by the registers of the Congregation, although there was no evidence of the exact date of establishment.[56]

The best explanation of the relation between the two Congregations that can be offered now is that Pope Sixtus V included in the new Congregation of Sacred Rites what had belonged to the Ceremonial Congregation prior to 1588, but that the latter regained its separate status shortly thereafter. This conclusion is confirmed by the name Sixtus gave to the Congregation, Sacred Rites *and Ceremonies*, as well as by the inclusion in its field of competence of those matters logically belonging to the Ceremonial Congregation. It is supported, moreover, by the fact that the new Congregation did not exercise any jurisdiction over matters of papal court ceremonial,[57] leaving these rather to the Ceremonial Congrega-

[54] *BRT*, VII, 990. This passage has reference to the profane or non-liturgical functions of the Papal Court. In the same document the liturgical ceremonies of the *Capella Pontificia* are also referred to the Congregation of Sacred Rites.

[55] Lega, *Praelectiones de Iudiciis Ecclesiasticis*, II, 235; Hilling, *Procedure at the Roman Curia*, p. 93; Cappello, *De Curia Romana*, I, 343; Grimaldi, *Les Congrégations Romaines*, p. 511; Simier, *La Curie Romaine*, p. 79.

[56] Haine, *Synopsis S.R.E. Cardinalium Congregationum* (Lovanii, 1857), p. 67, footnote n. 1; *De la Cour Romaine*, I, 65; Ojetti, *De Romana Curia*, p. 144; Monin, *De Curia Romana*, p. 29; Lalmant, "Cérémoniale (Sacrée Congrégation de la)," *Dictionnaire de Droit Canonique*, III, 258-260. Cappello, in his *Summa Iuris Canonici* (3 vols., Vol. I-II, 4. ed., Romae: Aedes Universitatis Gregorianae, 1945, I, 296, footnote n. 23), now speaks of "traces" of the Ceremonial Congregation during the pontificate of Gregory XIII.

[57] Monin, *De Curia Romana*, p. 29; cf. Coronata, *Institutiones Iuris Canonici*, I, 414.

tion.[58] From a historical point of view, the two Congregations may thus be said to be allied. Their juridical relation will be considered later.[59]

2. Congregation of Indulgences and Relics

The erection of this Congregation must be briefly considered because of its subsequent (temporary) union with the Congregation of Sacred Rites and because the latter ultimately fell heir to its jurisdiction over sacred relics.

In July of 1669 Pope Clement IX formally established the new Congregation *"Indulgentiis Sacrisque Reliquiis Praeposita,"*[60] although sessions of the members had been held previously, as early as 1667, and decrees had already been issued.[61] The Pontiff noted that no Congregation up to that time had the care of dispensing the sacred treasury of indulgences or of examining the relics of saints and making proper disposition of them. These matters he attributed to the new Congregation, together with the right to settle controversies and doubts concerning relics and indulgences.

The activity of this Congregation is shown in its collected decrees, which indicate that most of its decisions had to do with indulgences, not with sacred relics.[62] Its competence was redefined by Leo XIII in 1897. He confirmed some fourteen faculties belonging to the Congregation, in addition to the original concessions

---

[58] In liturgical matters the Congregation of Rites, at least in its early history, did issue decrees concerning the Papal Chapel. Cf. S.R.C., *Veneta*, 4 apr. 1626 — *AIP*, VII (1864), 182; S.R.C., *Urbis. Cappellae Pontificiae*, 19 iul. 1642 — *AIP*, VII (1864), 286; S.R.C., decr. 5 iul. 1653 — *AIP*, VII (1864), 319. It was presumably with such decrees in mind that Ojetti (1862-1932) suggested that the two Congregations had cumulative jurisdiction over liturgical functions of the Papal Chapel and Court, while the Ceremonial Congregation had exclusive jurisdiction over profane ceremonial. — *De Romana Curia*, p. 144.

[59] Cf. *infra*, pp. 101-102.

[60] Const. *In ipsis Pontificatus*, 6 iul. 1669 — *BRT*, XVII, 805-806.

[61] *Decreta Authentica Sacrae Congregationis Indulgentiis Sacrisque Reliquiis Praepositae ab anno 1668 ad annum 1882* (Ratisbon, 1883), p. viii.

[62] *Loc. cit.*; Dooley, *Church Law on Sacred Relics*, The Catholic University of America Canon Law Studies, n. 70 (Washington, D. C.: The Catholic University of America, 1931), p. 44.

of Clement IX. Of these faculties two pertained to jurisdiction over relics, while the others referred exclusively to indulgences.[63]

The work of this Congregation and that of the Congregation of Rites had overlapped to a certain extent, with regard to sacred relics, inasmuch as the latter was concerned with the relics of the Servants of God in the course of their processes and also regulated the use of relics in sacred functions, as well as the celebration of local offices in honor of relics.[64] For this reason and others, early in 1904 Pope Pius X united the independent Congregation of Indulgences and Relics to the Congregation of Sacred Rites.[65] This later proved to be the first step in the dissolution of the Congregation founded by Clement IX.

The Pontiff explained the union of the two Congregations as based on the similarity of matters handled and the benefits to be had from the co-ordination of their related activities. He therefore decreed that the Congregation of Indulgences would be permanently united to the Congregation of Rites, but that its duties, officials, and faculties would remain intact. To secure the unity of action he desired, Pius X made the rule that the Prefect of the Congregation of Indulgences would be Pro-Prefect of the Congregation of Rites in the future.

3. Commissions of the Congregation of Rites

The two Congregations just discussed were independent bodies but had a certain relation to the Congregation of Sacred Rites. More directly concerned with the Congregation and more important in the description of its historical development were the Commissions instituted at the end of the nineteenth and at the beginning of the twentieth centuries.

A partial reform of the Roman Curia was undertaken by Leo XIII over the years of his pontificate, largely by means of newly

[63] Leo XIII, litt. *Christianae Reipublicae*, 31 oct. 1897 — Galante, *Fontes Iuris Canonici Selecti* (Oeniponte, 1906), pp. 552-553; *Archiv für katholisches Kirchenrecht* (Innsbruck, 1857-1861; Mainz, 1862-   ), LXXVIII (1898), 337-340.

[64] Dooley, *Church Law on Sacred Relics*, p. 51.

[65] Pius X, motu propr. *Quae in Ecclesiae*, 28 ian. 1904 — *Pii X Pontificis Maximi Acta* (5 vols., Romae, 1905-1914), I, 141.

created Commissions of Cardinals. These were either independently constituted or attached to the existing Congregations. By the year 1900 there were such groups as the Commissions for Historical Studies, for the Election of the Bishops of Italy, for the Reunion of Dissident Churches, and for the Correction of the Oriental Liturgical Books.[66]

Toward the end of 1891, when the need for a new edition of the *Decreta Authentica* of the Congregation of Rites was felt, Pope Leo established a *Commissio Liturgica* and attached it to the Congregation.[67] The principal work of the Commission was the codification and publication of the decrees;[68] this was completed in 1901. In addition, the group of experts, six in number, acted as consultants to the Congregation. This is noted in decrees as early as 1893,[69] and it is the common practice by 1896, as shown by the individual decrees of that year,[70] although the first reference to the Commission in the pontifical yearbook is in 1898.[71]

In 1902 a second commission or *coetus*, as it was called, was added to the Congregation by the same Pope. Like the first one it consisted of a president, a secretary, and a small number of expert members.[72] This second board was called the *Commissio historico-liturgica* and was given the office of settling historical questions of hagiography and liturgy, with especial reference to the eventual emendation or reformation of the liturgical books.[73]

The creation of the two commissions filled a considerable need in the Congregation of Sacred Rites, even apart from their respective labors in connection with the new editions of the decrees (by the Liturgical Commission) and of the ritual books (by the

[66] *La Gerarchia Cattolica* for 1900, *passim.*

[67] *Decreta Authentica*, I, xii.

[68] Cf. *infra*, pp. 148-149.

[69] S.R.C., *Dubiorum*, 13 iun. 1893 — D. 3801.

[70] S.R.C., *Quebecen.*, 6 mart. 1896 — D. 3891; S.R.C., *Basileen.*, 14 mart. 1896 — D. 3892; S.R.C., *Dianen.*, 14 mart. 1896 — D. 3893; S.R.C., *Ordinis Minorum de Observantia S. Francisci*, 27 mart. 1896 — D. 3894.

[71] *La Gerarchia Cattolica* for 1898, p. 710; Ojetti, *De Romana Curia*, pp. 141-142.

[72] Monin, *De Curia Romana*, p. 314.

[73] S.R.C., decr. 28 nov. 1902 — *ASS*, XXXV (1902), 372-373.

Historico-Liturgical Commission). In the nineteenth century, problems concerning sacred rites had been decided by the Congregation with the advice of the Apostolic Masters of Ceremonies, since all the consultors attached to the Congregation were concerned exclusively with matters of beatification and canonization. There was, moreover, no one appointed to examine historical questions of ritual in a scientific manner, as was frequently necessary in view of the matters under consideration. With the changes introduced by Leo XIII, the Liturgical Commission had the duty of examining ceremonial matters and then offering an opinion or *votum* to the Congregation itself, while the Historico-Liturgical Commission was available "to consider, clarify, and explain" the historical questions beyond the province of the first board.[74]

Leo's successor, Pius X, made certain preliminary changes in the Roman Curia, even before his general rearrangement of the curial sytsem in 1908. Among these was the suppression of certain obsolete Congregations,[75] and the union of the Congregation of Indulgences with that of Rites, as already described. Another change was a continuation of the policy of Leo XIII by the increase of the number of Commissions attached to the Congregation of Rites.

 In 1904 Pius X established a permanent *coetus* or commission for ecclesiastical music,[76] and a particular, temporary commission for the Vatican edition of the liturgical books containing Gregorian chant.[77] The occasion for the first commission was the reform of church music and of the liturgical law governing music which the Pope initiated in his celebrated Motu Proprio of November, 1903.[78] The work of the other body was the examination and approval of the new editions of the books of chant. These were to be based on the studies of the Benedictines, especially those of

---

[74] *Loc. cit.*

[75] Motu propr. *Sacrae Congregationi,* 26 maii 1906 — *Pii X P. M. Acta,* III, 136-137.

[76] *"Per la musica e il canto sacro"* — *La Gerarchia Cattolica* for 1905, p. 520; Ojetti, *De Romana Curia,* p. 142-143; Monin, *De Curia Romana,* p. 314.

[77] Motu propr. *Nostro Motu proprio,* 25 apr. 1904 — *ASS,* XXXVI (1904), 589-590; D. 4134.

[78] Motu propr. *Inter pastoralis officii,* 22 nov. 1903 — D. 4121; *Fontes,* n. 654. S.R.C., decr. *Urbis et Orbis,* 8 ian. 1904 — D. 4131.

Solesmes, and the commission was directed to employ the services of the Historico-Liturgical Commission already in existence, if difficulties should arise concerning the liturgical texts themselves.[79]

Thus the Congregation of Sacred Rites, after the preliminary changes of Pius X, included three commissions of a stable character and one temporary commission,[80] in addition to its own members and consultors. It had, moreover, the Congregation of Indulgences and Sacred Relics united to it.

E. Apostolic Constitution 'Sapienti Consilio'

On the 29th of June, 1908, Pope Pius X issued the Constitution on the Roman Curia, *Sapienti consilio*, together with two subsidiary documents intended to put its provisions into effect. These were the *Lex Propria Sacrae Romanae Rotae et Signaturae* and the *Ordo Servandus in S. Congregationibus, Tribunalibus, Officiis Romanae Curiae, Pars Prima, Normae Communes.*[81] In the following September the second part of the *Ordo Servandus* was issued, containing the *Normae Peculiares.*[82] Taken together, these regulations effected a complete juridical reorganization of the Curia, with the purposes of facilitating its business and removing the serious problem of cumulative jurisdiction among the Congregations.

The new system may be briefly described as consisting of eleven Congregations, three Tribunals, and five Offices. New Congregations, for the discipline of the Sacraments and for the affairs of Religious, were established, while others were suppressed, including the Congregation of Bishops and Regulars and that of Indulgences and Sacred Relics. The Tribunal of the Roman Rota

---

[79] Motu propr. *Nostro Motu proprio*, 25 apr. 1904 — D. 4134.

[80] The Commission for the books of Gregorian chant does not appear in *La Gerarchia Cattolica* after 1908. Since that time, it has not been the practice to publish the names of members of temporary commissions set up within the Congregation for the revision of liturgical books or for other particular purposes.

[81] *AAS*, I (1909), 7-58; *Fontes*, n. 682, 6459, 6460.

[82] 29 sept. 1908 — *AAS*, I (1909), 59-108; *Fontes*, n. 6460.

was restored, together with the Apostolic Signatura, and the competence and faculties of the entire Curia were defined.

This was the first broad and indeed complete reform of the Roman Curia since the time of Sixtus V. Its principal accomplishment was the sharp division of competence among the Congregations. Although changes have been introduced since 1908, the pattern of organization established by Pius X has been maintained, as the plan set by Pope Sixtus had remained the basis for the curial system from 1588 to 1908.

The Congregation of Sacred Rites was affected in several ways by the new dispositions of the *Sapienti consilio* and the accompanying Norms. It was subject to the new regulations for officials and procedure, as will be explained below.[83] For the most part, these regulations were the same for all the Congregations. Of greater importance, the competence of the Congregation was redefined and, to a certain extent, limited. While its new scope need not be explained here, it may be summarized as follows:

1. Matters pertaining proximately to sacred rites.
2. Vigilance for the observance of rites and ceremonies.
3. Grants of dispensations, insignia, and privileges.
4. Beatification, canonization, and sacred relics.[84]

The principal restriction of the Congregation was in the clause, *quae sacros ritus .... proxime spectant.* This meant that matters remotely connected with the sacred liturgy would henceforth be determined by other Congregations, principally by the new Congregation for the Discipline of the Sacraments, the Congregation of the Council, and the Congregation of Religious. None of these restrictions, however, derogated from the power of the Congregation of Rites over the external rites and ceremonies, which it had held from its institution.

In addition, there were several other determinations made concerning the Congregation. The *Sapienti consilio* declared: "To this Congregation there are joined the *Coetus liturgicus,* the

---

[83] Cf. *infra*, pp. 118-120; 122-125.
[84] Pius X, const. *Sapienti consilio*, 29 iun. 1908, § I, n. 8° — *Fontes*, n. 682.

Coetus historico-liturgicus, and the *Coetus pro sacro concentu."* [85]
Thus the actual structure of the Congregation remained unchanged, with the confirmation of the three permanent commissions attached to it previously. The extension of the competence
of the Congregation to include sacred relics coincided with the
dissolution of the Congregation of Indulgences upon the publication of the *Sapienti consilio.* [86] This terminated the union of the
latter with the Congregation of Rites.

Finally, the *Normae Peculiares* issued after the Constitution
Sapienti consilio, but as an integral part of that legislation, gave
further details concerning the Congregation. It listed among the
specific powers of the Congregation of Sacred Rites the following:
approbation of liturgical books, concession of new offices and
calendars, settlement of liturgical questions, and, with restrictions,
the granting of indults according to its former discipline. [87] The
discussion of these matters belongs to the chapter on the Congregation's competence. [88] The same series of regulations also determined that the Congregation should retain, for the most part, its
constitution, nature, and norms of activity as before:

> The Congregation will retain its constitution and nature,
> as before, excepting the prescriptions of the Constitution
> *Sapienti consilio* and of this law, in those things which are
> referred to this Congregation.
>
> In cases of beatification and canonization the norms
> proper and peculiar to this matter are to be maintained,
> always preserving, however, the prescriptions of this law
> pertaining to this matter.
>
> Concerning sacred Relics, the Congregation of Rites will

---

[85] *Loc. cit.: Huic Congregationi adiunguntur Coetus* liturgicus, *Coetus* historico-
liturgicus *et Coetus* pro sancto concentu.

[86] The power of the Congregation of Indulgences and Sacred Relics over indulgences was transferred to the Holy Office in the *Sapienti consilio,* § I, n. 1°,
3°. This arrangement was later changed by Canon 258, § 2, which attributed the
power over indulgences to the Sacred Penitentiary.

[87] Ordo servandus in S. Congregationibus, Tribunalibus, Officiis Romanae
Curiae, 29 sept. 1908, Pars II, Normae Peculiares, cap. VII, art. VIII, n. 2° —
Fontes, n. 6460.

[88] Cf. *infra,* pp. 81-85.

adhere to the prescriptions of the Constitution *In ipsis,* 6
iul. 1699 . . . [89]

In summary, the reforms of Pius X in 1908 did not substantially
change the Congregation of Sacred Rites. Its nature and structure
remained unaltered, and the new definition of its competence
served to clarify its position in the Roman Curia and in the government of the Church universal.

F. Changes in the Congregation after 1908

The last matters to be considered in the history of the Congregation of Sacred Rites are the changes that have occurred subsequent to the general reform by Pope Pius X. While these have
been few, they have affected the structural organization of the
Congregation considerably.

After the restoration of the Sacred Roman Rota by Pius X, with
very extensive jurisdiction and activity, the Auditors of the Rota
were no longer available for hearing the minor cases in connection
with the processes of the Servants of God, which they had
examined and decided since 1878.[90] Accordingly, toward the end cf
1908 the Pontiff established a substitute procedure whereby these
lesser cases would be submitted to a *Congregatio particularis* or
Congregatio peculiaris within the Congregation of Rites itself. A
number of the Cardinals and officials were to be appointed for the
individual cases.[91]

[89] N. 1°, 4°-5°: 1. *Suam, quam hactenus, constitutionem retinet atque naturam,
salvis praescriptionibus Const.* Sapienti consilio *atque huius legis, in iis quae ad
Congregationem hanc referuntur.*

4. *In causis* Beatificationis *et* Canonizationis *standum normis eius rei propriis
ac peculiaribus, servatis tamen semper huius legis praescriptionibus ad hoc genus
materiae pertinentibus.*

5. *Circa sacras Reliquias, Congregatio Rituum inhaerebit praescriptis Const.*
In ipsis, *die VI mensis Iulii a. MDCLXIX, superius memoratae sub* art. I., *de
Sancto Officio.*

[90] Cf. *supra,* pp. 30-31.

[91] S.R.C., decr. 9 dec. 1908 — *AAS,* I (1909), 160. This group is mentioned,
in somewhat different form, in Canon 2100, § 1, of the Code, where it is to consider the validity of the apostolic process. Cf. Ojetti, *De Romana Curia,* pp.
137-138.

Of much greater importance was the radical alteration of the Congregation's structure by the same Pontiff in 1914. In a Motu Proprio issued at the beginning of that year, he abolished the three Commissions or *coetus* attached to the Congregation and rearranged the order of consultors to agree with the new disposition.[92]

The Pope explained, in the document mentioned, that in spite of the twofold character of the Congregation as created by Sixtus V the consultors had been principally concerned with matters of beatification and canonization. This left questions of rites and ceremonies either to the Apostolic Masters of Ceremonies or (since the time of Leo XIII) to the various Commissions, which had to be consulted by the Congregation. Since the three Commissions confirmed by the Constitution *Sapienti consilio* remained "external instruments" of the Congregation and were neither members nor consultors, the integrity and strength of the whole Congregation seemed to require a division into two sections, each with its own body of consultors. Those already belonging to the Congregation were named consultors of the first section, for beatification and canonization; new consultors were to be named for the second section, for sacred rites; and the commissions were suppressed.[93]

With this action the reorganization of the Congregation of Sacred Rites by Pope Pius X was complete, and its twofold character emphasized by the division into two sections of the single Congregation. The Code of Canon Law promulgated by his successor, Benedict XV, did not alter the constitution of this Congregation. With regard to the matters considered by the Congregation, the new Code included a lengthy series of laws on the processes of beatification and canonization,[94] but the liturgical law remained in force unless it was expressly corrected.[95] The terms of the *Sapienti consilio* defining the Congregation's competence were repeated almost verbatim,[96] and its discipline (like that of the other agen-

---

[92] Motu propr. *Quanta semper cura,* 26 ian. 1914 — *AAS,* VI (1914), 25-27.

[93] *Loc. cit.*

[94] Can. 1999-2142.

[95] Can. 2; 6, 6°.

[96] Can. 253.

cies of the Roman Curia) was confirmed according to the norms set by the Roman Pontiffs.[97]

A final note must be made of one further development in the history of the Congregation of Rites. In 1930 Pope Pius XI added a third section to the two determined in 1914, which were the *Sectio pro causis beatificationis et canonizationis* and the *Sectio pro sacra Liturgia.* This was the Historical Section which was established to consider the cases of the Servants of God which might involve historical problems; thus the results of its research assist the first section. Moreover, the new section was to provide the historical study necessary for the Congregation in its work of reforming, correcting, and publishing new editions of the liturgical books.[98] With this addition the structure of the Congregation of Sacred Rites is complete, and with this organization it functions today.

[97] Can. 243, § 1.
[98] Piux XI, motu propr. *Già da qualche tempo,* 6 febr. 1930 — *AAS,* XXII (1930), 87-88.

CHAPTER III

AUTHORITY OF THE CONGREGATION

A. Nature of the Power

The Sacred Roman Congregations are the organs of rule of the
Supreme Pontiffs, the immediate assistants of the Bishops of Rome
in the government of the universal Church. They act in the name
of and by authority of the Roman Pontiff;[1] in law they are included, together with the Tribunals and Offices of the Roman
Curia, under the name of Apostolic See or Holy See;[2] to them the
Pontiff communicates his supreme authority.[3] The Congregations
fulfill an obvious purpose in the life of the Church for the maintenance of ecclesiastical discipline and the administration of jus-
tice. Since the Popes cannot personally deal with the manifold
affairs brought to the Holy See, they have associated with them
the various agencies of the Curia, and principally the Roman Congregations, in the exercise of the sovereign power. This is made
clear by Sixtus V and Pius X, the two Pontiffs chiefly responsible
for the shaping of the Roman Curia.[4]

The decisions of these Congregations are by no means merely
doctrinal in value, but are truly authoritative, necessary, and of
obligatory force.[5] The nature of this power and the functions of
it must therefore be indicated. In part all the Congregations
share a similar power, in part they differ, as the character of their
competence and duties varies. The Congregation of Sacred Rites

---

[1] Can. 7; S.R.C., *Urbis et Orbis*, 13 mart. 1942—*AAS*, XXXIV (1942), 112.
Bargilliat, *Praelectiones Iuris Canonici* (37. ed., 2 vols., Parisiis, 1923), I, 370.

[2] Can. 7.

[3] Michiels, *Normae Generales Juris Canonici* (2. ed., 2 vols., Parisiis: Desclée,
1949), I, 148.

[4] Sixtus V, const. *Immensa aeterni Dei*, 22 ian. 1588—*BRT*, VIII, 986; Pius X,
const. *Sapienti consilio*, 29 iun. 1908—*AAS*, I (1909), 7; *Fontes*, n. 682.

[5] Reiffenstuel, *Ius Canonicum Universum* (5 vols in 7, Parisiis, 1864-1870),
Proemium, n. 130.

may thus be considered as enjoying a share in the same supreme power as the other Congregations, together with whatever aspects or functions of that power which are proper to it.

The jurisdictional power of the various authorities in the Church is either ordinary or delegated, according to its basis or according to the title by which it inheres in its subject.[6] The positive law gives a definition of the two: Ordinary power is that which is annexed by the law itself to an office; delegated power, that which is committed to a person.[7] Ordinary power thus comes through the office to the person who holds the office, and this because of the determination of the law establishing the office.[8] Delegated power, on the other hand, is, as its name explains, power conferred upon a given person by a superior, irrespective of any office held by the recipient. This second power is exercised not in view of one's office, but in view of the commission or delegation received.

The power of the Congregation of Sacred Rites is *ordinary*, like that of the other Congregations. This is clear from the establishment of the Congregations by law and from the fact that their specific powers are conferred upon them by law.[9] In the case of the Congregation of Rites its ordinary power derived first from Pope Sixtus V and was confirmed by Pius X, as described before.[10] Canon 253 confirms this anew and determines the present position of the Congregation. The discussion of the exact ambit of competence belongs to another chapter; here it is sufficient to note that the Congregation's power comes from the law itself.

It should be noted that the Congregations, and the Congregation of Sacred Rites in particular, may possess delegated power by concession of the Roman Pontiff. This would be by way of exception and in addition to the ordinary power held by law.[11] Yet

---

[6] Ottaviani, *Institutiones Iuris Publici Ecclesiastici*, I, 212.

[7] Can. 197, § 1.

[8] Regatillo, *Institutiones Iuris Canonici* (4. ed., 2 vols., Santander: Sal Terrae, 1951), I, 255.

[9] Can. 247-257.

[10] Cf. *supra*, pp. 24-28; 39-42.

[11] Badii, *Institutiones Iuris Canonici* (3. ed., 2 vols., Florentiae, 1921-1922), I, 157.

the requirement that matters be referred to the Roman Pontiff or that his approbation be secured by the Congregations[12] does not mean that the power then exercised is delegated. In such instances the acts are not performed by the Congregation in virtue of any new authority granted by the Pontiff and the acts remain those of the Congregation.[13]

There are several consequences of the possession of ordinary power by the Congregations. Powers which are ordinary are not extinguished so long as the office is held. Hence, so long as the Cardinals who form a Congregation hold this office, they enjoy, as a group, the ordinary power of jurisdiction within the scope of the Congregation's competence. The significance of this during the vacancy of the Holy See is considered below.[14] Moreover, the delegation of the ordinary power of the Congregations is ruled by the provisions of canon 199. An application of this, in the case of the Congregation of Sacred Rites, is the delegation of various liturgical faculties to local Ordinaries.[15]

With reference again to the basis of jurisdictional power, the Congregations may be said to enjoy *vicarious* power, in distinction to proper power. In this the Congregation of Rites does not differ from the others. Ordinary vicarious power is that which inheres in and which is exercised in the name of another;[16] it is attached to the office, but it is used by a secondary agent or substitute of the one possessing the proper power.[17] In the Apostolic See the power to act in his own name belongs personally to the occupant of the See, while the Congregations—and other agencies of the Curia—exercise their power in the name of the Sovereign

[12] Can. 244.

[13] Monin, *De Curia Romana*, p. 198; Regatillo, *Institutiones Iuris Canonici*, I, 291.

[14] Cf. *infra*, pp. 62-66.

[15] Index facultatum quinquennalium quae ordinariis nostris per tramitem S. C. Consistorialis tradi solent — Formula IV, cap. IV — Beste, *Introductio in Codicem* (3. ed., Collegeville, Minn.: St. John's Abbey Press, 1946), p. 1001; Bouscaren, *The Canon Law Digest* (2 vols., and Supplement through 1948, Milwaukee: Bruce, 1934-1949), II, 37-38.

[16] Regatillo, *Institutiones Iuris Canonici*, I, 256.

[17] Ottaviani, *Institutiones Iuris Publici Ecclesiastici*, I, 213.

Pontiff. This is shown by the restrictions placed upon the Congregations in the Code of Canon Law,[18] and by the definition of Canon 7: ". . . *Congregationes, Tribunalia, Officia, per quae idem Romanus Pontifex negotia Ecclesiae universae expedire solet.*" The very language used in decrees of the Congregation of Rites, for example, makes its vicarious power clear: *auctoritate Summi Pontificis,*[19] *utendo facultatibus sibi attributis,*[20] *vigore facultatum sibi specialiter ab Ipso Sanctissimo Domino Nostro Pio Papa XII tributarum.*[21]

This ordinary vicarious power of the Congregations is *supreme,* apostolic, and universal, that is, it is the power of the principal See.[22] Although a given Congregation can deal only with matters subject to it, the power itself is supreme, and the consideration of it is included in the title of the Code on the supreme power and those who share in it by ecclesiastical law.[23] Yet, even within its competence, a Congregation's power is not absolute, but is limited and dependent on the Roman Pontiff. In other words, it is a participated power, supreme but partial. The subordinate character of the power in question is clearly indicated by the nature and purpose of Congregations and by the canonical restrictions placed on the Congregations in Canon 244.

In summary, the Congregations, including the Congregation of Sacred Rites, must be said to have a supreme but limited power of jurisdiction which is ordinary and vicarious. This is to describe their power from the point of view of its basis or its manner of existing in the body exercising it; the next step is to examine the nature of the power as it functions.

[18] Can. 244.

[19] E.g., S.R.C., *Urbis et Orbis,* 13 mart. 1942—*AAS,* XXXIV (1942), 112.

[20] E.g., S.R.C., *Brugen.,* 28 febr. 1939—*Ephemerides Liturgicae,* LIII (1939), 87.

[21] E.g., S.R.C., *Congregationis Missionis,* 18 dec. 1939—*Ephemerides Liturgicae,* LIV (1940), 13.

[22] Bouix, *Tractatus de Jure Liturgico,* p. 151; Monin, *De Curia Romana,* p. 197; Chelodi, *Ius Canonicum de Personis* (3. ed., curavit Pius Ciprotti, Vicenza: Società Anonima Tipografica, 1942), p. 256; Oppenheim, *Institutiones in Sacram Liturgiam,* II, 106.

[23] Title VII, Sectio II, Pars Prima, of the second book of the Code.

B. Legislative Power

The classic division of social power is made, according to its threefold function, into legislative, judicial, and executive power. The legislative exercise of power refers to the proposal by law of the obligatory means to the common good, the judicial power has to do with the authoritative definition of controverted particular rights and violations of law, and the executive power promotes the means to the common end proposed by law.[24] While these functions are sufficiently distinct, they may overlap, especially in the case of the executive power.[25]

The extent to which jurisdictional power is exercised in these three ways by the Congregation of Sacred Rites must now be explained, beginning with the legislative power. This is the principal function and the most important function of authority. It is the power to make, change, and abrogate laws; from another point of view, it is the power to interpret those laws authentically.[26]

There is considerable dispute among canonists as to the existence of true legislative power in the Roman Congregations, considered in general. Those who deny it point to the restrictions placed upon these agencies of the Roman Curia. The law of Pius X had required that *nihil grave et extraordinarium* be considered by the Congregations unless the matter was previously referred to the Roman Pontiff, and that decisions and favors over and above special faculties be submitted for papal approval.[27]. Substantially, this is the law of the Code already referred to above.[28] Although neither the law of the Constitution *Sapienti consilio* nor the law of the Code was a change from the original statement of Sixtus V,[29] the following argument is made. Universal laws are always "grave

[24] Ottaviani, *Institutiones Iuris Publici Ecclesiastici*, I, 80-81.

[25] *Ibid.*, I, 108.

[26] Can. 17, § 1.

[27] Pius X, const. *Sapienti consilio*, 29 iun. 1908—*Fontes*, n. 682.

[28] Can. 244.

[29] Const. *Immensa aeterni Dei*, 22 ian. 1588—*BRT*, VIII, 985-999, where these words are found: ". . . . *Ita ut graviores difficilioresque consultationes ad nos referant.*" Cf. Ferreres, *Institutiones Canonicae iuxta Codicem Novissimum* (2. ed., 2 vols., Barcinone, 1920), I, 174.

and extraordinary"; therefore, they are so much beyond the power
of the Congregations that the latter cannot be said to have legislative power.[80]

A further reason for denying legislative power to the Congregations is taken from the terms of the Motu Proprio establishing the
Commission for the Interpretation of the Canons of the Code in
1917.[81] Having first determined the character of the Commission
itself, Pope Benedict XV described the position and duties of the
Roman Congregations, in these words:

> The Sacred Roman Congregations shall not hencefor-
> ward make *new General Decrees,* unless some grave
> necessity of the universal Church urges otherwise. Their
> ordinary duty, therefore, in this matter will be both to
> see that the prescriptions of the Code are religiously ob-
> served and to issue *Instructions,* if there is occasion,
> which will bring greater light to the precepts of the Code
> and produce greater effectiveness . . . . If, in the course of
> time, the good of the universal Church shall require that
> a new general decree be established by any Sacred Con-
> gregation shall warn the Supreme Pontiff of a discrep-
> it disagrees with the prescriptions of the Code, the Con-
> gregation, the latter shall itself make the decree; but if
> ancy of this kind . . . .[82]

The general decrees referred to are true laws; the Motu Proprio
indicates carefully the way in which they may be inserted in

---

[80] Wernz-Vidal, *Ius Canonicum,* II, 566; Cappello, *De Curia Romana,* I, 42;
Monin, *De Curia Romana,* p. 216; Jone, *Commentarium in Codicem Iuris Canonici,* Vol. I (Paderborn: Schöningh, 1950), p. 235.

[81] Benedictus XV, motu propr. *Cum iuris canonici,* 15 sept. 1917—*AAS,* IX
(1917), 483-484; printed in editions of the Code itself.

[82] *Sacrae Romanae Congregationes* nova Decreta Generalia *iamnunc ne ferant,
nisi qua gravis Ecclesiae universae necessitas aliud suadeat. Ordinarium igitur
earum munus in hoc genere erit tum curare ut Codicis praescripta religiose serventur, tum* Instructiones, *si res ferat, edere, quae iisdem Codicis praeceptis
maiorem et lucem afferant et efficientiam pariant. . . . Si quando, decursu
temporum, Ecclesiae universae bonum postulabit, ut novum generale decretum
ab aliqua Sacra Congregatione condatur, ea ipsa decretum conficiat, quod si a
Codicis praescriptis dissentiat, Summum Pontificem de eiusmodi discrepantia
moneat. . . .*

the Code.[33] From this it is argued that, since the making of such laws falls outside the power of the Congregations, the latter do not possess true legislative power. This conclusion is applied to the Congregations in general, and specifically to the Congregation of Sacred Rites.[34]

Those who oppose this view and argue that the Congregations do have legislative power always insist that the power is limited and imperfect.[35] Generally they state that the Congregations have "some legislative power."[36] This, according to Van Hove, is the more common opinion of canonists.[37]

Paradoxically, the strongest argument in favor of the legislative power of the Congregations is taken from the terms of the Motu Proprio quoted above. While that document limits the issuance of general decrees severely, it does allow such decrees when the serious need of the Church requires them and, moreover, gives directions for the making of such legislation by the Congregations. It seems incorrect to say that Benedict XV "suppressed" the use of general decrees,[38] or to say simply that the Congregations cannot issue decrees, without any mention of the clause, *nisi qua gravis Ecclesiae universae necessitas aliud suadeat.*[39] Instead it may be asserted that the Motu Proprio confirmed the legislative power, to be exercised under the limitations and restrictions of law.

To the further consideration, that the necessity of papal approval for general decrees destroys any legislative power of the Congregations, the distinction between approval *in forma communi*

---

[33] In the passage following the one quoted above.

[34] DeMeester, *Juris Canonici et Juris Canonico-Civilis Compendium* (3 vols. in 4, Brugis, 1921-1928), II, 64, where the S.R.C. is denied the *facultas condendi independentes et plane novas ordinationes.*

[35] Sipos, *Enchiridion Iuris Canonici* (3. ed., Pécs, 1936), p. 206; Oppenheim, *Institutiones in Sacram Liturgiam,* II, 107.

[36] Cicognani, *Canon Law* (2. ed., Reprint; Westminster, Maryland: Newman, 1949), p. 78; Maroto, *Institutiones Iuris Canonici ad Normam Novi Codicis* (2 vols., Vol. I, 3. ed., Romae, 1921), I, 411; Coronata, *Institutiones Iuris Canonici,* I, 399; Michiels, *Normae Generales,* I, 219; Vermeersch-Creusen, *Epitome Iuris Canonici* (3 vols., Vol. I, 7. ed., Mechliniae, Romae: Dessain, 1940), I, 304.

[37] *Prolegomena,* p. 74.

[38] Martin (*Les Congrégations Romaines,* p. 35) used this expression.

[39] As does Cappello, *Summa Iuris Canonici,* I, 286.

and *in forma specifica* may be urged. The Roman Pontiff may give
his approval to acts of legislation *in forma communi*, with the result that the acts remain those of the original legislator. This approval is generally indicated in one of the following formulas: *Ex
audientia Sanctissimi, Probante Sanctissimo Domino, In solita
audientia. . . . Sanctitas Sua resolutionem approbavit et con-
firmavit.* An example of this kind of approval is that given to the
legislation of plenary and provincial councils; their acts remain
the laws of the council and do not have the force of pontifical law.[40]
Approval *in forma specifica* differs from this in that the laws approved become true pontifical law, issuing directly from the pleni-
tude of papal power. This kind of approval is indicated by the
language used, commonly in the clauses: *Motu proprio, Ex certa
scientia, De apostolicae auctoritatis plenitudine.*[41]

The conclusion to be drawn is that the approval of the Sovereign
Pontiff, when given *in forma communi*, leaves the general decree
as the act of the respective Congregation, which therefore enjoys
true legislative power. There seems to be no reason to require
papal approval *in forma specifica*; this is not indicated in the Motu
Proprio of Benedict XV or in Canon 244.[42] It is true that the distinction can be urged too strongly and that the universal obligatory
force of the decrees in question is not affected,[43] but it is a way of
determining the precise character of the power communicated to
the Roman Congregations by the Supreme Pontiffs.

Additional reasons favoring true legislative power for the Congregations may be found in the reference to legislation by the Code
in connection with the competence of one of the Congregations,[44]

---

[40] Can. 291, § 1. Cf. Regatillo, *Institutiones Iuris Canonici*, I, 305.

[41] Coronata, *Institutiones Iuris Canonici*, I, 405, footnote n. 4; Cicognani,
Canon Law, p. 80; Chelodi, *Ius Canonicum de Personis*, p. 256; Sipos, *Enchiridion
Iuris Canonici*, p. 204; Regatillo, *op. cit.*, I, 291.

[42] Coronata, *op. cit.*, I, 406.

[43] Brys, *Juris Canonici Compendium* (10. ed., 2 vols., Brugis: Desclée, 1947-
1949), I, 336, Prümmer, *Manuale Iuris Canonici* (5. ed., Friburgi Brisgoviae,
1927), p. 137.

[44] Can. 249, § 1. Jone (*Commentarium in Codicem Iuris Canonici*, I, 237)
opposes this view, saying that the *legislatio* in the competence of the Congregation
of the Sacraments is "passive" legislation, *leges latae non leges ferendae.*

as well as in the laws issued by Pius X in the reformation of the Curia. These laws remain the norms by which the Curia is governed, unless abrogated or changed by the Code or by subsequent action of the Roman Pontiff.[45] Pius X, in decreeing the promulgation of laws in the *Acta Apostolicae Sedis,* indicated the work of the Congregations *ad leges iam latas declarandas aut ad novas constituendas.*[46] In the *Normae Peculiares* issued at the same time, the procedure was determined for legislation by the Congregations.[47] Coronata, in explaining the modern division of the dicasteries of the Roman Curia, found in the legislative power the point of difference between the Congregations and the Offices, and also between the Congregations and the Tribunals.[48]

What has been said concerning the Congregations in general applies to the Congregation of Sacred Rites as well, but, with regard to the latter, a further case can be adduced. The Congregation of Rites is unique in that its principal concern, liturgical law, is for the most part excluded from the legislation of the Code. The liturgical laws retain their force, unless they are expressly corrected in the Code;[49] unlike other disciplinary laws omitted from the Code, the laws found in the liturgical books do not lose their force on account of the publication of the Code.[50] Thus, although the Congregation of Sacred Rites is bound by Canon 244, its activity is broader than that of the other Congregations. In reference to laws not contained in the Code and belonging to its competence, the Congregation of Rites does not come under the provisions of the Motu Proprio *Cum iuris canonici,*[51] and need not submit its new general decrees in these matters to the Commission for the Interpretation of the Code.

[45] Can. 243, § 1.

[46] Const. *Promulgandi,* 29 sept. 1908 — *AAS,* I (1909), 1.

[47] Ordo servandus in S. Congregationibus, Tribunalibus, Officiis Romanae Curiae, 29 sept. 1908, Pars II, Normae Peculiares, cap. II, n. 1°: . . . . . *Acta denique omnia publici ordinis et communis, sive praeceptiones ea sint sive praescriptiones.* — *Fontes,* n. 6460.

[48] *Institutiones Iuris Canonici,* I, 399.

[49] Can. 2.

[50] Can. 6, 6°.

[51] Cf. *supra,* pp. 50-51; Coronata, *Institutiones Iuris Canonici,* I, 405, footnote n. 3.

Prior to the reform of the Curia in 1908, the Congregation of Rites had the broadest legislative power. In 1846 an *Affirmative* answer was given to the question: Whether the Decrees issued by the S.R.C. and any responses, formally published in writing by it, to doubts proposed, have the same authority as if they came from the Supreme Pontiff himself, even though no report of the same matters was made to His Holiness?[52] This response was confirmed by Pope Pius IX on July 17, 1846;[53] it was renewed in a different connection in 1854;[54] and it was included in the authentic collection of decrees published by authority of Leo XIII.

The power of the Congregation of Rites to legislate without reporting to the Roman Pontiff, as indicated in the decree of 1846, cannot be said to exist after the restrictions placed upon the entire Curia by the Constitution *Sapienti consilio*[55] and by Canon 244. Apart from this limitation, however, that grave and extraordinary matters must be referred to the Pope, the legislative power of the Congregation remains in force, and its decrees have the same authority as if they came from the Supreme Pontiff himself.[56] The nature of true legislative power is not changed by the required papal approval. As noted before,[57] the usual approval *in forma communi* given to a general decree does not make that decree a pontifical act; it remains the act of the Congregation and issues from the lawmaking power of the Congregation.

With reference to the Congregation of Sacred Rites, a further argument in favor of its power to legislate is derived from the expression *ius statuendi* in the enumeration of its fields of competence in the Code.[58] This is said of no other Congregation and may in-

[52] S.R.C., *Ordinis Praedicatorum*, 23 maii 1846 — D. 2916.

[53] *ASS*, III (1867), 864.

[54] S.R.C., *Romana*, 8 apr. 1854 — D. 3023, ad 1. This decree denied any necessity of promulgating the *Decreta et Responsiones* other than with the signatures of the Prefect and Secretary and under the seal of the Congregation.

[55] Cf. *supra*, p. 49.

[56] Van Hove, *Commentarium Lovaniense in Codicem Iuris Canonici*, Vol. I, Tom. II, *De Legibus Ecclesiasticis* (Mechliniae, Romae: Dessain, 1930), p. 253. Crnica, *Commentarium Theoretico-practicum Codicis Iuris Canonici*, Vol. I, (Šibenik: Kačic, 1940), p. 242.

[57] Cf. *supra*, pp. 51-52.

[58] Can. 253, § 1.

dicate a difference between the Congregation of Rites and the others.[59] The use of the word is even held to confirm the legislative power of this Congregation, to the exclusion of the others.[60]

A similar indication of the legislative power of the Congregation of Rites is found in a recent declaration of the present Pontiff. In his encyclical letter on the sacred liturgy, Pope Pius XII speaks of the competence of the Congregation and uses the word, *decernere*. Like *ius statuendi*, this is a further reference to an act of legislation.[61]

It seems clear that this Congregation possesses true legislative power. Whether this fact may be used to establish the existence of similar power in the other Congregations, in the minds of those denying them such power, is not here at issue. It is at least the more common opinion that all the Roman Congregations enjoy some legislative power; if they do not, it may in any event be attributed to the Congregation of Sacred Rites.

The other aspect of the legislative power is that of the interpretation of law. It bears close affinity to the executive power, since the interpretation of law, especially in particular cases, is part of the enforcement of law. Interpretation in particular cases is better called an application of the law.[62] There is no question concerning the power of the Roman Congregations, including the Congregation of Sacred Rites, to give authentic interpretations by means of particular rescripts. These, however, do not have the force of law and bind only the persons and affect the matters for which they are given.[63]

With regard to the authentic interpretation spoken of in Canon 17, § 2, of the Code, several distinctions must be made. The reform of the Curia instituted by the Constitution *Sapienti consilio* had abrogated the power of the Congregation of the Council to

---

[59] Eichmann, *Lehrbuch des Kirchenrechts* (2. ed., Paderborn, 1926), p. 158; Blat, *Commentarium Textus Codicis Iuris Canonici* (5 vols. in 6, Romae, 1919-1927), II, 269.

[60] Chelodi, *Ius Canonicum de Personis*, p. 266, footnote n. 2. Jone (*Commentarium in Codicem Iuris Canonici*, I, 237) argues against this.

[61] *Mediator Dei* — *AAS*, XXXIX (1947), 543.

[62] Michiels, *Normae Generales*, I, 501.

[63] Can. 17, § 3.

interpret the law of the Council of Trent.[64] This had been the original purpose for the creation of that Congregation,[65] confirmed by Sixtus V.[66] Pope Pius X gave the interpretative power to the individual Congregations according to their competence,[67] and a decision of the Sacred Consistorial Congregation (to which the *Sapienti consilio* had given the right to settle doubts of competence between Congregations)[68] made it certain that, before the Code, all the Congregations had full interpretative power, limited to their fields of competence.[69]

The new Code declared that authentic interpretation belongs to the legislator, his successor, and the one to whom either of these commits the power of giving an authentic interpretation.[70] Thus, to the extent that they possess true legislative authority, the Congregations would appear to have the power of authentic interpretation *per modum legis exhibita*, in general cases.[71] This is strengthened by the terms of Canon 243, § 1, confirming the norms set by the Roman Pontiffs for the Curia.

On the other hand, the interpretative power with relation to the canons of the Code was expressly granted in 1917 to the new Commission for the Interpretation of the Canons of the Code. The right was exclusive, even though the Commission was directed to hear the proper Sacred Congregation in important matters before givng the interpretation.[72] With reference to the law of the Code, therefore, the Congregations may at best be said to have

[64] Pius X, const. *Sapienti consilio*, 29 iun. 1908, § I, n. 4° — *Fontes*, n. 682.

[65] Pius IV, motu propr. *Alias nos*, 2 aug. 1564 — *BRT*, VII, 300-301.

[66] Const. *Immensa aeterni Dei*, 22 ian. 1588 — *BRT*, VIII, 987.

[67] Ordo servandus in S. Congregationibus, Tribunalibus, Officiis Romanae Curiae, 29 sept. 1908, Pars II, Normae peculiares, cap. II, n. 1°. — *Fontes*, n. 6460.

[68] § I, n. 2°, 4.

[69] S. C. Consist., *Romana*, 11 febr. 1911 — *AAS*, III (1911), 99-100; Van Hove, *De Legibus*, p. 253, footnote n. 1.

[70] Can. 17, § 1.

[71] Can. 17, § 2.

[72] Benedictus XV, motu propr. *Cum iuris canonici*, 15 sept. 1917, § I: . . . . *cui uni ius erit Codicis authentice interpretandi, audita tamen, in rebus maioris momenti, Sacra ea Congregatione cuius propria res sit, quae Consilio disceptanda proponitur.* — *AAS*, IX (1917), 483.

the power of giving merely declarative interpretations through the Instructions which they are to issue.[73]

Since the Code abrogated, for the most part, disciplinary laws not contained in it at least implicitly,[74] the interpretative power of the Congregations was reduced to particular cases, merely declarative interpretations, and the interpretation of whatever legislation might appear after the Code. Thus far what has been said applies equally to the Congregation of Sacred Rites; its right to interpret the law of the Code is subject to the same limitations as that of the other Congregations.[75]

With regard to liturgical law, on the other hand, the Code is largely silent. The laws of the liturgy retain their force unless they have been expressly corrected.[76] From this prescription of the Code it may be deduced that the Congregation of Rites retains its former power of giving general interpretations of liturgical law, with the exception of those laws which are now included in the Code.[77] A similar power of interpretation for the matters within its competence is shared by the Congregation for the Oriental Church in virtue of Canon 1, which excludes the Oriental Church, for the most part, from the prescriptions of the Latin Code.[78]

It may be added that authentic interpretations of liturgical law, given in general matters, must be promulgated according to the norms of Canons 9 and 17, § 2. This applies to interpretations

[73] Michiels, *Normae Generales,* I, 502. The Motu Proprio of Benedict XV, cited above, describes the "Instructions" in these words: *"Eiusmodi vero documenta sic conficiantur, ut non modo sint, sed appareant etiam quasi quaedam explanationes et complementa canonum, qui idcirco in documentorum contextu peropportune afferentur. —* § II.

[74] Can. 6, 6°.

[75] The S.R.C. did not hesitate, however, to interpret the law of the Code where a doubt had arisen, on account of the provisions of the Code, concerning the insertion of names in the Canon of Mass; cf. S.R.C., *Dubia,* 8 mart. 1919 — *AAS,* XI (1919), 145. See also S.R.C., *Urbis et Orbis,* 13 mart. 1942 — *AAS,* XXXIV (1942), 112.

[76] Can. 2.

[77] Van Hove, *De Legibus,* pp. 252-253; Michiels, *Normae Generales,* I, 503.

[78] Toso, *Ad Codicem Juris Canonici Commentaria Minora* (5 vols., Romae, 1921-1927), III, 64.

made by the Congregation of Sacred Rites; although liturgical law is largely excluded from the Code, the Congregation is subject to the general norms of Book I of the Code.[79]

The Congregation of Sacred Rites thus possesses true legislative power, limited in the making of law by the terms of Canon 244. In addition, it has the full power to give authentic interpretations of the liturgical law, not only in particular cases but in general cases as well, *per modum legis.* The Motu Proprio *Cum iuris canonici* has the effect of excluding from the interpretative power of the Congregation only those liturgical laws, comparatively few in number, which are contained in the Code.

C. Judicial Power

The judicial function of jurisdictional power is the right to define what actions conform or do not conform, in the concrete, to the law, and to declare the legitimate effects of this conformity or difformity. The judicial power settles controversies in particular cases by determining authoritatively the true meaning of a law and the relation of the fact or action in question to that law.[80] All the Roman Congregations have the power to settle controversies in particular cases; this is their common practice and to this extent they may be said to exercise judicial power.[81]

The definition of controverted matters, however, is better referred to the executive or administrative power of the Congregations, inasmuch as the reform of the Curia, confirmed by the Code of Canon Law, deliberately removed judicial power from the Congregations and centered it in the Tribunals. It was the intention of Pius X to restore the Sacred Roman Rota and the Apostolic Signatura by ordering "that the Sacred Congregations no longer receive or hear contentious cases, civil or criminal, requiring the judiciary order with a process and proofs."[82] This distinction was maintained in the Code, so that the "discussion and

---

[79] Van Hove, *De Legibus,* p. 13.
[80] Ottaviani, *Institutiones Iuris Publici Ecclesiastici,* I, 92.
[81] Wernz-Vidal, *Ius Canonicum,* II, 566.
[82] Pius X, const. *Sapienti consilio,* 29 iun. 1908 — *Fontes,* n. 682.

definition of a controversy" by one of the Congregations cannot be considered as a use of true or strict judicial power.[83]

With exceptions to be noticed below,[84] the Congregations, including the Congregation of Sacred Rites, determine controversies in an administrative manner, *"in linea disciplinari."* Neither the Constitution *Sapienti consilio* with the accompanying *Ordo servandus* of 1908 nor the Code itself determines precisely what matters must be decided administratively, what judicially. Although it belongs properly to the Tribunals to judge in cases where strict rights are involved, yet the difference between Tribunals and Congregations is largely one of the mode of procedure, and the same matter may often be settled administratively or judicially.[85]

There are many indications given of the difference in the two modes of procedure. In the administrative process, the judicial formalities are omitted: joinder of issue (*litis contestatio*), hearing of witnesses, arguments on behalf of the parties. Instead, only the interested parties are heard and the documents submitted by them are examined.[86] Moreover, the administrative decision of the Congregations may be based on the principles of equity rather than on a specific law.[87]

The distinction between the two types of procedure is repeatedly confirmed in the Code, in the enumeration of the powers of the Congregations,[88] as well as subsequently.[89] Both the *Sapienti consilio* and the Code require pontifical approval for important

---

[83] Can. 1552, § 1.

[84] Cf. *infra*, pp. 60-61.

[85] Coronata, *Institutiones Iuris Canonici*, I, 402-403; Wernz-Vidal, *Ius Canonicum*, II, 569.

[86] Ordo servandus in S. Congregationibus, Tribunalibus, Officiis Romanae Curiae, 29 sept. 1908, Pars II, Normae peculiares, cap. III, art. II, n. 7°. The title of the chapter is: *De modo tractandi negotia non stricte iudicialia.* — *Fontes*, n. 6460.

[87] Monin, *De Curia Romana*, p. 200.

[88] Can. 249, § 3 (S.C.Sac.); 250, § 5 (S.C.C.); 251, § 2 (S.C.Rel.); 253, § 1 (S.R.C.); 257, § 3 (S.C.Or.); 259; 1993.

[89] Pont. Commissio ad Codicis Canones authentice Interpretandos, *Romana*, 8 iul. 1940 — *AAS*, XXXII (1940), 317.

decisions of the Congregations, while insisting on the autonomy of the Tribunals in deciding cases lawfully heard by them.[90]

Whether a given controversy is to be decided administratively or judicially may be determined by the Sacred Congregation to which the controversy is referred, or by the Rota if the case is first presented to it.[91] In addition, the same *Normae Peculiares* which give this rule state that once a case is begun before a Congregation according to the administrative or disciplinary procedure—as agreed to by the parties, or at least not refused by them—the strictly judicial process may not be used, even though the Congregation has the right at any time to refer the case to a Tribunal.[92] The opposite is also true.[93]

What has been said so far applies to the Congregation of Sacred Rites as well as to the other Congregations: it may determine controversies administratively, provided they fall within its competence. Besides this, and by way of exception, the Congregation of Rites possesses strictly judicial power with reference to the causes of the Servants of God. This it shares with the Holy Office alone, which also has judicial power in matters proper to it.[94] That these two Congregations are the only ones to use the judicial procedure is made clear by the Code, where the power of the Roman Tribunals over cases demanding the *ordo iudiciarius* is limited by these words: *salvo iure Congregationis S. Officii et Congregationis Sacrorum Rituum in causas sibi proprias.*[95]

The Congregation of Sacred Rites has had judicial power in the cases of beatification and canonization since its institution.[96] For this reason precise norms of judicial procedure have been set up

[90] Can. 244, § 2.

[91] Ordo servandus in S. Congregationibus, Tribunalibus, Officiis Romanae Curiae, 29 sept. 1908, Pars II, Normae peculiares, cap. I, n. 3°. — *Fontes*, n. 6460. Cf. Coronata, *Institutiones Iuris Canonici*, I, 403. Cf. can. 1993.

[92] Cap. III, n. 10°.

[93] Pont. Commissio ad Codicis Canones authentice Interpretandos, *Romana*, 8 iul. 1940 — *AAS*, XXXII (1940), 317.

[94] Can. 247, § 1-3.

[95] Can. 259.

[96] Cf. *supra*, p. 29. See also Sipos, *Enchiridion Iuris Canonici*, p. 212; Toso, *Ad Codicem Juris Canonici Commentaria Minora*, III, 64.

to govern these cases; they are included in the Code in the Book
De Processibus.[97] And the judicial character of the process is not
altered by the requirement that the various steps must be confirmed by the Roman Pontiff.[98] This need for confirmation is explained by the fact that canonization is ultimately an exercise of
the indirect power of infallibility, a prerogative personal to the
Pope.[99]

D. Executive Power

The last function of social power, which is also called administrative power, is the right to exact the fulfillment of laws. It is
accomplished by the direction of persons and things, and by the
removal of obstacles to the concrete application of law.[100] To the
extent that it is the power to relax laws, it is called dispensative
power; with reference to the grant of favors it is *potestas gratiosa;*[101] and in connection with the infliction of penalties or the com-
pulsory enforcement of law it is coactive or coercive power.[102]

In the Roman Curia administrative or executive power is generally exercised by the Congregations in the name of the Pope,
preserving, except as already noted, the non-judicial character of
the Congregations as distinguished from the Tribunals. This term,
"non-judicial," is in fact sometimes used to indicate the nature of
the Congregations' activity.[103] And it is also called disciplinary
power, a name which is confirmed by the usage of Holy See.[104]

The executive or administrative power of the Congregation of
Sacred Rites does not differ in kind from that of the other Congregations, although the matters treated differ. Much of this
power has been indicated already in connection with the judicial

[97] Can. 1999-2141.

[98] E. g., can. 2071; 2083, § 1; 2100, § 3.

[99] Parente, *Theologia Fundamentalis*, pp. 167-168.

[100] Ottaviani, *Institutiones Iuris Publici Ecclesiastici*, I, 108.

[101] Monin, *De Curia Romana*, p. 200.

[102] Wernz, *Ius Decretalium*, II, 762; Ottaviani, *op. cit.*, I, 113.

[103] Brys, *Juris Canonici Compendium*, I, 325. Monin (*op. cit.*, p. 198) calls
the power of the Congregations "extra-judicial."

[104] Cappello, *Summa Iuris Canonici*, I, 285. Cf. can. 250, § 5; 251, § 2; 253, § 1;
257, § 3; 1993. § 1.

and legislative power. Thus, with relation to judicial power, the administrative definition and settlement of controverted cases belongs properly to the executive power; with relation to legislative power, the interpretation and application of law in particular cases belongs to the executive power. Similarly, the issuance of Instructions which do not have the character of law is an exercise of administrative power.[105] The purpose of such Instructions is to explain and complement the law itself;[106] although intended for universal application, they resemble the responses and replies given to individual questions.

In practice the administrative power is the basis of the routine activities of the Congregations and includes whatever does not belong to true legislative power (confined to the establishment of general laws) or strict judicial power (limited, in the Congregation of Rites, to the cases of beatification and canonization and absent in the other Congregations, with the exception of the Holy Office).[107] To it may thus be referred the concession of favors, the. granting of dispensations, the issuances of particular decrees and rescripts, the solutions given to doubts, and the like.

E. Sede Vacante

The power of the Congregation of Sacred Rites during the vacancy of the Holy See is not different from that of the other Congregations of the Curia in that period. In general, the power of the Congregations remains upon the death or resignation of the Roman Pontiff, but it is somewhat restricted.

Before the reform of the Curia it was taught that the ordinary power of the Congregations was not extinguished *Sede vacante* in any way; delegated power which the Congregations might possess was extinguished, at least *per se*.[108] Yet even the ordinary power was said to be quiescent and to be used licitly only. in ex-

---

[105] Regatillo, *Institutiones Iuris Canonici*, I, 291.

[106] Benedictus XV, motu propr. *Cum iuris canonici*, 15 sept. 1917 — *AAS*, IX (1917), 483-484.

[107] Naz, *ed.*, *Traité de Droit Canonique* (4 vols., Paris: Letouzey et Ané, 1948-1949), I, 385.

[108] Cappello, *De Curia Romana*, II, 79-80.

traordinary cases.[109] The same expression, "quiescence" of power, is used today.[110] A confirmation offered for the perseverance of power was the fact that the authority of the Congregations needed no new concession upon the election of a Pontiff to fill the vacancy.[111]

In 1904 Pope Pius X issued a Constitution containing the law to be observed while the Apostolic See was vacant. It included provisions for the powers of the Cardinals, the duties of certain officals, and the regulations for the election of the new Pope.[112] One chapter of this document had to do with the Roman Congregations and their faculties during the vacancy of the See.[113]

The law of Pius X was not changed by the Code, but rather confirmed,[114] and the Constitution was printed as the first of the documents appended to the Code. In 1945 a new Constitution was issued by authority of Pius XII to govern the same matters; this has been given in subsequent printings of the Code, in place of the Constitution of Pius X.[115] Even in this, however, the chapter referring to the Congregations of the Curia was not altered. The text of the earlier Constitution in this regard was repeated verbatim.[116]

The basis of the power belonging to the Congregations when the Apostolic See is vacant is the principle that ordinary power is not extinguished by the loss of authority on the part of the one conceding the office to which the power is attached.[117] Since the Congregations, including the Congregation of Rites, act in virtue

[109] Cappello, *op. cit.*, II, 81.

[110] Wernz-Vidal, *Ius Canonicum*, II, 564.

[111] Bouix, *Tractatus de Jure Liturgico*, p. 152; Cappello, *op. cit.*, II, 81.

[112] Pius X, const. *Vacante Sede Apostolica*, 25 dec. 1904 — *Pii X Pontificis Maximi Acta* (5 vols., Romae, 1905-1914), III, 239.

[113] Chapter IV of Title I, *De Sacris Romanis Congregationibus earumque facultatibus Sede Apostolica vacante.*

[114] Can. 241.

[115] Pius XII, const. *Vacantis Apostolicae Sedis*, 8 dec. 1945 — *AAS*, XXXVIII (1946), 65-99.

[116] *AAS*, XXXVIII (1946), 74.

[117] Can. 208; cf. can. 183, § 2.

of ordinary power, they do not lose this power upon the death or resignation of the Roman Pontiff.[118]

The positive law places certain restrictions upon the power of the Congregations. They may be stated in the terms of the two Constitutions already mentioned, which need little commentary in the part referring to the Congregations.

1. During the vacancy of the See the Sacred Congregations have no power in those matters which, when the See is occupied, they cannot do or expedite except *facto verbo cum SS.mo,* or *ex audientia SS.mi,* or *vigore specialium et extraordinariarum facultatum,* which faculties are usually granted to the Prefects or Secretaries of the Congregations by the Roman Pontiff.

In the case of the Congregation of Sacred Rites, its published decrees often indicate matters granted in virtue of special and extraordinary faculties. Such would be beyond the power of the Congregation during the vacancy of the See, and in them it could not act validly: *nullam potestatem habent in iis.*

2. But faculties which have been attributed to the Congregations by Apostolic Letters and are, therefore, considered as ordinary and as proper to the Congregations, are not extinguished by the death of the Roman Pontiff.

This is in accordance with the law that habitual faculties are placed in the class of privileges *praeter ius,*[119] and that, as such, they do not cease upon the loss of power by the one who granted the faculties.[120] The Congregation of Sacred Rites has many ordinary faculties which are not lost upon the vacancy of the Holy See.[121]

These two paragraphs determine the general norms of action, that extraordinary powers requiring the consultation and approval of the Roman Pontiff may not be validly used during an inter-

---

[118] Badii, *Institutiones Iuris Canonici,* I, 159; Cance, *Le Codé de Droit Canonique* (7. ed., 3 vols., Paris: Gabalda, 1946), I, 249.

[119] Can. 66, § 1.

[120] Can. 73, which adds: *nisi data cum clausula:* ad beneplacitum nostrum, *vel alia aequipollenti.*

[121] Cf. *infra,* pp. 109-114.

regnum, and that the ordinary faculties are not lost. A further qualification is then added with regard to the use of ordinary power:

> 3. We will, nevertheless, that the Sacred Congregations use these ordinary faculties only in conceding those favors which are of lesser importance, according to the circumstances. But in expediting or defining matters which seem to be graver or controverted, we decree: if the matter is such that it can be deferred to another time, it is entirely reserved to the future Pontiff; but if it allows no delay, then we grant to the Sacred College of Cardinals that it can commit the matter to the Prefect and some other Cardinals of that Congregation to which the Pontiff had similarly committed such an affair for examination. After the matter has been carefully discussed, they can decree—*per modum provisionis*, until a Pontiff is chosen—what, according to the prudence given to them by the Lord, they consider apt and agreeable to the preservation and protection of law and ecclesiastical ordinances.[122]

The restrictions played upon the Congregations follow logically from the requirement of Canon 244 that matters of graver moment should be referred to the Roman Pontiff.[123] During the vacancy of the Holy See a similar reservation of power is made, either to the future Pontiff or to the College of Cardinals, in the latter case for a provisional determination only.

In summary, the Congregations may use their ordinary faculties freely in matters of lesser importance during the time of the vacancy. In more serious cases and in those that are likely to be controverted, the decision must be left to the future Pope if possible; otherwise, when delay is not possible, the Sacred College

---

[122] Pius XII, const. *Vacantis Apostolicae Sedis*, 8 dec. 1945 — *AAS*, XXXVIII (1946), 74. The language of this paragraph is taken from the Constitution of Clement XIII, *Apostolatus officium*, 4 oct. 1732, § 18 — *BRT*, XXIII, 450. Cf. Monin, *De Curia Romana*, p. 375.

[123] Pius X, const. *Sapienti consilio*, 29 iun. 1908 — *Fontes*, n. 682.

may depute the proper Congregation to act. Their decision in turn is subject to the approval or disapproval of the new Pontiff, who is in no way bound by it. In other words, the ordinary power is neither extinguished nor suspended in ordinary cases; it is suspended in the more difficult cases.[124]

The nature of the power of the Congregation of Rites has been described, as the exercise of the three functions of social power, during the occupancy and during the vacancy of the Apostolic See. Next to be considered is the object of the power of the Congregation, which is its scope or competence; then the subject exercising it, namely, the members and personnel according to their mode of procedure; and, finally, the decrees in which the exercise of power is embodied.

[124] Coronata, *Institutiones Iuris Canonici*, I, 380; Sipos, *Enchiridion Iuris Canonici*, p. 204.

CHAPTER IV

COMPETENCE OF THE CONGREGATION

A. Competence before the Code of Canon Law

By competence is meant limited or restricted jurisdiction. It is lawful social authority or power in the concrete, according to the nature and circumstances of operation by the one possessing the authority.[1] With reference to the Roman Congregations, the term indicates the scope of matters placed within their power and under their authority by the Roman Pontiffs.

The field of competence of the Congregation of Sacred Rites has twice been defined, once at the time of its creation in 1588, and again in 1908. The first enumeration of the Congregation's powers has already been summarized; the following are the words of the bull *Immensa aeterni Dei* giving the duties of the Cardinal members of the Congregation:

> They are to take care that the ancient sacred rites be carefully observed by all persons in every place, in all the churches of the City and the World, even in our Pontifical Chapel, at Mass, the divine Office, the administration of the sacraments, and in other matters pertaining to divine worship; and
>
> that ceremonies be restored, if they have become obsolete, and reformed, if they have been corrupted.
>
> They are to reform and emend the books of sacred rites and ceremonies, to the extent necessary, especially the Pontifical, Ritual, and Ceremonial,
>
> and to examine and grant the divine Offices of patron Saints, having first consulted Us.

---

[1] Oesterle, *Praelectiones Iuris Canonici*, Vol. I (Romae, 1931), p. 137.

> In addition, they are to use great care concerning the canonization of Saints, and the celebration of feast days, that all may be done correctly and properly, according to the tradition of the Fathers.
>
> They are to consider and provide carefully that Kings, Princes, their Ambassadors, and other persons, even ecclesiastics, who come to the City and the Roman Curia, be ceremoniously received in accordance with the dignity and kindness of the Apostolic See, in the manner of the past.
>
> Let them examine, conclude summarily, and settle controversies over precedence in processions or elsewhere, and other difficulties incident to rites and ceremonies of this kind.[2]

With the exception of matters properly belonging to the Ceremonial Congregation, the original competence of the Congregation of Sacred Rites remained intact until the present century according to the form given it by Pope Sixtus V. The exception in favor of the Ceremonial Congregation may be indicated by the removal of the phrase, "even in our Pontifical Chapel," from the competence over sacred rites and by the removal of the statement concerning the reception of Kings and Princes.

---

[2] Sixtus V, const. *Immensa aeterni Dei*, 22 ian. 1588: . . . . *quibus haec praecipue cura incumbere debeat ut veteres ritus sacri ubivis locorum, in omnibus Urbis, orbisque ecclesiis, etiam in capella nostra pontificia, in missis, divinis officiis, sacramentorum administratione, caeterisque ad divinum cultum pertinentibus, a quibusvis personis diligenter observentur; caeremoniae si exoleverint, restituantur, si depravatae fuerint, reformentur, libros de sacris ritibus et caeremoniis, inprimis Pontificale, Rituale, Caeremoniale, prout opus fuerit, reforment et emendent; officia divina de sanctis patronis examinent, et nobis prius consultis, concedant. Diligentem quoque curam adhibeant circa sanctorum canonizationem, festorumque dierum celebritatem, ut omnia rite et recte et ex Patrum traditione fiant, et ut reges et principes eorumque oratores, aliaeque personae, etiam Ecclesiasticae, ad Urbem Curiamque Romanam venientes, pro Sedis Apostolicae dignitate ac benignitate honorifice more maiorum excipiantur, cogitationem suscipiant seduloque provideant. Controversias de praecedentia in processionibus, aut alibi, caeterasque in huiusmodi sacris ritibus et caeremoniis incidentes difficultates cognoscant, summarie terminent et componant. — BRT, VIII, 989-900.*

If, in addition, the reference to precedence is taken from the mention of questions to be decided by the Congregation, the text of the *Immensa aeterni Dei* might be used of the Congregation of Rites in the present law. It would be necessary only to define the terms in a somewhat stricter sense than was understood prior to 1908, when Pope Pius X restated the competence of the various Roman Congregations.

In the reform of Pius X, the power of the Congregation of Rites was defined in these words:

> 1. This Sacred Congregation has the right of providing for and establishing all those things which pertain proximately to the sacred rites and ceremonies of the Latin Church, but not those which are more widely referred to sacred rites, such as the rights of precedence and other matters of this kind, concerning which there may be dispute, whether the judicial order or the disciplinary form, that is, *in linea disciplinari*, as it is called, be observed.

> 2. Moreover, to this Congregation belong especially vigilance that the sacred rites and ceremonies be diligently observed in the celebration of Mass, in the administration of the sacraments, in the performance of the Divine Office, and finally in all that pertains to the worship of the Latin Church; concession of opportune dispensations; grant of insignia and honorary privileges, both those that are personal and temporary and those that are local and perpetual, which may refer to sacred rites or ceremonies, and care that abuses do not creep into these.

> 3. Lastly, it must carry out all those things which pertain to the beatification and canonization of Saints or to Sacred Relics.[3]

---

[3] Pius X, const. *Sapienti consilio*, 29 iun. 1908, § I, n. 8°: 1. *Haec Sacra Congregatio ius habet videndi et statuendi ea omnia, quae sacros ritus et caeremonias Ecclesiae Latinae proxime spectant, non autem quae latius ad sacros ritus referuntur, cuiusmodi sunt praecedentiae iura, aliaque id genus, de quibus, sive servato*

The text of the Constitution *Sapienti consilio* was further clarified by the *Normae Peculiares*, which supplied the omission of any direct reference to the Congregation's other powers, namely, over the liturgical books and the calendar, and the resolution of doubts and disputes:

> And so, since the office of seeing that, in the entire Latin Church, sacred rites and ceremonies be diligently observed in the celebration of Mass, in the administration of the sacraments, in the performance of the divine Offices, is proper to this Congregation and not held in common with others, it must on this account:
>
> a) exercise vigilance over the liturgical books of every kind belonging to the Latin Church, inspect, correct, or disapprove them, while preserving the competence of the Holy Office in those things which pertain to the articles of faith, or dogmas;
>
> b) examine and approve new divine Offices and calendars;
>
> c) judge and decide doubts concerning rites;
>
> d) grant concessions, indults, faculties which seem to be necessary in this matter, according to the old catalogue, but as circumscribed by the new norms of discipline, especially those already given with regard to the Con-

---

iudiciario ordine sive ratione disciplinae, hoc est, uti aiunt, in linea disciplinari disceptetur. 2. Eius proinde est praesertim advigilare ut sacri ritus ac caeremoniae diligenter serventur in Sacro celebrando, in Sacramentis administrandis, in divinis officiis persolvendis, in iis denique omnibus quae Ecclesiae Latinae cultum respiciunt; dispensationes opportunas concedere; insignia et honoris privilegia tam personalia et ad tempus, quam localia et perpetua, quae ad sacros ritus vel caeremonias pertineant, elargiri, et cavere ne in haec abusus irrepant. 3. Denique ea omnia exequi debet, quae ad beatificationem et canonizationem Sanctorum vel ad Sacras Reliquias quoquo modo referuntur. — Fontes, n. 682. The fourth paragraph concerning the Congregation has to do with the three permanent Commissions at that time attached to the Congregation. This confirmation of the Congregation's structure has already been mentioned in connection with its general history. Cf. *supra,* pp. 40-41.

gregation of the Sacraments (n. 10) and the Congregation of the Council (n. 4).[4]

B. Present Competence of the Congregation

At the present time the competence of the Congregation of Sacred Rites is based primarily upon Canon 253 of the Code. This canon repeats the law of the Constitution *Sapienti consilio,* with only verbal variations.[5] In addition, the laws of the *Sapienti consilio* and the *Ordo servandus* are confirmed by the Code as "the norms, both general and particular, which the Roman Pontiff himself shall have established."[6] These are the positive declarations of the Congregation's competence. From a negative point of view, much can be learned from a consideration of the powers of other Roman Congregations which may touch upon liturgical matters.[7]

---

[4] Ordo servandus in S. Congregationibus, Tribunalibus, Officiis Romanae Curiae, 29 sept. 1908, Pars II, Normae peculiares, cap. VII, art. VIII, n. 2°: *Itaque quum huius proprium et cum aliis non commune sit munus curandi ut, in universa Ecclesia latina, sacri ritus ac caeremoniae diligenter serventur in Sacro celebrando, in Sacramentis administrandis, in divinis officiis persolvendis; idcirco debet: a) advigilare liturgicis omne genus libris Ecclesiae latinae, eos inspicere, corrigere aut reprobare, salva Sancti Officii competentia in iis quae fidei capita, seu dogmata, respiciunt; b) excutere atque approbare nova officia divina et calendaria; c) dubia de ritibus iudicare ac dirimere; d) quae hac in re necessaria videantur temperamenta, indulta, facultates concedere, veteri retento catalogo, novis tamen disciplinae normis circumscripto, iis praesertim quae superius allata sunt,* num. 10., *de Congregatione Sacramentorum, et* num. 4 et 5., *de Congregatione Concilii.* — *Fontes,* n. 6460.

[5] Outside of variations of punctuation and word order not affecting the meaning, the following are the only changes: (1) The name of the Congregation is inserted in the first paragraph, *Congregatio Sacrorum Rituum* for *Haec Sacra Congregatio.* (2) In the place of the term *ratione disciplinae,* with its explanation in apposition: *"hoc est, uti aiunt, in linea disciplinari,"* only the latter phrase is used, so that the whole expression is simplified and reads: *sive servato ordine iudiciario sive in linea disciplinari.* (3) In the third paragraph, with reference to beatification and canonization, *agit* is substituted for *exequi debet,* and *Servorum Dei* for *Sanctorum,* as more accurate. None of these creates any change in the law governing the Congregation.

[6] Can. 243, § 1. See also Abbo-Hannan, *The Sacred Canons,* I, 301; Coronata, *Institutiones Iuris Canonici,* I, 404; Regatillo, *Institutiones Iuris Canonici,* I, 289.

[7] Cf. *infra,* "Relation to the Other Congregations," pp. 91-102.

The ways in which jurisdiction may be restricted by the measure of competence are several: according to the nature of the power, the persons subject to the authority, the territory affected, and the matters attributed to it.[8]

With regard to the Congregation of Sacred Rites, the kind of jurisdiction which it possesses has already been considered.[9] The only restriction on its authority as to persons is that based on rite; just as the faithful of the Oriental Churches are not subject to the common law of the Western Church,[10] so they are not bound by the jurisdictional power of the Congregation of Rites. This limitation of the Congregation to the Latin Church is found in the determination of its material competence.[11] An exception similar to that of Canon 1 of the Latin Code may be made: Orientals do not come under the decrees of the Congregation of Rites, unless the nature of the case so requires. Thus, for example, an Oriental allowed by apostolic indult to receive Orders in a Latin rite[12] would be obliged to observe any decrees of the Congregation governing the ceremonies of that ordination.

The restriction of competence on the basis of territory is specifically determined for the Roman Curia in the legislation of Pius X, but there was no change affecting the Congregation of Rites. The law states that, for the affairs of its competence, no territorial limits are set for the Congregation.[13]

The determination of competence based on the scope of matters or business considered is the most significant. In this respect the Code did not change the definition of the Congregation's power given by Pope Pius X, and it may be best considered next, according to the three paragraphs of Canon 253.

Can. 253, § 1. Congregatio Sacrorum Rituum ius

[8] Monin, *De Curia Romana*, p. 174.
[9] Cf. *supra*, "The Authority of the Congregation," pp. 45-66.
[10] Can. 1.
[11] Can. 253, § 1-2.
[12] Can. 1004.
[13] Ordo servandus in S. Congregationibus, Tribunalibus, Officiis Romanae Curiae, 29 sept. 1908, Pars II, Normae peculiares, cap. I, n. 1°, g) — *Fontes*, n. 6460.

habet videndi et statuendi ea omnia quae sacros ritus et caeremonias Ecclesiae Latinae proxime spectant, non autem quae latius ad sacros ritus referuntur, cuiusmodi sunt praecedentiae iura aliaque id genus, de quibus sive servato ordine iudiciario sive in linea disciplinari disceptetur.

This paragraph first describes the kind of power which the Congregation of Rites possesses, namely the *"ius videndi et statuendi,"* the right of providing and establishing. The nature of this power has been considered earlier.[14] Its object is "all those things which pertain proximately to the sacred rites and ceremonies of the Latin Church." This is a statement in the most general terms of the power to regulate the entire liturgy of the Latin Church.

The use of the expression, *sacros ritus et caeremonias,* is the equivalent of the sacred liturgy, that is, the worship of God by His Church. While "ceremonies" refers to the outward and accidental acts of worship, "sacred rites" embraces the entire order of services and functions which make up the liturgy.[15] In the Code the expression is used in several places in the most general sense, to include the whole of liturgical law, that is, the rubrics and the rules which govern the performance of Catholic worship.[16] This includes all the ritual law of the Mass, the sacraments, the divine Offices, and all that may be referred to by the name of sacramentals.[17] Under the latter fall the prayers, blessings, and exorcisms not contained in the functions of Mass, sacraments, and Office. These are principally sacred words and actions; there are, besides, the things used and necessary for the celebration of the

---

[14] Cf. *supra,* "The Authority of the Congregation," pp. 54-55.

[15] Oppenheim, *Institutiones in Sacram Liturgiam,* III, 41-42; Menghini, *Elementa Iuris Liturgici,* p. 27.

[16] Michiels, *Normae Generales,* I, 57-58. Cf. can. 2; 249, § 1; 733, § 1; 2378. The phrase also appears as the rubric of chapters in the law of sacraments: Cap. III of Title I (Baptism), Liber III; Cap. III of Title V (Extreme Unction), Liber III; Cap. IV of Title VI (Orders), Liber III. In the same book of the Code, in Title III (on the Holy Eucharist), the rubric of Art. II of Cap. I is: *De Missae ritibus et caeremoniis.*

[17] Can. 1144. Cf. Monin, *De Curia Romana,* p. 301.

holy liturgy, such as churches and altars, sacred furnishings, vessels and vesture.[18]   Moreover, there must be added the regulation of the ecclesiastical arts employed in the liturgy or in the adornment of sacred things, including liturgical music.

This interpretation of "sacred rites and ceremonies" to embrace the government of the entire liturgy is confirmed by the elaboration of the phrase in the second paragraph of Canon 253, which speaks more specifically of the Congregation's competence as "the celebration of Mass, the administration of the sacraments, the performance of the divine Office, and finally all that pertains to the worship of the Latin Church." It is in harmony also with a recent declaration and description of the Congregation of Rites by Pope Pius XII:

> The Church has used the right in liturgical matters of protecting the sacredness of divine worship against the abuses temerariously and imprudently introduced by private individuals and particular churches. And so it happened that, since in the sixteenth century uses and customs of this kind had increased so greatly and the inventions of private persons in this matter endangered the integrity of faith and piety, with great profit to heretics and wide propagation of their false teachings, Our Predecessor of immortal memory, Sixtus V, established the Congregation of Sacred Rites in the year 1588, in order to defend the lawful rites of the Church and to prohibit in them any corruption that might have been introduced. Even in our age it pertains to the official function of that institution to ordain and decree with vigilant concern all those things that have to do with the sacred Liturgy.[19]

[18] Crnica, *Commentarium Theoretico-practicum*, I, 242.

[19] *Mediator Dei: . . . . Tum Decessor Noster imm. mem. Sixtus V, ut legitimos Ecclesiae ritus defenderet, ab iisdemque quidquid impurum inductum fuisset prohiberet, anno MDLXXXVIII Sacrum constituit tuendis ritibus Consilium; ad quod quidem institutum nostra etiam aetate ex credito munere pertinet ea omnia vigilanti cura ordinare ac decernere, quae ad sacram Liturgiam spectant. — AAS,* XXXIX (1947), 543.

The competence of the Congregation over matters touching the sacred liturgy is limited, however, in several ways. It is restricted by Canon 253, § 1, to the sacred rites and ceremonies of the Latin Church;[20] it has no authority in liturgical matters when questions of doctrine arise; and its power over the liturgy itself is confined to things pertaining proximately to the actual rites of worship.

First of all, the term "Latin Church," as used here, has reference to the Western Church, that is, to all the churches which belong to the patriarchate of the West. It is used in distinction to the Oriental Churches and is the equivalent of non-Oriental Church. The competence of the Congregation extends to the liturgy of the entire Latin Church and to it alone. Just as the Oriental Churches are excluded from the Latin Code, which is the Code of the Western Church, so their sacred rites are excluded from the power of the Congregation.

Although the enumeration of the powers of the Congregation of Sacred Rites before 1908 did not mention this limitation of its scope to the Latin Church, it should not be thought that this forms a new restriction upon the Congregation. In the seventeenth and eighteenth centuries, for example, there were particular Congregations appointed to deal with the liturgies of the East, the *Congregatio super correctione Euchologii Graecorum* (1636-1645) and the *Congregatio super correctione librorum Ecclesiae Orientalis* (1717).[21] The same was true in the nineteenth century, when Pius IX directed that the examination of the liturgical books of the East be handled by the section of the Congregation for the Propagation of the Faith which concerned itself with the affairs of the oriental rites.[22] In other words, the competence of the Congregation of Sacred Rites is and has been in the past logically confined to the Latin Church.

[20] § 2 makes the same reference: *Ecclesiae Latinae cultum.*

[21] *Statistica della Gerarchia e dei Fedeli di Rito Orientale* (Roma, 1932), p. 12. Cf. Benedictus XIV, litt. *Ex quo,* 1 mart. 1756 — *Fontes,* n. 438.

[22] Dziob, *The Sacred Congregation for the Oriental Church,* The Catholic University of America Canon Law Studies, n. 214 (Washington, D. C.: The Catholic University of America Press, 1945), pp. 55-56.

A further exception must be made. Even within the Latin Church, the Congregation of Rites is not competent with regard to the particular liturgical rites celebrated in the Pontifical Chapel, or celebrated by Cardinals even outside the Pontifical Chapel.[23] Although there is no mention of it in Canon 253, this limitation is clear from the competence of the Ceremonial Congregation.[24] The restriction does not materially affect the competence of the Congregation of Rites, which is still properly said to extend to the entire Latin Church.

The principal rite of the Latin Church is, of course, the Roman. It is followed by the greatest number of members of the Western Church, so that the non-Roman rites of the West appear to be exceptions, however distinct and independent may be their origin. For the most part, the other rites of the West have Latin as their official liturgical language, and from this fact the term, Latin Church, derives.[25] It is not accurate, however, to say that the Latin Church is that in which the liturgy uses the Latin language.[26] An exception is to be found in the liturgical use of the Paleo-Slavonic or Glagolitic language in certain parts of Jugoslavia;[27] this is nonetheless a rite of the Latin Church, and its liturgy is subject to the Congregation of Rites, as may be seen from the decrees of the latter.[28]

Among the non-Roman rites of the West, the independent rites of Milan and Toledo are the most venerable. The former is the Ambrosian Rite and is used in many parishes of Milan, as well as in other dioceses of Northern Italy and Italian Switzerland;[29] the latter is called the Mozarabic Rite, and is now very little used.[30]

---

[23] Monin, *De Curia Romana*, p. 299.

[24] Can. 254; cf. *infra*, pp. 101-102.

[25] Cicognani, *Canon Law*, p. 446.

[26] Blat (*Commentarium Textus Codicis Iuris Canonici*, II, 269) makes this statement.

[27] In the provinces of Gorizia, Zagreb, and Zara.

[28] E.g., S.R.C., *Resolutiones*, 13 febr. 1892 — D. 3768; S.R.C., decr. 18 dec. 1906 — D. 4196.

[29] Van Hove, *De Legibus*, p. 12.

[30] Ferreres, *Institutiones Canonicae*, I, 309-311; King, *Notes on the Catholic Liturgies*, p. 253.

There are also certain lesser Roman rites, largely derived from medieval usages, in Braga and Lyons, and in various religious institutes. The latter include the monastic rites of the Benedictines, Cistercians, and Carthusians, and those of the Premonstratensians, Dominicans, and Carmelites.[81]

All of these rites, Roman and non-Roman, fall within the competence of the Congregation of Sacred Rites. This may be observed in many of its decrees.[82] Because of the comparatively small numbers belonging to the various rites, they are of lesser importance in the activity of the Congregation of Sacred Rites. On the other hand, the Holy See encourages their preservation and continuance, at least with reference to those of ancient origin. In the sixteenth century unification of the liturgy in the Western Church, those rites which dated from antiquity or which could prove a usage of two centuries were expressly allowed to continue without change.[83]

Another restriction upon the competence of the Congregation of Rites, different from the above, exists with regard to matters of faith. In the regulation of the liturgy, the Congregation of Rites must always yield to the Congregation of the Holy Office in what pertains to the articles of faith. This limitation is not mentioned in Canon 253,[84] but is evident from the absolute nature of the Holy Office's power among the Roman Congregation in doctrinal matters.[85] It is specifically declared (with reference to the approval

[81] Monin, *De Curia Romana*, p. 299; Van Hove, *De Legibus*, p. 12, footnote n. 5.

[82] E.g., S.R.C., *Ordinis Carthusianorum*, 22 nov. 1687 (on the Carthusian Breviary and Missal) — *AIP*, VIII (1865), 1292-1295; S.R.C., *Novarien.*, 3 apr. 1821 (on the Ambrosian Rite) — D. 2614; S.R.C., *Mediolanen.*, 16 mart. 1939 (on a new edition of the *Vesperale Ambrosianum*) — *Ephemerides Liturgicae*, LIII (1939), 138; *Ephemerides Liturgicae*, XXXIV (1920), 430-436 (on the liturgical books of Braga in Portugal).

[83] Pius V, litt. ap., *Quod a Nobis*, 9 iul. 1568 — *BRT*, VII, 685-688; litt. ap. *Quo primum tempore*, 14 iul. 1570 — *BRT*, VII, 839-841.

[84] The meaning of *"proxime"* in this Canon, which is to be considered next, does not directly exclude doctrinal truths as found in sacred rites from the competence of the Congregation of Rites. These are in fact intimately bound up with the practice of worship.

[85] Can. 247, § 1; 249, § 1; 251, § 2; 257, § 2. Cf. *infra*, pp. 91-92.

of liturgical books) in the *Normae Peculiares* of 1908, in these words: *salva Sancti Officii competentia in iis quae fidei capita, seu dogmata, respiciunt.*[36]

In practice, no difficulty arises from this. The Congregation of Rites is incompetent when questions arise bearing on the rites essential to the validity of the Mass or the sacraments,[37] nor can it decide doctrinal questions as such merely because these are found in the text or actions of sacred rites. Its broad power to correct abuses in the practice of the liturgy,[38] moreover, does not give it competence to settle doubts which concern errors of doctrine or superstitious rites.

The third and final restriction to be noted in the examination of the first paragraph of Canon 253 arises from the use of the word *"proxime."* The Congregation is to exercise its authority over sacred rites and ceremonies, but only in those things which pertain *proximately* to them. To this is contrasted (and excluded from the competence of the Congregation) whatever refers only more broadly to sacred rites. Lastly, an example is offered of what belongs to sacred rites only *latius,* namely, rights of precedence and other things of this kind. In such cases, whether the question is to be settled judicially or administratively, the Congregation is not competent.[39]

The insistence in the terms of this Canon (and in the Constitution *Sapienti consilio*) that "sacred rites and ceremonies" must be considered strictly was in fact a change in the actual power of the Congregation of Rites. For several reasons the Congregation had exercised authority, in practice, over some matters only remotely connected with the celebration of rites. There was no Congregation in the Curia before 1908 competent as to the general discipline

---

[36] Cap. VII, art. VIII, n. 2°, *a*).

[37] Monin, *De Curia Romana*, p. 300.

[38] Can. 253, § 2.

[39] The reason for the phrase, *sive servato ordine iudiciario sive in linea disciplinari,* in this paragraph of Canon 253 seems to be the complete exclusion from the competence of the Congregation of Rites of anything not proximately connected with sacred rites. If the judicial order is observed, such cases belong to the Roman Rota; if the disciplinary or administrative order is used, such cases belong to one of the other Roman Congregations.

of the Mass and the sacraments, over and above the rites and ceremonies; there are many matters which have an accidental or material connection with the liturgy itself;[40] and there was in the system of Congregations a considerable degree of cumulative jurisdiction. Thus the terms of Canon 253 restore the Congregation of Rites to its original competence, at least for the most part, by limiting its scope to things pertaining directly to rites and ceremonies.

Because the Congregation had concerned itself to a large extent with questions of precedence,[41] even outside of liturgical functions,[42] precedence is used as an example of a matter no longer to be considered as strictly liturgical, but merely as something more widely connected with sacred rites. Henceforward questions of precedence would belong, not to the Congregation of Rites,[43] but to the Congregation of the Council, the Ceremonial Congregation, and the Congregation of Religious;[44] they belong to the Roman Rota, if they are to be decided judicially.

Many other matters are connected with the liturgy in a broad sense only, for example, what pertains to the discipline of the Mass and the sacraments. This includes the various elements of time, place, and conditions of celebration, administration, and reception. None of these is proximately connected with the sacred function itself; they belong rather to the discipline of the clergy and the

[40] Monin, *De Curia Romana*, p. 300, footnote n. 1.

[41] This, of course, belonged properly to the Congregation according to the terms of the *Immensa aeterni Dei* of Sixtus V.

[42] Monin (*op. cit.*, p. 28) explains that in the old Curia the Congregation of Rites considered questions of precedence in liturgical functions to the exclusion of the other Congregations, and had cumulative jurisdiction over such questions in extra-liturgical matters with the Congregation of Bishops and Regulars, the Congregation of the Council, and the Roman Rota.

[43] Toso (*Ad Codicem Juris Canonici Commentaria Minora*, III, 64) makes the reasonable distinction between liturgical precedence, when one enjoys precedence according to liturgical laws, celebrating or ministering at the altar, and personal precedence which flows from one's juridic status. The former, he maintains, still falls within the competence of the Congregation of Rites. This would mean that the Congregation would have the right to determine the position of ministers and servers in a liturgical procession, but not the right to settle the order of those who walk in the same procession according to their rank, dignity, or power.

[44] Cf. *infra*, pp. 98-100; 101-102.

people on the occasion of the sacred function.[45] Authors give such specific examples as the regulation of bination, the juridic effects of absence from choir, the *Missa pro populo,* the monastic enclosure, the *iura funeralia.*[46] To these may be added further instances: Of the law on churches and altars, only that part belongs to the competence of the Congregation of Rites which is a part of the function of consecration or blessing; the liturgical observance of vigils and fasts belongs to the care of the Congregation, the law of fasting does not; and the form of blessing to be used for sacramentals is determined by the Congregation, although it may not attach indulgences to the same sacramentals.

The distinction between matters pertaining proximately to sacred rites and matters pertaining less directly is best made by examples, such as those just given. This is in fact the means of distinction employed by Pius X and by the Code, in an attempt to make certain that each Congregation has exclusive jurisdiction over its own field.[47] Further illustration, besides the initial determinations of competence, is afforded by the faculties belonging to a given Congregation, in this case the Congregation of Rites.[48]

By way of summary, it may be said that the Congregation of Rites enjoys competence over whatever touches the execution of the acts of divine worship in the Latin Church.[49]

[45] Monin, *De Curia Romana,* pp. 299-300.

[46] Simier, *La Curie Romaine,* p. 70, footnote n. 1; DeMeester, *Juris Canonici et Juris Canonico-Civilis Compendium,* II, 87.

[47] Pius X (const. *Sapienti consilio,* 29 iun. 1908) saw in his reform of the Curia and the elimination of the confusion of cumulative jurisdiction the beginning of the collection of ecclesiastical law: *Quo factum est ut hodie singularum iurisdictio, seu* competentia, *non omnibus perspicua nec bene divisa evaserit; plures ex Sacris Congregationibus eadem de re ius dicere valeant, et nonnullae ad pauca tantum negotia expedienda redactae sunt, dum aliae negotiis obruuntur. . . . Cum vero in praesenti res quoque sit de ecclesiasticis legibus in unum colligendis, maxime opportunum visum est a Romana Curia ducere initium, ut ipsa, modo apto et omnibus perspicuo ordinata, Romano Pontifici Ecclesiaeque operam suam praestare facilius valeat et suppetias ferre perfectius.* — *Fontes,* n. 682. For the consideration of matters referring only in a broad sense to sacred rites, which are the concern of Congregations other than the Congregation of Rites, cf. *infra,* "Relation to the Other Congregations," pp. 91-102.

[48] Cf. *infra,* pp. 105-115.

[49] Martin, *Les Congrégations Romaines,* p. 154.

After this general consideration of the competence of the Con-grègation of Sacred Rites as given in the first paragraph of Canon 253, and as further defined by the principal limitations set forth there, certain more specific powers need to be mentioned. Some of these, of less significant character, are enumerated in the second paragraph of the same canon; others are given expressly by Pius X[50] and fall logically under this discussion of the Congrega-tion's jurisdiction.

The first of the latter powers is the regulation of the liturgical books of the Latin Church, a power possessed by the Congregation of Rites from its institution and one of the highest importance. Concerning these books and their publication, the Code legislates in several places, reserving the right to approve them in Canon 1257,[51] requiring proper attestation that editions of them conform to the texts approved, according to Canon 1390,[52] and including in-correct editions among prohibited books, in Canon 1399, 10°.[53]

Much of the activity of the Congregation of Rites is concerned with the preparation of liturgical books.[54] It has enlarged upon the prescriptions of Canon 1390 in two general decrees, one prior to the Code, one issued in 1946. The first determines the differ-ence between an *Editio Typica* of a liturgical book, one submitted page by page for the approval of the Congregation and thus made authentic in every way, and an *Editio iuxta Typicam*, published with the attestation of the respective Ordinary that the text con-

[50] Ordo servandus in S. Congregationibus, Tribunalibus, Officiis Romanae Curiae, 29 sept. 1908, Pars II, Normae peculiares, cap. VII, art. VIII, n. 2° — *Fontes*, n. 6460. As has been mentioned several times, Canon 243, § 1, confirms these norms, unless they are modified by other legislation.

[51] *Unius Apostolicae Sedis est tum sacram ordinare liturgiam, tum liturgicos approbare libros.*

[52] *In edendis libris liturgicis eorumque partibus, itemque litaniis a Sancta Sede approbatis, debet de concordantia cum editionibus approbatis constare ex attesta-tione Ordinarii loci in quo imprimuntur aut publici iuris fiunt.*

[53] *Editiones librorum liturgicorum a Sede Apostolica approbatorum, in quibus quidpiam immutatum fuerit, ita ut cum authenticis editionibus a Sancta Sede approbatis non congruant.*

[54] Research of a historical nature in this connection was included among the duties of the new *Sectio Historica* created in 1930 — Pius XI, motu propr. *Già da qualche tempo,* 6 febr. 1930, III, 8 — *AAS*, XXII (1930), 87-88.

forms perfectly to the Typical Edition.[55]   In 1946 the Congregation made a further restriction, to the effect that its permission was necessary for the publication of any liturgical books, and this over and above the certification of concordance given by the Ordinary.[56]

The following are the liturgical books of the Roman Rite,[57] as enumerated in 1946 by the Congregation itself:[58]

Brevarium Romanum—the text for the canonical hours of the Divine Office.[59]

Missale Romanum—the text for the Sacrifice of the Mass and functions directly connected with it.[60]

---

[55] S.R.C., decr. 17 maii 1911 — D. 4266. The terms of Canon 1390 summarize and confirm what is given in detail in this decree. The decree, among other things, restricts the publication of Typical Editions to the Vatican Press and other Pontifical Printers, who obtain the permission of the Congregation.

[56] S.R.C., decr. 10 aug. 1946 — *AAS*, XXXVIII (1946), 371-372. This decree determines that only the Vatican Press has the right to publish liturgical books; all other publishers and printers, including those who hold a pontifical certificate, require permission as often as they desire to publish such books.

[57] The liturgical books of the other rites of the Latin Church, which also need the approbation of the Congregation, correspond in general to the more important Roman books, that is, they include Missal, Breviary, etc. Cf. S.R.C., decr. 6 febr. 1920 — *AAS*, XII (1920), 333-334 (for Braga); S.R.C., *Mediolanen.*, 16 mart. 1939 — *Ephemerides Liturgicae*, LIII (1939), 138 (for the Ambrosian Rite).

[58] S.R.C., decr. 10 aug. 1946 — *AAS*, XXXVIII (1946), 371-372. The decree of 1911 cited above gives a similar enumeration; it does not mention the *Octavarium Romanum* (which may be included under the Breviary), but it adds specifically the *Instructio Clementina* (included in the collection of decrees of the S.R.C.) and the Propers "of Offices and Masses of any Diocese, Order, or Religious Congregation" (which fall under the Missal and Breviary, in the listing of 1946). — S.R.C., decr. 17 maii 1911 — D. 4266.

[59] A new typical edition appeared in 1948 — S.R.C., decr. 21 dec. 1948; *Ephemerides Liturgicae*, LXIV (1950), 301. The previous typical edition was published in 1914, after the liturgical reform of Pius X — S.R.C., decr. 25 mart. 1914 — *AAS*, V (1914), 192-193; 672. The corresponding liturgical book containing the chant of the Divine Office is the *Antiphonale Diurnum*, approved in 1912 — S.R.C., decr. 8 dec. 1912 — *AAS*, IV (1913), 727; a Vatican edition of the chants of Matins has not appeared since the reform of Pius X.

[60] Typical edition 1920 — S.R.C., decr. 25 iul. 1920 — *AAS*, XII (1920), 448-449. Several editions *post Typicam* have since been published, with minor changes. The *Kyriale* (1905) and *Graduale* (1907) are the principal corresponding books of chant.

Rituale Romanum—the text for the administration of the sacraments, blessings, exsequies, processions, litanies, and exorcisms.[61]

Pontificale Romanum—the text for the celebration of pontifical functions, corresponding to the *Rituale* for the priest.[62]

Martyrologium Romanum—the text, used liturgically in the hour of Prime, containing notices of feasts and saints.[63]

Caeremoniale Episcoporum—a book of ceremonial directions for the celebration of the functions of the Missal and the Breviary in pontifical rite; it does not contain the texts of these rites.[64]

Memoriale Rituum—a book of ceremonial for use in smaller churches on certain occasions.[65]

Octavarium Romanum—the text of lessons (for the second and

[61] Only the sacrament of Orders is omitted from this book, as belonging exclusively to the *Pontificale;* much of the law of the Code on the sacraments is included in the Ritual, even though it does not pertain strictly to the rites themselves, but to the general discipline of the sacraments. Typical edition 1952 — S.R.C., decr. 25 ian. 1952. A typical edition was published after the Code, in order that the new law might be introduced into the Ritual (S.R.C., decr. 10 iun. 1925 — *AAS*, XVII [1925], 326). The 1952 edition rearranges the order of the Ritual, without making extensive changes in any of the rites.

[62] A typical edition has not been published since 1888, during the pontificate of Leo XIII — Oppenheim, *Institutiones in Sacram Liturgiam*, IV, 115-116; Callewaert, *Liturgicae Institutiones*, I, 103. A commission to emend the *Pontificale* was set up in 1931, but a new edition has not yet appeared. Cf. *Ephemerides Liturgicae*, XLVIII (1934), 591; Nabuco, *Pontificalis Romani Expositio Juridico-Practica* (3 vols., Petropolis, Brazil: Vozes, 1945), I, 30-31.

[63] This forms a kind of supplement to the Breviary. Typical edition 1914 — S.R.C., decr. 23 apr. 1914 — *AAS*, V (1914), 278. Revised editions have since been published. Cf. Oppenheim, *Institutiones in Sacram Liturgiam*, IV, 118; Moretti, *Caeremoniale iuxta Ritum Romanum seu De Sacris Functionibus* (4 vols., Taurini: Marietti, 1936-1939), I, 4.

[64] The regulations for the functions whose text is found in the *Pontificale* are not given in this book. On the other hand, much of the book is applicable to non-pontifical rites and obliges in such cases, according to repeated decrees of the S.R.C. (*Senen.*, 19 apr. 1681 — D. 1666; *Limburgen.*, 14 iun. 1845 — D. 2888, ad 2; *Angelopolitana*, 17 aug. 1894 — D. 3839, ad 1). The last typical edition dates from the time of Leo XIII and was published in 1886 — Oppenheim, *op. cit.*, IV, 119-120.

[65] The *Memoriale Rituum* is supplementary to the rubrics of the Missal. After the Code, in 1920, a typical edition was published — S.R.C., decr. 14 ian. 1920 — *AAS*, XII (1920), 448.

third nocturns of Matins) to be used during octaves celebrated in particular churches but not universally.[66]

Collectio Decretorum—the decrees of the Congregation of Sacred Rites, as authentically collected.[67]

In addition to these books, there are various excerpts taken from them and so published, for example, *Horae Diurnae* or *Missae Defunctorum.* There are, moreover, the Propers of moral persons, containing formularies for particular dioceses and religious institutes. These may be considered as supplements to the Missal and the Breviary. All such publications are equally subject to the authority of the Congregation of Sacred Rites.

The second of the powers listed in the *Normae Peculiares* of Pius X is the examination and approval of new divine Offices and calendars.[68] This matter is intimately connected with the Congregation's competence over the liturgical books. Although there have been few changes in the Roman liturgy since the time of Pius V, the addition and subtraction of feasts has gone on intermittently in these last centuries. This is true of the calendar of the universal Church and also of the calendars of particular churches.

With the institution of a new feast, the preparation of a new Mass and Office is done by the Congregation or by a commission within it,[69] just as is the case with new texts to be added, for ex-

[66] The last typical edition of this book appeared in 1883 — Oppenheim, *op. cit.,* IV, 119; Callewaert, *Liturgicae Institutiones,* I, 103. Another book of lessons appeared, in a typical edition, in 1914, to be used in last place at Matins for the commemoration of feasts. It was called *Lectiones Contractae pro Festis Universalis Ecclesiae ad Matutinum Legendae* — S.R.C., decr. 24 iun. 1914 — *Ephemerides Liturgicae,* XXVIII (1914), 641-642.

[67] Cf. *infra,* "Collections of Decrees," pp. 148-149. These appeared in 1898-1901 (5 vols.), 1912 (Vol. VI), and 1927 (Vol. VII), under the title, *Decreta Authentica Sacrae Congregationis Sacrorum Rituum.* Volume IV (pp. 3-151) contains the *Instructio Clementina,* giving directions for the celebration of the Forty Hours' Prayer. The *Instructio* has been subsequently modified somewhat by the Congregation in the decree *Romana,* 27 apr. 1927 — *AAS,* XIX (1927), 192.

[68] Cap. VII, art. VIII, n. 2°, b).

[69] E. g., S.R.C., *Urbis et Orbis,* 9 ian. 1942 — *AAS,* XXXIV (1942), 25; S.R.C., *Urbis et Orbis,* 4 maii 1944 — *AAS,* XXXVII (1945), 44.

ample, to the Ritual.[70]   Likewise, it belongs to the Congregation to approve local calendars and the adoption of proper feasts by dioceses and religious institutes.[71]

The third matter mentioned in the *Normae Peculiares* is the power of the Congregation to judge and decide doubts concerning rites.[72]   This is, of course, a restatement of the original competence of the Congregation—"to examine, conclude summarily, and settle controversies"—with all reference to precedence now omitted, since it has been eliminated from the Congregation's scope. There is no need to describe in any detail this power; its exercise is apparent from the collected decrees which deal for the most part with the settlement of questions and doubts arising in liturgical law. It should be noted that the doubts which are to be decided concerning rites must fall strictly within the competence of the Congregation, as already described, and not pertain only broadly to the liturgical rites.

Thus an examination of the first paragraph of Canon 253 gives a general view of the competence of the Congregation of Rites. In summary, it includes all matters belonging proximately to sacred rites and ceremonies. This includes the powers just enumerated specifically, namely, over the liturgical books, new offices and calendars, and the resolution of doubts. It is restricted to the Latin Church, and it excludes questions that are strictly dogmatic and also whatever relates to the sacred functions in a broad sense only.

Can. 253, § 2.   Eius proinde est praesertim advigilare, ut sacri ritus ac caeremoniae diligenter serventur in Sacro celebrando, in Sacramentis administrandis, in divinis officiis persolvendis, in iis denique omnibus quae Ecclesiae Latinae cultum respiciunt; dispensationes concedere opportunas; in-

---

[70] A blessing for mountain-climbing equipment was approved in 1931 — S.R.C., decr. 14 oct. 1931 — *AAS*, XXIII (1931), 446; for hospitals in 1939 — S.R.C., *Urbis et Orbis*, 18 iul. 1939 — *AAS*, XXXII (1940), 197.

[71] Some of the exact powers of the Congregation are best seen by an examination of its faculties in this regard. Cf. *infra*, pp. 107-108; 110; 113.

[72] Cap. VII, art. VIII, n. 2°, *c*).

signia et honoris privilegia tam personalia et ad tempus, quam localia et perpetua, quae ad sacros ritus vel caeremonias pertineant, elargiri, et cavere ne in haec abusus irrepant.

There is much less to be said concerning this second paragraph of Canon 253. It gives three specific areas of competence belonging to the Congregation of Sacred Rites, which are determinations of the general terms of the first paragraph rather than an enlargement of them.

The first clause imposes upon the Congregation the duty and office of vigilance over the observance of sacred rites and ceremonies, and it defines the liturgical services intended. These are the celebration of Mass, the administration of the sacraments, the performance of the divine Office, and all other matters touching upon the cult offered to God by the Latin Church. The enumeration is not materially different from the general competence defined in the first paragraph of the same canon.

In fulfilling the office of vigilance over sacred rites, the Congregation has both positive and negative powers: positive, to see that the rites of worship are carried out properly and in accordance with the text and rubrics of the liturgical books; negative, to remove any erroneous usages or abuses. Both aspects belonged to the original competence of the Congregation: to take care that ancient sacred rites be carefully observed and that ceremonies be restored, if they had become obsolete, and reformed, if they had been corrupted.[73]

To see how the Congregation of Rites has exercised its powers to require observance of ritual law, it would be necessary to review its entire competence. The Congregation's decrees give many examples where it has insisted upon compliance with the rubrics[74] and where it has removed corruptions or abuses.[75]

[73] Sixtus V, const. *Immensa aeterni Dei*, 22 ian. 1588 — *BRT*, VIII, 989-900.

[74] E. g., S.R.C., *Sanctorien.*, 12 sept. 1884 — D. 3622, ad 5; S.R.C., *Portus Principis*, 11 aug. 1888 — D. 3694, ad 2; S.R.C., *Pacen.*, 24 ian. 1890 — D. 3722, ad 5; *Macaonen.*, 10 maii 1895 — D. 3854, ad 2, 6, 9.

[75] E.g., S.R.C., decr. gen. 3 apr. 1821 — D. 2613, ad 6; S.R.C., *Taurinen.*, 22 iun. 1874 — D. 3333, ad 2; S.R.C., *Lucionen.*, 29 dec. 1884 — D. 3624, ad 11.

The next clause of the second paragraph deals with the concession of dispensations. This must, of course, be interpreted in the light of what has been said of the competence of the Congregation of Rites. The dispensations must fall within the field of what pertains proximately to sacred rites and ceremonies. In practice, such dispensations will be those found in the Congregation's catalogue of faculties, or others which are similar to them.[76]

The third clause of Canon 253, § 2, refers to the kinds of insignia and honorary privileges which the Congregation may grant. Concerning them a restriction in keeping with the scope of the Congregation's competence is made: they must pertain to sacred rites and ceremonies. Moreover, the Congregation is to take care that there is no abuse of such favors.

There should be no difficulty offered by the kinds of insignia and privileges. Those which are local and permanent are attached to churches or places, for example, the title of minor basilica conceded to a church or the naming of a patron for a place or group. Those which are personal and temporary are granted to individuals, for example, the permission to use *pontificalia* or to perform reserved blessings.[77] The same distinction is found in the Code in connection with the law on privileges.[78]

Can. 253, § 3. Denique ea omnia agit quae ad beatificationem et canonizationem Servorum Dei vel ad sacras reliquias quoquo modo referuntur.

The third paragraph of Canon 253 concedes a twofold competence to the Congregation of Rites—over the causes of the Servants of God and over relics. This is done in the broadest terms. Whatever pertains to either of these matters in any way comes within the competence of the Congregation.

Processes of beatification and canonization are *causae maiores*.[79]

---

[76] Cf. *infra*, "Faculties of the Congregation," pp. 105-115.

[77] Monin, *De Curia Romana*, p. 302.

[78] Can. 74-75.

[79] Reiffenstuel, *Ius Canonicum Universum*, Lib. III, tit. 45, n. 6; Schmalzgrüber, *Ius Ecclesiasticum Universum*, Lib. III, tit. 45, n. 3.

As such, they are reserved to the Apostolic See,[80] and the Roman Pontiffs have entirely excluded them, in spite of their judicial character, from the competence of the Roman Rota.[81]   Canon 1999, § 2, repeats the designation of the Congregation of Rites as the sole competent authority in these cases: . . . . *una Sacrorum Rituum Congregatio in his causis competens est.*

Little need be said concerning the Congregation's power in the causes of the Servants of God, although it is of the greatest importance and occupies a large part in the Congregation's activity. Since its power is complete, it is rather with the special modes of procedure employed for the processes that any discussion should be concerned.

The competence of the Congregation over these cases does not extend to any general doctrinal decisions, which are reserved to the Holy Office.[82]   An important feature of the procedure is also a limitation upon the Congregation, namely, the fact that all the major steps in the process must be referred to the Roman Pontiff personally for approval.[83]

In the nature of its work, the Congregation is largely concerned with the individual causes of the Servants of God proposed to its consideration. And in this its procedure is governed by the lengthy norms of *Pars Secunda* of the fourth Book of the Code.[84]   In addition, the Congregation on occasion publishes further norms of a general character to govern its own procedure and that of those who approach the Congregation in connection with these processes.[85]   It also is given a specific power by the Code to examine and approve books dealing with the causes of the Servants of God: "Whatever pertains in any way to the causes of beatification

---

[80] Can. 1999, § 1.

[81] Can. 259; Lex propria S. R. Rotae et Signaturae Ap., 29 iun. 1908, can. 15. — *Fontes,* n. 682.

[82] Can. 247, § 1.

[83] Can. 2071; 2083, § 1; 2100, §3; 2107; 2111; 2132.

[84] *De Causis Beatificationis Servorum Dei et Canonizationis Beatorum.*

[85] Before the Code, these were not infrequent; the Code summarized the earlier procedure. A more recent example is S.R.C., decr. 15 ian. 1935 — *AAS,* XXVII (1935), 58.

and canonization of the Servants of God cannot be published without the permission of the Congregation of Sacred Rites."[86]

With reference to the other matter mentioned in the last paragraph of Canon 253, sacred relics, the Congregation of Rites is in part the heir of the competence of the Congregation of Indulgences and Sacred Relics, with which it was united from 1904 to 1908.[87] Yet it must not be supposed that such matters were not considered by the Congregation of Rites during its earlier history. Even in the early seventeenth century it gave frequent decisions regarding sacred relics.[88] What may be called the native right of the Congregation over relics arose in three ways: the decisions made regarding relics in connection with its exclusive competence over beatification and canonization; the concession of the Mass and Offices of relics;[89] and the regulation of the use of relics in the course of sacred functions.[90] Thus the Congregation possessed a large share of power over sacred relics even during the existence of the special Congregation of Indulgences and Relics founded in 1669 by Clement IX.[91]

The latter Congregation received the right to examine and dispose of sacred relics, in order that abuses in connection with them might be eliminated. It was empowered to settle controversies and doubts concerning relics, except dogmatic questions (within the province of the Holy Office), graver and more difficult cases (to be submitted to the Roman Pontiff), and matters which required judicial trial (to be referred to the proper judges).[92] At a later

[86] Can. 1387: *Quae ad causas beatificationum et canonizationum Servorum Dei quoquo modo pertinent, sine licentia Sacrorum Rituum Congregationis edi nequeunt.*

[87] Cf. *supra*, p. 36.

[88] E.g., S.R.C., *Urbis*, 8 apr. 1628 — D. 460, ad 3; S.R.C., *Urbis*, 16 oct. 1628 — D. 477, ad 4; S.R.C., *Urbis et Orbis*, 13 ian. 1631 — D. 555.

[89] E.g., S.R.C., decr. 13 febr. 1666 — D. 1334; S.R.C., decr. gen. 19 oct. 1691 — D. 1853; S.R.C., *Toletana*, 20 sept. 1806 — D. 2564, ad 1; S.R.C., decr. 5 nov. 1914 — *AAS*, VI (1914), 193-195.

[90] E.g., S.R.C., *Brixien.*, 15 sept. 1736 — D. 2324, ad 1-3; S.R.C., *Lucionen.*, 23 maii 1835 — D. 2722, ad 1, 3; S.R.C., *Florentina*, 14 iun. 1845 — D. 2887, ad 4.

[91] Dooley, *Church Law on Sacred Relics*, p. 51.

[92] Clement IX, const. *In ipsis Pontificatus*, 6 iul. 1669: . . . . *Cum facultate omnem difficultatem ac dubietatem in Sanctorum Reliquiis aut Indulgentiis*

period, Leo XIII confirmed certain faculties of the Congregation of Indulgences and Relics, namely, the right to interpret all rescripts concerning relics, and the right to decide questions of lesser moment without reference to the full Congregation.[93]

All of this power, formerly that of the Congregation of Indulgences and Sacred Relics, now belongs properly to the Congregation of Rites. It is a logical conclusion to the history of the two Congregations and gives the Congregation of Rites exclusive competence over sacred relics, so closely related to its original purpose, as Pius X noted.[94] The law governing sacred relics, according to which the Congregation proceeds, is given in a special Title of the Code,[95] as well as in the ritual books and the decrees of the Congregation. It should be added that the Congregation of Rites does not have the office of distributing relics, which is left to the Vicariate of Rome and to others.[96]

Thus the third paragraph of Canon 253 embraces the causes of the Servants of God and sacred relics within the competence of

---

emergentem, quae ad fidei dogmata non pertineat (Nobis tamen et Romano Pontifice pro tempore existenti circa graviora difficilioraque consultis) ·expediendi; ac, si qui abusus in eis irrepserint, illos iudicii forma plane postposita, corrigendi et emendandi; causas vero iudicialem formam requirentes ad proprios Iudices remittendi; . . . . Reliquias de novo inventas, quas rec. mem. Innocentius Papa III. Praedecessor Noster in generali Concilio Lateranensi publica veneratione coli nisi prius auctoritate Romani Pontificis approbatis prohibuit, recognoscendi quoque et examinandi; ac in concedendis indulgentiis, Sanctorumque Reliquiis donandis moderationem adhiberi, omniaque pie, sancte et incorrupte fieri curandi. — *BRT,* XVII, 805.

· [93] Leo XIII, litt. *Christianae Reipublicae,* 31 oct. 1897 — Galante, *Fontes Iuris Canonici Selecti,* pp. 552-553; *Archiv für katholisches Kirchenrecht* (Innsbruck, 1857-1861; Mainz, 1862-   ), LXXVIII (1898), 337-340. This in no way detracted from the competence of the Congregation of Rites at the time, and the Congregation retained the right to determine the authenticity of relics and the cult due them, in connection with the processes of beatification and canonization, as well as the right to grant Offices for sacred relics. Cf. Simier, *La Curie Romaine,* p. 70.

[94] Motu propr. *Sacrae Congregationi,* 26 maii 1906 — *Pii X Pontificis Maximi Acta,* III, 136-137.

[95] Can. 1276 - 1289.

· [96] Monin, *De Curia Romana,* pp. 78-79, footnote n. 3; Simier, *La Curie Romaine,* p. 70, footnote n. 2; Dooley, *Church Law on Sacred Relics,* p. 52.

the Congregation of Rites. They are matters related to its more general power, as expressed in the first two paragraphs, over the sacred rites and ceremonies of the Latin Church.

All of this is a positive consideration of the Congregation's jurisdiction in itself; it remains to describe its relation, with regard to competence, to the other Roman Congregations. A description of their powers in matters affecting the sacred liturgy in a broad sense will illustrate and, in part, repeat what has been said of the competence of the Congregation of Sacred Rites.

C. Relation to the Other Congregations

It is necessary to mention only those Congregations of the Roman Curia whose competence bears some relation to that of the Congregation of Sacred Rites, and to enumerate briefly the pertinent powers. The principal sources are the Code itself (repeating, in large part, what was determined by the Constitution *Sapienti consilio* of Pius X)[97] and the *Normae Peculiares* of 1908.

1. Congregation of the Holy Office

The competence of the Holy Office with reference to matters considered by the Congregation of Rites is the same as its power in relation to all the other Roman Congregations, namely, the protection of "the doctrine of faith and morals."[98] In the liturgy the truths of faith are expressed through the ritual texts. Should questions arise in the preparation or publication of the liturgical books touching upon the dogmatic truths of the Church, the competence to determine the questions would belong exclusively to the Holy Office. The terms of the *Normae Peculiares* make this clear in describing the rights of the Congregation of Sacred Rites over the liturgical books.[99]

[97] The principal changes in the Curia introduced by the Code were the suppression of the Congregation of the Index (with its competence assigned by Canon 247, § 4, to the Holy Office) and the institution of the Congregation for the Oriental Church in Canon 257. Other changes did not affect the congregational structure of the Curia.

[98] Can. 247, § 1: *Congregatio . . . . tutatur doctrinam fidei et morum.*

[99] Cap. VII, art. VIII, n. 2°, *a*).

The relation of the celebration of the liturgy to Christian belief is explained in the statement, *Lex supplicandi statuat legem credendi.*[100] This saying has been used repeatedly through the centuries as a catchword suggesting that the truths of faith are to be found in the liturgical texts. Recently Pius XII carefully clarified the real meaning of the phrase, not that the holy liturgy determines the doctrines of faith, but rather that it illustrates and professes them; in an absolute sense, the law of belief establishes the law of prayer.[101] In this sense it is plain that in matters of faith the Congregation of the Holy Office takes precedence over the others. This is especially the case with matters affecting the essentials of the Mass and the sacraments.

In the Code the Holy Office is also given competence over a specific law governing the discipline of the Holy Eucharist, the law of the Eucharistic fast for priests who are the celebrants of Mass.[102] According to the principle that matters involving the discipline of the sacraments belong to the Congregation of the Sacraments, this is an exception,[103] and the latter Congregation retains its power over the Eucharistic fast in all other cases.[104] In none of this does the Congregation of Rites have any part.

2. Congregation for the Oriental Church

Just as sacred rites and ceremonies fall under the power of the Congregation of Rites in the Latin Church, the Congregation for the Oriental Church has the same competence over the rites of the East. It has, in addition, far greater powers with regard to things remotely pertaining to ritual, such as the entire discipline of the

---

[100] Long ascribed to Pope St. Celestine I (422-432) and now with greater likelihood to St. Prosper of Aquitaine. Cf. Oppenheim, *Institutiones in Sacram Liturgiam*, II, 71-72.

[101] *Mediator Dei* — *AAS*, XXXIX (1947), 541.

[102] Can. 247, § 5.

[103] Can. 249, § 1.

[104] Another exception, made with the approbation of the Supreme Pontiff, is the recent issuance by the Holy Office of an Instruction on the entire discipline of the Eucharistic fast, for priests and lay people alike, in connection with the Apostolic Constitution *Christus Dominus* of January 6, 1953 — *AAS*, XLV (1953), 15-32; 47-56.

Eucharistic Liturgy and the sacraments. This is included in the general jurisdiction of this Congregation over all matters of persons, discipline, or rites in the Oriental Churches.[105] Its competence and faculties are the same for persons subject to it as the competence and faculties of all the other Roman Congregations, the Holy Office alone excepted, in matters within the latter's scope.[106]

From this it is clear that the Congregation of Sacred Rites has no authority over the worship of the Eastern Churches, but that the Congregation which is given their charge exercises similar authority, among its many other functions, over the oriental sacred rites. The language of Canon 253, in any case, confines the Congregation of Rites to the members of the Latin (or non-Oriental) Church.

In 1938 the competence of the Congregation of the Oriental Church was increased by Pius XI. Having determined the territories over which the Congregation was to have full and exclusive jurisdiction (in addition to its authority over Orientals outside those territories), the Pontiff decreed that it should also exercise jurisdiction over Latin Catholics in these lands.[107] Moreover, with regard to the members of the Latin Church who are thus subjected to the Congregation of the Oriental Church, the Congregation possesses the same faculties which the other Roman Congregations have for the faithful outside the territories of the East.

By itself this appears to be a restriction upon the Congregation of Sacred Rites, although the numbers of Latin Catholics in the various places are not large. The Motu Proprio establishing the new competence, however, stated that the faculties enjoyed by the Congregation of the Oriental Church were to be considered "without any lessening of the reservations which have been made to the

---

[105] Can. 257, § 1.

[106] Can. 257, § 2.

[107] Pius XI, motu propr. *Sancta Dei Ecclesia*, 25 mart. 1938 — *AAS*, XXX (1938), 157-158. The countries included are the following: Egypt and the Peninsula of Sinai, Eritrea and Northern Ethiopia, Southern Albania, Bulgaria, Cyprus, Greece, the Dodecanese Islands, Iran, Iraq, Lebanon, Palestine, Syria, Transjordan, Asiatic Turkey, and Thrace subject to Turkey. It is obvious that Latins in these countries will be a small minority among the total number of Catholics.

S. Congregation of Sacred Rites."[108]   In practice, this means that the Congregation for the Oriental Church has the same faculties and powers over the persons concerned as the Congregation for the Propagation of the Faith has for persons in its territories.[109] With regard to sacred rites, these powers are limited to the matters mentioned in Canon 253, § 2, namely, the office of seeing to the observance of liturgical law and the concession of dispensations and favors. The Congregation for the Oriental Church has no power to give or interpret the general norms of Latin sacred rites, which are strictly reserved to the Congregation of Rites, even in the case of Latins subject to the former Congregation.[110]

All of what has been said refers to the competence over sacred rites. In this the two Congregations exercise the same power over the Latin and Oriental Churches, respectively; the Oriental Congregation has in addition the right to make use of faculties in liturgical matters where Latin Catholics within its territories are concerned, but only in particular cases. A final note must be added; it has to do with the processes of the Servants of God.

The Congregation of Sacred Rites has exclusive competence over all that pertains to the beatification and canonization of the Servants of God, even in the cases of members of the Oriental Churches and in places where the Congregation for the Oriental Church is otherwise competent. This is clear positively from the use of *"quoquo modo"* in the definition of the authority of the Congregation of Rites in this regard.[111] It is clear negatively from the restriction of the Congregation for the Oriental Church to the handling of cases in the administrative order; if the Congregation judges that matters must be settled judicially, it is to send them to a tribunal of its own designation.[112] Since the causes of the Serv-

---

[108] *Loc. cit.* The text also makes special mention of the rights of the Holy Office, and refers to other Congregations whose powers, as lawfully reserved, are not diminished by the increased competence of the Congregation for the Oriental Church.

[109] Dziob, *The Sacred Congregation for the Oriental Church*, p. 132.

[110] Cf. can. 252, § 4; Dziob, *op. cit.*, p. 135.

[111] Can. 253, § 3.

[112] Can. 257, § 3.

ants of God must always be determined according to their proper
and unique judicial procedure, the Congregation for the Oriental
Church lacks all competence over them.[113]

3.   Congregation for the Discipline of the Sacraments

The relation of this Congregation to the Congregation of Sacred
Rites is principally based upon a distinction already made, between the discipline of the sacraments and the sacred rites as they
are performed or executed.   The discipline of the Mass and the
sacraments, which belongs to the Congregation being considered,
consists in matters of time, place, conditions, and circumstances;
it includes the rights and obligations of clergy and faithful which
arise on the occasion of the Mass and the sacraments.[114] In short,
and from a negative viewpoint, it is the law of the Mass and the
sacraments, exclusive of the regulation of sacred rites and ceremonies.

According to the Code, the Congregation of the Sacraments[115]
has as its field of competence all legislation concerning the discipline
of the seven sacraments, with the exception of what belongs to
the Holy Office[116] and to the Congregation of Sacred Rites. The
latter's jurisdiction is referred to in these words: *circa ritus et
caeremonias quae in Sacramentis conficiendis, ministrandis et re-
cipiendis servari debent.*[117]

The competence of the Congregation of the Sacraments extends
to the discipline of the Sacrifice of the Mass as well as to the dis-

---

[113] Cf. Dziob, *The Sacred Congregation for the Oriental Church*, pp. 111, 120-
123, where a similar conclusion is reached.

[114] Monin, *De Curia Romana*, p. 300.

[115] Either name is correct; the *Normae Peculiares* use the expressions *Congre-
gatio de Sacramentis* and *Congregatio Sacramentorum*, while the Constitution
Sapienti consilio and the Code use the longer name, *Congregatio de disciplina
Sacramentorum.*

[116] Namely, matters of faith and morals and the discipline of the Eucharistic
fast in the case of the celebrant of Mass. — Can. 247, § 1 and 5.

[117] Can. 249, § 1.

cipline of the sacraments.[118] Its principal concerns are enumerated in the Code as cases of non-consummation of matrimony, matrimonial impediments, the obligations of major Orders, the validity of sacred ordination.[119] All of these matters pertain indirectly to the sacred liturgy, but they do not touch proximately upon the rites and ceremonies which are the concern of the Congregation of Rites.

The faculties which are conceded by the Congregation of the Sacraments give a clear picture of its function in things belonging to the discipline of the sacraments. For example, it gives permission for the celebration of Mass by a blind priest or by one losing his sight; the manner of celebration, on the other hand, and the rules to be followed by such a priest are regulated by the Congregation of Rites.[120] The *Normae Peculiares* of 1908 provided a list of such faculties as pertained to the discipline of the sacraments, as follows:

1. Reservation of the Holy Eucharist in churches or in chapels lacking this right.

2. Celebration of Mass in private chapels, and other privileges which are customarily granted in this regard, taking care to see to the decency of the chapel.

3. Erection of an altar for celebration *sub dio*.

4. Celebration before dawn and after noon.[121]

5. Celebration of Mass on Holy Thursday, and likewise of three Masses Christmas night, in private chapels, with the distribution of the Holy Eucharist.[122]

[118] Can. 249, § 2. The paragraph excepts matters reserved to other Congregations. Thus, it includes the discipline of the Mass as found in Canon 802-844, in addition to the discipline of the Eucharist as a sacrament (Can. 845-869), with the exception of dogmatic questions (Holy Office), sacred rites (Can. 814-819 — Congregation of Sacred Rites), and Mass stipends (Can. 824-844 — Congregation of the Council).

[119] Can. 249, § 3.

[120] S.R.C., *Instructio*, 12 ian. 1921 — D. 4363.

[121] The need for concessions in this matter is lessened by Canon 821, § 1.

[122] The last phrase is rendered unnecessary, in most circumstances, by Canon 869. Because the terms of the *Normae Peculiares*, given here, mentioned only

6. Use of a skull-cap or other head covering in the celebration of Mass or in carrying the Holy Eucharist.

7. Permission for a blind priest or one growing blind
to celebrate with the faculty of using the votive
Mass of the Blessed Virgin Mary or the Mass for
the Dead.[123]

8. Celebration of Mass on ships.

9. Consecration of a Bishop on a day other than those
which are established in the *Pontificale Romanum*.

10. Conferral of sacred Orders *extra tempora*.

11. Exemption of the faithful, and also of religious, as
often as there is need, from the law of the Eucharistic fast.[124]

The section of the *Normae Peculiares* which follows this enumeration of faculties refers to the power of the Congregation of the
Sacraments in matrimonial cases and in dispensations from irregu-
larities for Orders, and then speaks of "questions of law concerning the place, the time, the necessary conditions for celebrating
Mass, for bination, and for the custody of the Holy Eucharist;
likewise questions of the place, the time, the conditions required
by ecclesiastical discipline for the lawful administration and reception of the other sacraments; and, at the same time, extraordinary
dispensations sought in this matter."[125]

---

private chapels, the question arose as to the right to allow the three Masses
Christmas night in other chapels and churches. In 1910 the Sacred Consistorial
Congregation — which, from the time of the Constitution *Sapienti consilio* to
the Code, had power to settle questions of controverted competence between Congregations — decided that this faculty also belonged to the Congregation of the
Sacraments, and not to the Congregation of Sacred Rites — S. C. Consist., decr.
14 mart. 1910 — *AAS*, II (1910), 56. This decision helped to clarify any doubts
as to the competence of the new Congregation for the Discipline of the Sacraments.

[123] This faculty may be conceded in other cases, for an aged or sick priest, and
for Masses other than the two mentioned. S. C. Consist., 16 aug. 1910 — *AAS*,
II (1910), 649.

[124] Cap. VII, art. III, n. 10°.

[125] Cap. VII, art. III, n. 11°, *b*).

Thus the competence of the Congregation of the Sacraments is seen to be very wide with reference to the discipline governing the Mass and the sacraments, but it has no authority over the sacred rites and ceremonies themselves, which belong to the competence of the Congregation of Rites.

4. Congregation of the Council

The Congregation of the Council must be considered at this point because it does have competence over certain matters related to the discipline of liturgical matters, and also because it deals with questions that formerly were within the competence of the Congregation of Sacred Rites.

The fundamental competence of the Congregation of the Council (which in 1908 lost its original jurisdiction, namely, that of interpreting the laws of the Council of Trent) comprises whatever refers to the discipline of the secular. clergy and the Christian people.[126] When this is made more specific, in the second paragraph of Canon 250, the Congregation's scope includes the power to dispense from the common law and to regulate whatever pertains to parish priests and canons, various kinds of societies, pious legacies and works, Mass stipends, benefices, etc. The inclusion here of whatever has to do with the chapters of canons removed from the Congregation of Rites a competence that only indirectly touched on the holy liturgy.[127]

In addition, the question of precedence is attributed to the Congregation of the Council, with the exception of the precedence of religious, which belongs to the Congregation of Religious, and the precedence of members of the Papal Court, which belongs to the Ceremonial Congregation.[128] This is a change, introduced by Pius X, taking all controversies about precedence away from the authority of the Congregation of Rites; after that time these questions were not to be considered as bearing proximately on sacred

---

[126] Can. 250, § 1.

[127] The Congregation of Rites had issued decrees, for example, concerning the erection of chapters (S.R.C., *Montis Regalis*, 4 aug. 1657 — D. ·1034), the *distributiones* received by canons (S.R.C., *Romana*, 12 iul. 1892 — D. 3780, ad 13), and absence from choir (S.R.C., *Asculana*, 30 aug. 1664 — D. 1299, ad 8).

[128] Can. 250, § 3.

rites. The rank or position of various persons, which must be observed in the course of sacred functions, is thus based upon the determination of extra-liturgical precedence.

The *Normae Peculiares* illustrate the competence of the Congregation of the Council in things broadly related to sacred rites or belonging to the discipline of liturgical functions with an enumeration of these faculties:

1. Dispensations for colleges of canons or chapters from the obligation of celebrating the Mass of a *feria* or a vigil; of chanting and applying the conventual Mass; of chanting and reciting in choir the canonical hours.

2. Anticipation of the recitation of the Office of Matins and Lauds by chapters and by individuals of the secular clergy.

3. Anticipation of Vespers and Compline before noon by chapters.

4. Commutation of the recitation of the Office with other prayers for priests of the secular clergy.

5. Dispensations from the fast prescribed before the consecration of sacred buildings.

6. Faculty of making a window in the internal wall of a church or public chapel, or of erecting a small choir, or of constructing a door, by which a private entrance is afforded.[129]

5. Congregation for Religious

Little need be said concerning the powers of this Congregation in relation to matters treated by the Congregation of Sacred Rites. It has no competence in this connection, but enjoys a jurisdiction like that of the Congregation of the Council in cases where religious persons are affected. This includes specifically dispensa-

---

[129] Cap. VII, art. IV, n. 4°. The paragraph following this repeats the competence concerning precedence or *potior dignitatis locus,* and distinguishes the matters to be reserved to the Congregation of Religious and to the Ceremonial Congregation.

tions from the common law, with the exception of the Eucharistic fast for the celebrant of Mass.[130] The faculties noted above as belonging to the Congregation of the Council, and referring to the general discipline of the liturgy, belong also to the Congregation of Religious, to the extent that they are applicable.

6. Congregation for the Propagation of the Faith

The Congregation for the Propagation of the Faith has jurisdiction over the missions and over those regions where a missionary status still remains.[131] The breadth of its competence would include as well an authority over sacred rites and ceremonies in its territories, except for the express restrictions in the Code: "But this Congregation is bound to defer to the competent Congregations affairs which touch the faith,[132] or matrimonial causes, [133] or the general norms to be handed down or interpreted concerning the discipline of sacred rites." [134]

This is an important restriction on the competence of the Congregation of Sacred Rites in those places which are subject to the Congregation for the Propagation of the Faith, since in those territories the latter Congregation is competent when "general norms" are not concerned. An examination of Canon 253, on the jurisdiction of the Congregation of Rites, suggests, however, that the powers which the Congregation for the Propagation of the Faith enjoys over sacred rites may be reduced to what is contained in the second paragraph: vigilance over the observance of rites, dispensations, and concessions of favors. Only these may be said to belong to the Congregation in particular cases, and not in cases where a general norm is to be decreed or interpreted.[135]

---

[130] Can. 251, § 3. The second paragraph requires that the Congregation transmit to the other Congregations any mixed matters, between a religious and a nonreligious, if it deems this equitable.

[131] Can. 252, § 1, 3.

[132] Holy Office.

[133] Congregation of the Sacraments.

[134] Congregation of Sacred Rites. The text is Canon 252, § 4.

[135] It is certainly incorrect to say, as Callewaert (*Liturgicae Institutiones*, I, 112, footnote n. 3) did, that the Congregation for the Propagation of the Faith enjoys in missionary places the same competence (*eadem competentia*) as the Congregation of Rites.

The principal power of the Congregation for the Propagation of the Faith in ritual matters is to be found in the faculties which it grants, of which there are several lengthy formulas, all including some that have to do with rites and ceremonies.[136] Its relation to the Congregation of Rites is seen in the inclusion of the latter's decrees in its own collections, whenever there is question of general norms of rites and ceremonies.[137] It is confirmed, moreover, by a decision of the Consistorial Congregation in 1909, which declared that while the Congregation for the Propagation of the Faith retained all its faculties referring to the Mass, Office, etc., it must defer to the Congregation of Rites in those matters which are attributed to that Congregation in the Constitution *Sapienti consilio*.[138] This was not altered by the Code.

By way of summary it may be repeated that the Congregation for the Propagation of the Faith may, in places subject to its jurisdiction, act with regard to particular cases of sacred rites and ceremonies, leaving all other matters of sacred functions to the Congregation of Rites.

7. Ceremonial Congregation

This Congregation enjoys a competence entirely distinct from that of the Congregation of Sacred Rites as to persons subject to its authority. The historical relation of the two Congregations has already been described.[139]

Sacred rites and ceremonies, in the same meaning of the expression used with regard to the Congregation of Rites, fall within the jurisdiction of the Ceremonial Congregation when these rites are celebrated in the Pontifical Chapel and also when they are celebrated by Cardinals outside the Pontifical Chapel.[140] Thus

---

[136] *Sylloge Praecipuorum Documentorum Recentium Summorum Pontificum et S. Congregationis de Propaganda Fide* (Romae: Typis Polyglottis Vaticanis, 1939), pp. 581-583, 585, 586.

[137] *Collectanea S. Congregationis de Propaganda Fide* (2 vols., Romae, 1907), *passim; Sylloge Praecipuorum Documentorum Recentium, passim.*

[138] S. C. Consist., *Dubia de competentia,* 7 ian. 1909, ad IV — *AAS,* I (1909), 148-152.

[139] Cf. *supra*, pp. 32-35.

[140] Can. 254.

such rites are entirely removed from the province of the Congregation of Sacred Rites.

In addition, the Ceremonial Congregation regulates the non-liturgical ceremonies of the Pontifical Court, and has competence over certain cases of precedence, namely, that of Cardinals and of legates which states send to the Holy See.[141] In this the Congregation of Rites has no part. From its competence are excluded the sacred functions of the Pontifical Chapel, the matters of ritual affecting Cardinals of the Holy Roman Church, and questions of precedence settled by the Ceremonial Congregation.

D. Faculties of the Congregation

The scope of the activity of the Congregation of Sacred Rites is indicated in part by the catalogue of faculties attributed to it by the Roman Pontiffs. Over and above the field of competence determined by law, specific faculties belong to the Congregation, either for its own use or for concession to petitioners.

A listing of these faculties may, in addition to its practical usefulness, help to clarify the competence of the Congregation, especially in the light of the restrictions introduced or restored by the Constitution *Sapienti consilio* and the Code. Some of the faculties, moreover, reveal the nature of the routine private replies of the Congregation, which would not usually be found in the *Decreta Authentica.*

Although mention is made in earlier decrees of the faculties possessed or especially attributed to the Congregation,[142] it was not until 1903 that a catalogue of them was made public by authority of Pius X.[143] This consisted of three series of faculties and ap-

---

[141] Can. 254. There are not many recent published decrees of this Congregation. Those which have appeared exhibit the several aspects of its competence, for example: S.C.Caer., decr. 7 iul. 1925 — *AAS*, XVIII (1926), 350-363; S.C.Caer., decr. 2 dec. 1930 — *AAS*, XXIII (1931), 56-59; S.C.Caer., decr. 27 maii 1934 — *AAS*, XXVI (1934), 522; S.C.Caer., decr. 24 iul. 1934 — *AAS*, XXVI (1934), 523-524.

[142] E.g., S.R.C., *Calaguritana et Calceaten.*, 13 febr. 1892 — D. 3767, ad 29; S.R.C., *Urbis Eiusque Districtus*, 21 iul. 1893 — D. 3809.

[143] The Pontiff actually confirmed an earlier group of concessions made by Leo XIII on July 13, 1896, which had not been published.

peared in the *Acta Sanctae Sedis.*[144] First were twelve "extraordinary faculties which can be obtained through the Sacred Congregation of Rites in audience with the Holy Father." They have
not been changed subsequently.[145] All deal with the cases of beatification and canonization; they are listed here for the sake of com-
pleteness.

1.   Extraordinary Faculties — Cases of the Servants of God

1.   Deputation of Bishops, in the number designated by the
General Decrees, for drawing up Apostolic Processes.

2.   Prorogation of the *terminus* for completing Apostolic Processes.

3.   Permission to open Processes, drawn up by Ordinary or by
Apostolic Authority, with the clause added: *servatis servandis.*

4.   Proposal in Ordinary Congregation, without the intervention and *votum* of the Consultors, of the Doubts: I. Validity of
Processes; II. Signing of the Commission of Introduction of the
Cause; III. Reassumption of the Cause for Canonization; IV. Individual doubts, which are commonly considered *minor;* V. Causes
of approval or confirmation of immemorial *Cultus.*

5.   Proposal in Ordinary Congregation of the Doubt, Signing
of the Commission of Introduction of the Cause, although the required period of ten years has not passed since the presentation
of the Processes drawn up by Ordinary Authority.

6.   Proposal of the Doubt *super Virtutibus*, although the required period of fifty years has not passed since the death of the
Servants of God in question.

7.   Concession of particular Letters of the Congregation of
Sacred Rites with Instructions of the Promotor of Faith: I. For
obtaining the writings of the Servants of God; II. For examining
or transferring their bodies or relics; III. For extracting relics for
Beatification . . . .

[144] *ASS*, XXXVI (1903), 412-419.
[145] Cappello, *De Curia Romana*, I, 333-334; Oppenheim, *Institutiones in Sacram
Liturgiam*, II, 128-129.

8. Concession of the same particular Letters as often as they refer to the execution of some Decree of the Congregation of Sacred Rites, or pertain to some information which the Promotor of Faith requires to be sought, even in enclosed Monasteries.

9. Permission to change Informative Processes into Apostolic Processes.

10. Concession of Remissorial Letters for the drawing up of Processes, *ne pereant probationes,* before the examination of the Doubts *de Cultu non exhibito* and *de Fama sanctitatis.*

11. Concession of Remissorial Letters for the drawing up of Processes by Apostolic authority, directing not only Bishops according to the General Decrees, but others . . . . according to the circumstances.

12. Deputation of Cardinals of the Congregation of Sacred Rites required by Postulators as *Ponens* or *Relator* in the Causes of Beatification and Canonization.

A note at the end of this first series of faculties states that, while they must be obtained in audience with the Supreme Pontiff, they can be conceded immediately by virtue of faculties especially granted to the Congregation, provided it is a case of necessity and access cannot be had to the Holy Father.

The other series of faculties are of greater interest. They deal with the liturgical matters handled by the Congregation and are of two kinds, extraordinary and ordinary, the former requiring the approval of the Roman Pontiff. When the Curia was reformed in 1908, some of these faculties, originally granted to the Congregation of Rites, were redistributed to other Roman Congregations. The *Normae Peculiares* set down "that the old catalogue of faculties is to be retained, but as circumscribed by the new disciplinary norms,"[146] and the relation of the various Congregations is shown by the redistribution of the faculties.

In the lists which follow, the faculties withdrawn from the juris-

---

[146] Ordo servandus in S. Congregationibus, Tribunalibus, Officiis Romanae Curiae, 29 sept. 1908, Pars II, Normae peculiares, cap. VII, art. VIII, n. 2° — *Fontes,* n. 6460.

diction of the Congregation of Rites in 1908[147] (as well as some which have become obsolete in other ways) are placed in parentheses. The indication of the Sacred Congregation to which a given faculty now pertains will suggest the realignment of competence in the reform of Pius X.[148] When both the Congregation of the Council and the Congregation of Religious are named, the former has competence with regard to the secular clergy and the faithful, the latter with regard to religious.[149]

2.   Other Extraordinary Faculties

1. Consecration of fixed altars by a priest.
2. Consecration of portable altars by a priest.
3. For Bishops: Subdelegation for the consecration of altars.
(4. Erection of a portable altar *sub dio.*—S.C.Sac.)
5. Change of title of consecrated altars.
6. Change of the images of consecrated altars.
7. Taking the ablutions at Mass with water alone.[150]
8. Imparting the *Absolutio* at funerals after a low Mass.
9. Approbation of proper formulas for blessings.
10. Blessing of a new abbot on a ferial day.
11. Solemn blessing in the name of the Supreme Pontiff (in general).[151]

[147] Lists of these are given by Cappello (*De Curia Romana*, I, 333-339) and by Oppenheim (*Institutiones in Sacram Liturgiam*, II, 126-130). Monin (*De Curia Romana*, p. 302, footnote n. 1) repeated Cappello's listing.

[148] Ordo servandus in S. Congregationibus, Tribunalibus, Officiis, Romanae Curiae, 29 sept. 1908, Pars II, Normae peculiares, cap. VII, art. III, n. 10° (for faculties transferred to the Congregation of the Sacraments); art. IV, n. 4°-5° (for faculties transferred to the Congregation of the Council). Pius X, const. *Sapienti consilio,* 29 iun. 1908, § I, n. 5°, 3 (for faculties transferred to the Congregation of Religious, in these words: *Huic denique Congregationi reservatur concessio dispensationum a iure communi pro sodalibus religiosis*). — *Fontes,* n. 682, 6460.

[149] Cappello, *De Curia Romana,* I, 339.

[150] E.g., S.R.C., *Urbis et Orbis,* 12 maii 1944 — *AAS,* XXXVI (1944), 154.

[151] Oppenheim, *Institutiones in Sacram Liturgiam,* II, 130.

12. Solemn blessing in the name of the Supreme Pontiff after Pontifical Mass.

13. Solemn blessing in the name of the Supreme Pontiff outside of Mass.

14. Same blessing with dispensation from the reading of the Brief.

(15. Wearing of a beard.—S.C.C. and S.C.Rel.)[152]

16. Concession of the title of minor basilica.

17. Exposition of the images of *beati.*

18. Solemn procession of the relics of *beati,* in accordance with the instruction of the promoter of the faith.

19. Dedication of altars to *beati.*

20. For Bishops: Subdelegation for the consecration of fixed and portable altars.

(21. Consecration of bishops on a ferial day.—S.C.Sac.)[153]

22. Consecration of a church with dispensations.[154]

(23. Opening of a small choir in churches and oratories. —S.C.C.)

24. Reduction of the number of candles for the Exposition of the Blessed Sacrament.

25. Celebration of the anniversary of Dedication on one and the same day by all the churches of a diocese, Order, Congregation, etc.[155]

(26. For a Chapter: Dispensation from the Mass of a feria, a vigil, etc.—S.C.C.)

[152] Cappello, *De Curia Romana,* I, 339.

[153] The fact that this faculty was lost to the S.C.Sac., as pertaining to the discipline of the sacraments, while n. 10 *supra* was retained, indicates that the competence of the S.R.C. extends to the discipline of the sacramentals, as well as to their actual rite. Monin (*De Curia Romana,* p. 301) maintained this, on the basis that the discipline of the sacramentals is nowhere given to another Congregation.

[154] I.e., with dispensations which pertain to the *rite* of consecration. — Oppenheim, *Institutiones in Sacram Liturgiam,* II, 130.

[155] This indult is not required by Ordinaries, according to S.R.C., decr. gen. 28 oct. 1913, I, 1, f. — D. 4308.

(27. Dispensation from the fast before the consecration of
altars.—S.C.C. and S.C.Rel.)

28. Extension of the feasts of *beati* to dioceses and
churches.

29. Elevation of the rite of feasts to *duplex maius, duplex secundae et primae classis.*

30. Reduction of the rite of feasts from *duplex maius,
duplex secundae et primae classis* to a lower rank.

(31. Dwelling above a church.—As a servitude, it pertains to the S.C.C.; otherwise, if by reason of decency or reverence only, it belongs to the S.C.Sac.)[156]

32. Concession of special insignia to bishops, canons,
parish priests, dignitaries, and of the use of a throne
to a Coadjutor Bishop.

33. Concession and reformation of particular calendars.

(34. Concession of a low conventual Mass or the omission
of the conventual Mass.—S.C.C. and S.C.Rel.)

35. Concession and approval of proper Masses, according to the practice of the Congregation.

36. Celebration of Mass with dispensations.[157]

37. Celebration of a proper Mass for a period of four
days.[158]

38. Celebration of a proper Mass for a period of eight
days.[159]

(39. Celebration of Mass in the interior chapel of a
cloister.—S.C.Sac.)

40. Celebration of a votive Mass of the Blessed Virgin
Mary in sanctuaries.

41. Celebration of the votive Mass of any saint in sanctuaries.

42. Celebration of the Mass *Rorate* during Advent.

---

[156] Cappello, *De Curia Romana*, I, 339.

[157] I.e., with dispensations which pertain to the *rite* of Mass. — Cappello, *op.
cit.*, I, 339; Oppenheim, *Institutiones in Sacram Liturgiam*, II, 130.

[158] With the same restriction as in n. 36.

[159] With the same restriction as in n. 36.

(43. Celebration of Mass two hours before dawn and after noon.—S.C.Sac.)

(44. Celebration of Mass for a community on Holy Thursday, together with the fulfillment of the precept of Paschal Communion.—S.C.Sac.)

(45. Commutation of the ferial Office into another.—S. C.C. and S.C.Rel.)

(46. Anticipation of the Office in choir.—S.C.C. and S.C.Rel.)

(47. Anticipation of the Office before 2 p.m. for any ecclesiastic.—S.C.C. and S.C.Rel.)

48. Concession, extension, and suppression of Offices.

49. Selection and approval of patrons.

50. Selection and approval of patrons for an entire class or University.

51. Transferral of the feast of the Purification of the Blessed Virgin Mary, together with the blessing of candles.

(52. Wearing a skull-cap or a covering for a head wound. —during Mass, S.C.Sac.; at other times, S.C.C. and S.C.Rel.)

(53. Opening of an entrance next to a church.—S.C.C.)

54. Transferral of the Corpus Christi procession to the afternoon hours.

55. Concession of the use of the *pontificalia* to canons, etc.

(56. For Regular Bishops: Use of the rochet.)[100]

57. Approbation of rites and ceremonies and of the liturgical books, according to the practice of the Congregation.

(58. Reservation of the Holy Eucharist temporarily in the private oratory of communities and nuns.—S.C.Sac.)

---

[100] This was made obsolete by the concession of the rochet to all regular bishops in a *motu proprio* of Benedict XV, 25 apr. 1920 — D. 4360.

(59. Reservation of the Holy Eucharist in the oratory of a bishop.—S.C.Sac.)

(60. Carrying the Blessed Sacrament within a city, with the head covered by a hat, cap, or skull-cap.—S.C. Sac.)

(61. Anticipation of Vespers, with or without Compline, in choir before noon.—S.C.C. and S.C. Rel.)

(62. Erection of oratories other than the principal one in religious houses.—S.C.Sac.)

3. Ordinary Faculties

1. Erection of a portable altar before the images of *beati.*

2. For Nuns: Washing of sacred linens.

3. Solemn blessing of water performed on the vigil of Epiphany.

4. Use of approved formulas of blessings which require apostolic permission.

5. Blessing of candles in honor of St. Joseph.

6. Blessing of cinctures and candles in honor of St. Joseph.

7. Blessing of rings and candles in honor of St. Joseph.

8. Blessing of the angelic *coronae* of St. Michael.

9. Blessing of water in honor of St. Ignatius.

10. Blessing of the medals of St. Benedict, Abbot.

11. Blessing of all scapulars.

12. Blessing of four scapulars under one formula.

13. Blessing of the small image, in the form of a scapular, of the Sacred Heart of Jesus.

14. Blessing of bells.

15. Blessing of bells, *non exclusa aqua.*

16. Blessing of sacred furnishings, in which anointing is not used.

17. Blessing or reconciling churches and cemeteries by a priest.

18. Blessing or reconciling churches and cemeteries by a priest, with water blessed by a priest.

19. Blessings reserved to the bishop, in which anointing is not used.

20. Blessing given to the sick in honor of St. Anne.

21. For Bishops: Subdelegation of the consecration of chalices and patens.

22. Consecration of altars performed privately with the short formula.

23. Consecration of the Holy Oils with a lesser number of ministers.

(24. Wearing a wig.—at Mass, S.C.Sac.; outside of Mass, S.C.C. and S.C.Rel.)

(25. Sacramental confession in a private oratory.)[161]

(26. For Nuns: Dispensation from reciting the ninth lesson of a simplified office.—S.C.Rel.)

(27. Dispensation for any ecclesiastical community from additions to the ferial office, namely, Penitential and Gradual Psalms, Small Office of the Blessed Virgin Mary, Office of the Dead.—S.C.C. and S.C.Rel.)

28. Extension of feasts to dioceses and churches.

29. Extension of feasts to *duplex minus* rite.

30. Reduction of feasts from *duplex minus* to lower rite.

31. Celebration of the functions of Holy Week in the oratories of nuns, religious, etc.[162]

32. Celebration of the functions of Holy Week and the like, according to the *Memoriale* of Benedict XIII, in churches and oratories, especially of nuns, religious, etc.

33. Uncovering the images in Passion time.

34. Use of vestments made of wool or cotton until they are worn out.

[161] Can. 909.
[162] Cf. can. 1193.

(35. Anticipation of the private recitation of Matins.—
S.C.C. and S.C.Rel.)

(36. Celebration of the Midnight Mass of Christmas in
the oratories of nuns and communities and in private
oratories.—S.C.Sac.)[163]

(37. For blind priests: Celebration of all votive Masses.
—S.C.Sac.)

(38. For priests with failing sight: Celebration of all
votive Masses.—S.C.Sac.)[164]

39. Celebration of proper Masses during a triduum.

40. Celebration of a proper Mass on any day, especially
for a new priest.

(41. Celebration of a proper Mass in an oratory, even a
private oratory.—S.C.Sac.)

(42. Celebration of several Masses in a private oratory
three times in the year.—S.C.Sac.)

(43. Celebration of several Masses in a private oratory,
on the feast day of the Titular.—S.C.Sac.)

(44. Several Masses in a private oratory on the occasion
of the infirmity of those enjoying the indult.—
S.C.Sac.)

(45. Celebration of Mass on the sea.—S.C.Sac.)

(46. Celebration of Mass in prison.—S.C.Sac.)

47. For priest-pilgrims and leaders of pilgrimages: Celebration of the votive Mass of the Blessed Virgin
Mary or of any saint, etc., in sanctuaries.

48. Votive Mass of the Passion in Holy Week.

49. Requiem Mass *cum cantu* several times in the week
for churches.

50. Low Requiem Mass upon the announcement of death.

(51. Mass one hour before dawn or after noon.—S.C.Sac.)[165]

[163] Cf. can. 821; Oppenheim, *Institutiones in Sacram Liturgiam*, II, 126.

[164] Oppenheim (*op. cit.*, II, 127) held that the only reservation to the S.C.Sac.
was the concession of the Votive Mass of the Blessed Virgin Mary and of the
Requiem Mass. But see S.C.Consist., decr. 16 aug. 1910 — *AAS*, II (1910), 649.

[165] Can. 821, § 1.

(52. For Priests: Mass on Holy Thursday.—S.C.Sac.)[166]

53. Incensation at *Missa cantata* without ministers.

54. Solemn Mass and low Masses on the occasion of the extrinsic festivity of any saint, *beatus,* or martyr, according to the practice of the Congregation.

55. Solemn Mass from the *Commune,* in a place where there is preserved the body of a martyr, with a proper name.

56. Low Masses from the *Commune,* as above.

(57. For Regulars, if they are living in the world and are deprived, for a just cause, of the habit of their religious institute: Recitation of the Office and celebration of Mass according to the calendar of their own religious institute.)[167]

(58. Commutation and dispensation of the divine Office. —S.C.C. and S.C.Rel.)

(59. Anticipation of the divine Office.—S.C.C. and S.C. Rel.)

60. Transferral of Offices.

61. Use of Holy Oil blessed in the previous year.

(62. For infirm priests: Erection of a private oratory at home or in the country.—S.C.Sac.)

(63. As above, with the fulfillment of the precept of hearing Mass by the members of the household, except on the more solemn days.—S.C.Sac.)

(64. As above, for another priest, when the one possessing the indult is impeded.—S.C.Sac.)

(65. Erection of private oratories in cemeteries belonging to families or to communities.—S.C.Sac.)

[166] Oppenheim (*Institutiones in Sacram Liturgiam,* II, 126-127) stated that faculties n. 41-46 and 52 are still granted in practice by the S.R.C., but he offered no proof of this.

[167] This is made obsolete by S.C.Rel., decr. 15 iun. 1909 — *AAS,* I (1909), 523. Cf. Cappello, *De Curia Romana,* I, 339.

66. For Spain and regions now or in the past subject to Spain: Permission for vestments of blue color in the festal or votive Mass of the Immaculate Conception.

(67. Reservation of the Holy Eucharist under the usual conditions in non-parochial churches, public and semi-public oratories.—S.C.Sac.)

(68. Reservation of the Holy Eucharist with a dispensation from the daily celebration of Mass, according to the practice of the Congregation.—S.C.Sac.)

(69. Distribution of the Holy Eucharist in a private oratory, except at Easter.)[168]

(70. Carrying the Blessed Sacrament outside a city, with the head covered by a hat, cap, or skull-cap.—S.C. Sac.)

71. Exposition of the Blessed Sacrament in the form of the Forty Hours' Prayer, with a dispensation from the night hours.

72. Extensions of proper and approved Offices and Masses.

73. Elevation of feasts to the rite of *duplex maius*.

(74. Fulfillment of precept of hearing Mass in private oratories for members of the household, guests, relatives by blood and marriage.—S.C.Sac.)

(75. Second Mass in private oratories for a single priest-guest, six times in the year.—S.C.Sac.)

(76. Anticipation of the private recitation of Matins and Lauds from 1 p.m. with some reasonable cause.—S.C.C. and S.C.Rel.)

(77. Second Mass in private oratories, as often as those enjoying the indult go to Holy Communion.—S.C. Sac.)

(78. Mass in a private oratory on the more solemn days. —S.C.Sac.)

---

[168] Cf. can. 869.

> (79. Mass in a private oratory on the feasts of the Assumption and of the patron.—S.C.Sac.)
>
> (80. Fulfillment of the precept of hearing Mass in a private oratory by *commensales* and *coloni.*—S.C.Sac.)

The faculties granted by the Congregation of Sacred Rites to Nuncios and Ordinaries fall, for the most part, within the limits of the above catalogue. Several additional powers, evidently belonging to the Congregation, may be derived from the published faculties:

1. Blessing of bells and consecration of churches, with notice given to the Ordinary and not against his will.[169]

2. Recitation of the divine Office and the celebration of Mass according to the Roman calendar for the clergy of the City.[170]

3. To permit, in the Mass of Holy Week when the Passion is said, that priests who, having obtained the faculty, celebrate two Masses read only the latter part of the Passion (*Altera autem die,* etc.) in one of them, saying before it: *Munda cor meum,* etc.—*Sequentia sancti evangelii secundum* (*Matthaeum*).

4. To bless marriages outside of Mass, or to recite the prayers over the spouses, according to the approved formulas, with power to subdelegate.

5. To bless and impose the five scapulars with a single formula, with power to subdelegate.

6. To bless and impose the five scapulars with a single formula, without recourse to the competent Ordinaries or religious Congregations, and without the obligation of inscribing the names in cases of a great gathering of people, during spiritual exercises and missions, with the power to subdelegate.

7. To bless objects of piety with the sign of the cross, observing the rites prescribed by the Church. But on the occasion of the pastoral visitation, when many people ask for the blessing of

---

[169] Index facultatum quas pro locis Missionis suae Nuntiis, Internuntiis et delegatis Apostolicis penes civitates seu nationes post Codicis Iuris Canonici publicationem tribuere SS.mus Dominus Noster Pius XI decrevit ceteris abrogatis, cap. IV, n. 45 — Coronata, *Institutiones Iuris Canonici,* V, 185.

[170] Index facultatum, cap. VI, n. 51 — Coronata, *op. cit.,* V, 186.

various objects of this kind, often requiring different formulas, in these cases a single short formula is permitted when the sign of the cross is made over the objects: *Benedicat haec omnia Deus, Pater et Filius et Spiritus Sanctus. Amen.*[171]

This listing of the Congregation's faculties concludes the consideration of the competence enjoyed by the Congregation of Sacred Rites. The field of competence may be seen from several points of view: negatively, from the relation to the other Roman Congregations which consider similar matters; practically, from its activity as revealed in specific faculties and decrees; juridically, from the determinations of Canon 253 and the legislation of Pope Pius X, to whom the Congregation owes its present character. Acting on behalf of the Roman Pontiffs, the Congregation of Sacred Rites has the supreme charge of the worship of the Latin Church, including all that pertains proximately to rites and ceremonies, as well as complete authority over the causes of the Servants of God.

---

[171] Index facultatum quinquennalium quae ordinariis nostris per tramitem S. C. Consistorialis tradi solent — Formula IV, cap. V, n. 4-7, 11. — Beste, *Introductio in Codicem,* p. 1001; Bouscaren, *The Canon Law Digest,* II, 37-38. Cf. Oppenheim, *Institutiones in Sacram Liturgiam,* II, 131-132.

CHAPTER V

CONSTITUTION AND PROCEDURE OF THE CONGREGATION

A. Personnel of the Congregation

While the officials and assistants of the Congregation of Sacred Rites have increased in number and activity over the period of its existence, the fundamental structure was apparent from the beginning: a group of Cardinals together with those who would advise and assist them.

Juridically the Congregation of Rites, like the other Roman Congregations, consists of the Cardinal members alone, since they have the sole decisive vote in the conduct of its affairs.[1] Thus the Congregation, as a moral person constituted by the Roman Pontiffs, may be considered a *collegium* of the several Cardinals appointed to it.[2] Of their number, one serves as presiding and governing officer and is called the Cardinal Prefect. While the position was not specifically mentioned by Pope Sixtus V in setting up this and other Congregations, there has always been a Prefect, and the lists of Cardinals holding the office go back to its institution.[3]

The same is true of the principal official of the Congregation after the Cardinals, the Secretary,[4] and other officials were gradually added. Cardinal DeLuca described the personnel of the Congregation as including, besides the Cardinals whose number was at the will of the Roman Pontiff, a group of prelates and learned

---

[1] Monin, *De Curia Romana*, p. 196.

[2] Cappello, *Summa Iuris Canonici*, I, 285; Jombart, *Manuel de Droit Canon* (Paris: Beauchesne, 1949), p. 110.

[3] Phillips, *Kirchenrecht*, VI, 566; Moroni, *Dizionario di Erudizione Storico-Ecclesiastica*, XVI, 267; *AIP*, VII (1864), 13-14.

[4] *AIP*, VII (1864), 11-13, where, in the preface to the second book of the decrees there published, the names of the early Secretaries are given. This preface was written by Mucante, who was himself appointed Secretary in 1609.

theologians as consultants. He mentioned the Secretary and, among the advisers, the Sacristan of the Pope, the Master of the Sacred Palace (an Augustinian and a Dominican, respectively), and one or more papal Masters of Ceremonies, in addition to those officials concerned with beatification and canonization.[5]

Benedict XIV, writing of the Congregation in the eighteenth century, devoted his attention to the processes of the Servants of God for the most part. He described the duties of the Protonotary[6] and the Secretary,[7] the three Auditors of the Rota who acted as consultors,[8] the Promoter of the Faith and the Subpromoter of the Faith,[9] as well as the principal Notary (who had the duty of supervising the archives) and the other Consultors.[10]

In the late eighteenth century and during the nineteenth century the personnel of the Congregation of Rites could be divided into the Cardinals, the *Praelati* (Sacristan, Rotal Auditors, Master of the Sacred Palace, Promoter of the Faith, Secretary), the Consultors, and the minor Assistants.[11] Among the latter were included various Substitutes, the Hymnographer, the Notary and Chancellor, and the like.[12] Among the Consultors there regularly were representatives of certain religious orders: a Dominican, a Friar Minor, a Jesuit, a Conventual, a Barnabite, and a Servite.[13]

The reform of Pius X clarified the positions and responsibilities of the officials serving the Roman Congregations. In general they are divided into two classes, major and minor. The major

---

[5] *Theatrum Veritatis et Justitiae*, Relatio Romanae Curiae Forensis, Disc. XVIII, n. 2.

[6] As early as 1604 the need for one of the Protonotaries *de numero participantium* to act because of the judicial character of the processes was recognized. —S.R.C., *Deputatio Protonotarii*, 8 maii 1604 — *AIP*, VII (1864), 118.

[7] *Opera Omnia*, De Servorum Dei Beatificatione, Lib. I, cap. XVII, n. 2, 4.

[8] *Op. cit.*, Lib. I, cap. XVII, n. 6.

[9] *Op. cit.*, Lib. I, cap. XVIII, n. 1, 11.

[10] *Op. cit.*, Lib. I, cap. XIX, n. 1, 24.

[11] *Notizie* for 1792, pp. 136-137.

[12] *Notizie* for 1822, pp. 68-70.

[13] Bouix, *Tractatus de Curia Romana*, p. 186; Hilling, *Procedure at the Roman Curia*, p. 87; Ojetti, *De Romana Curia*, p. 136.

officials are the Cardinal Prefect, the Secretary (or whoever holds
the first administrative position after the Prefect), and the Substitute, while the minor officials include the Assistants (*studii
adiutores* or *minutanti*), the Amanuenses, Protocolists, Archivists,
and lesser ministers or servants.[14]

An important distinction between the major and minor officials
of the Congregations is in the manner of their appointment. The
major officials are freely named by the Pope, according to the
Normae Communes,[15] while the minor officials are appointed after
a written examination and a *scrutinium* by the Prefect, Secretary,
and Substitute.[16] The results of the voting by these three officials
are reported to the Pope for approval and for the nomination of
the minor officials.[17] Before taking office, they are required to
take a threefold oath, to fulfill the office faithfully, not to accept
gifts even if offered spontaneously, and to observe secrecy in the
conduct of the affairs of the Congregation.[18]

In addition to this general division of the officials, the Congregation of Sacred Rites retained, in the reform of Pius X, the four-
fold classification of members and personnel it had previously:

1. Cardinals (with whom were listed the Secretary and
   the Substitute, as had become the practice before
   the issuance of the *Sapienti consilio*).[19]

2. *Praelati Officiales* (who were concerned with the
   processes of the Servants of God, and included the
   Promoter of the Faith and the Subpromoter. The
   latter was also the Assessor of the Congregation).

3. Consultors.

---

[14] Ordo servandus in S. Congregationibus, Tribunalibus, Officiis Romanae
Curiae, 29 iun. 1908, Pars I, Normae communes, cap. I, n. 1°; 29 sept. 1908, Pars
II, Normae peculiares, cap. VI — *Fontes*, n. 6460; Naz, "Congrégations Ro-
maines," *Dictionnaire de Droit Canonique*, IV, 208-209.

[15] Cap. II, n. 1°.

[16] Cap. II, n. 4°-8°.

[17] Cap. II, n. 9°.

[18] Cap. III. Canon 243, § 2, also enjoins this secrecy.

[19] *La Gerarchia Cattolica* for 1906, p. 443.

4. Lesser officials (of whom there were eight at the time of the reform by Pius X: the Hymnographer, the first and second *adiutores,* the archivist, the amanuensis or *scriptor,* the protocolist, the notary and chancellor, and the substitute chancellor).[20]

Over and above this enumeration of personnel, the three Commissions at that time attached to the Congregation of Rites should be noted. Each had a President, a Secretary, and several members.[21]

A few words concerning the more important of these officials will indicate their duties, as determined by the *Normae Peculiares* issued in 1908 and still in effect. To the *Secretary* belongs, under the Cardinal Prefect, the supervision of the Congregation's business. He is to expedite matters, to submit cases to the consultors, and to summon the latter as may prove necessary. Moreover, he is to see to the publication of decrees in the *Acta Apostolicae Sedis,* and to administer the funds of the Congregation.[22] The *Substitute* is to assist the Secretary, in addition to other duties he may have, and also to act for the Secretary in the latters' absence.[23]

The *Normae Peculiares* also determined carefully the work of the *Studii Adiutores* or Assistants: to prepare *compendia* or summaries of cases assigned to them, to be present at the discussion of the cases, to write letters and rescripts, to prepare formal summaries of important matters to be considered by the Cardinals. In the actual work of writing they are assisted by the clerks or *Scriptores Amanuenses.*[24] The duties of the latter, as well as of the *Archivist,* the *Protocolist,* and the *Notary* and *Chancellor,* are clear from their titles. One of the minor officials peculiar to the Congregation of Rites is the *Hymnographer,* assigned to prepare hymns for new Offices.[25]

---

[20] Index Praepositorum et Officialium in SS. Congregationibus, Tribunalibus, Officiis Romanae Curiae, S. Congregazione dei Riti — *AAS,* I (1909), 124-126.

[21] *Loc. cit.*

[22] Cap. VI, n. 1°.

[23] Cap. VI, n. 2°.

[24] Cap. VI, n. 3°-4°, 6°.

[25] Cappello, *De Curia Romana,* I, 315.

The dissolution of the three Commissions of the Congregation in 1914, with the redistribution of the labors of the Congregation into two sections, altered the constitution of officials. The same was true, to a lesser degree, of the addition of the Historical Section of the Congregation by Pius XI in 1930.[26] In neither case was the distinction between major and minor officials lost, nor was there any substantial change in the nature of the various offices of the Congregation.

The present structure or constitution of the personnel of the Congregation of Sacred Rites is as follows, according to the *Annuario Pontificio*:[27]

1. *Cardinals*—The Cardinal *Prefect* and the Cardinal members are listed, together with the *Secretary* (a titular archbishop) and the *Substitute*. (At times the Congregation of Rites has had an assistant to the Substitute, the *Sostituto Aggiunto*, who ranked with the major officials.)[28]

2. *Sectiones*—In the first Section (for beatification and canonization) the general officials are given: the *Promotor Generalis Fidei*, the *Assessor* and *Subpromotor Generalis*, four *Assistants*, and a *Scriptor*. Next come the *Praelati Officiales* who are *ex-officio* attached to the Congregation for cases of beatification and canonization. Among them are the following, according to the tradition of the Congregation: the Dean of the Rota, the Sacristan of the Holy Father,[29] a Protonotary Apostolic, two Auditors of the Rota,[30] the Master of the Sacred Apostolic Palace,[31]

---

[26] This *Sectio Historica* should not be confused with the *Commissio historico-liturgica* which was suppressed in 1914. Such an error was made by Cavigioli (*Manuale di Diritto Canonico* [3. ed., Torino: Società Editrice Internazionale, 1946], p. 236), who spoke of the Commission founded in 1902 as if still in existence.

[27] For the year 1954, pp. 879-881.

[28] *Annuario Pontificio* for 1926, p. 479.

[29] An Augustinian.

[30] The two senior Auditors after the Dean.

[31] A Dominican.

and the Relator General of the Historical Section.[82] Finally the Consultors are listed; they include representatives of the various religious orders.

The second Section (for the sacred liturgy) includes only an enumeration of the Consultors dealing with ritual matters, since the secretarial work of this section is handled by the general secretariat of the Congregation. The Pontifical Masters of Ceremonies are the first of the Consultors of this Section.

The third Section (for the historical cases of the Servants of God and the emendation of the liturgical books) has its own officials: the *Relator General*, the *Vice-Relator General*, and three *Assistants*. In addition there is a third body of Consultors belonging to this Section.

3. *Other Officials*—The minor officials who transact the business of the entire Congregation are divided into those of the secretariat and those of the chancery. The former include the *Hymnographer*, two *Assistants*, the *Archivist*, the *Protocolist* and *Assistant Archivist*, and a second *Assistant Archivist*. The chancery includes the *Notary* and *Chancellor*, and an *Assistant to the Chancellor*.

This description of the personnel of the Congregation of Sacred Rites may serve to indicate the orderly and efficient constitution it has acquired, largely through the changes effected in 1914 and 1930 by Pius X and Pius XI, respectively.

B. Procedure of the Congregation

The detailed norms which accompanied the Constitution *Sapienti consilio* determined not merely the jurisdiction of the Congregations and the responsibilities of the officials, but also the mode of their procedure. One of the most important aspects of the pro-

----

[82] A new addition to the *Praelati Officiales*. The presence of this official among the *Praelati* indicates the connection between the first and third Sections of the Congregation.

cedural regulations was the division between the *Congregatio plena* and the *Congressus*. While this distinction was not new to the Roman Curia,[33] Pope Pius X drew a careful line between matters to be handled by one or the other.

The *Congressus* of a Congregation consists of the Cardinal Prefect, the Prelate who supervises the Congregation, and the Substitute. In the case of the Congregation of Sacred Rites, the *Congressus* includes the Prefect, Secretary, and Substitute. In general, this body or group examines and expedites minor matters, and arranges and prepares more serious affairs for the consideration of the entire Congregation of Cardinals.[34] This is defined in the words of the *Normae Peculiares*:

> To the *Congressus* pertains the preparation of what must be referred to the full Congregation; the execution of the Congregation's decisions after the approval of the Supreme Pontiff; the adaptation of the same decisions to similar cases, where the matter is clear, obvious, and subject to no controversy; the concession of faculties, favors, indults, which are customary and easy, in accordance with the power granted by the Roman Pontiff; provision that the affairs of the Congregation's office proceed properly, according to the common norms and the peculiar norms of this law and of the Constitution *Sapienti consilio*.[35]

Negatively the powers of the *Congressus* are limited by the reservation of authority to the *Congregatio plena*, as described below.

The same *Normae Peculiares* determine that the Secretary should preside over the *Congressus* in the absence of the Prefect, and direct that the Assistants (*Studii Adiutores*) should be present, to propose their opinions regarding the questions assigned to them.[36] It is thus made clear that the routine business and de-

---

[33] Hilling, *Procedure at the Roman Curia*, p. 84.

[34] Ordo servandus in S. Congregationibus, Tribunalibus, Officiis Romanae Curiae, 29 iun. 1908, Pars I, Normae communes, cap. I, n. 3°-4° — *Fontes*, n. 6460.

[35] Cap. II, n. 2°.

[36] Cap. VI, n. 1°, 3°.

cisions of the Congregation belong to the *Congressus*. In addition it examines the *vota* or opinions of the Consultors in more important matters and decides what recommendation should be made to the full body of Cardinals.[37]

The *Congregatio plena* is made up of all the Cardinals of the Congregation, presided over by the Cardinal Prefect.[38] Regulations are given in the *Normae Peculiares* for their procedure: In the preparatory stage the questions to be considered may be submitted to one or more Consultors, or to the entire body of Consultors meeting as a *collegium*.[39] Their *vota* are given to the Cardinals, together with the documents pertinent to the case. The meetings of the *Congregatio plena* of the Congregation of Sacred Rites take place on Tuesdays in the Vatican Palace.[40] At these meetings the Cardinals may require further recommendations from the Consultors. Then the Cardinals present their own opinions, the Cardinal *Ponens* of the case (if there is one) speaking first, the Cardinal Prefect last.[41]

In general, the *Congregatio plena* is to consider all business of greater importance. The following matters are reserved to it in the *Normae Peculiares*:

> . . . . the solution of all doubts and questions concerning the interpretation of law; the examination of controversies referring to administration or discipline which are more serious, either in themselves or because of circumstances; decisions concerning favors or faculties of greater moment and which are unusual in themselves or by reason of their form; finally, all acts of the public and common order, whether instructions or precepts.[42]

[37] Oppenheim, *Introductio in Sacram Liturgiam,* II, 119; cf. S.R.C., decr. 13 iul. 1896 — D. 3926.

[38] As used here, the term *Congregatio plena* refers to the actual meeting of the Cardinal members, in whom, as a *collegium,* reposes the authority of the Congregation.

[39] Cap. IV, n. 2°-3°, 6°.

[40] Cap. IV, n. 1°-3°; *Annuario Pontificio* for 1954, p. 881.

[41] Cap. IV, n. 7°-8°.

[42] Cap. II, n. 1°; Monin, *De Curia Romana,* p. 204.

The Constitution *Sapienti consilio* and Canon 244, § 1, require that nothing "grave and extraordinary" should be decided by the Congregations (or Tribunals and Offices) unless it has already been reported to the Roman Pontiff. The *Normae Peculiares* add that such reports should be accompanied by a summary of the matter and the resolution of the *Congregatio plena*. Should the Pope change anything determined by the Congregation, the Cardinal members are to be informed at the next meeting.[43]

The formal procedure just described, of the ordinary meetings of the *Congregatio plena,* is the proper manner in which the Congregation of Sacred Rites exercises its supreme authority. It is to be used in deciding such matters as rites and ceremonies, the approval of liturgical books, the concession of important favors and privileges, questions concerning sacred relics, and the like. Depending on the nature of the question under consideration, the *vota* of Consultors from one or more of the three Sections are presented to the Cardinals of the Congregation.

C. Processes of the Servants of God

The procedure of the Congregation of Rites just described is that which it follows in the conduct of its ordinary affairs, with the exception of the cases of beatification and canonization. For the latter there is the special judicial procedure given in Book IV of the Code.[44] This is too lengthy and too elaborate to be discussed here in any detail, but it may be briefly indicated, with especial reference to the members or personnel of the Congregation who take part in the various stages of the process.

According to the Code, causes of this kind may be handled in one of two ways: *via ordinaria non cultus,* in which proof is offered that no public cult has been shown to the Servant of God or, if there has been public veneration, this has been removed as an abuse; and *via extraordinaria casus excepti seu cultus,* in which proof is offered that the Servant of God is in possession of public

[43] Cap. V, n. 1°-2°.
[44] Can. 1999-2141.

ecclesiastical veneration.[45]   In either case there are three general
stages: the processes conducted by a local Ordinary on his own
authority, the introduction of the cause before the Congregation
of Rites and its consideration, and the apostolic processes conducted on the authority of the Congregation and then judged
by it.

In the preliminary stages of the cause of a Servant of God before
the Congregation of Rites, the *Congregatio plena* acts at its regular meetings (*comitia ordinaria*)[46] and examines there the processes
completed by the local Ordinary.[47]   This takes place in three steps:

1. Consideration of the writings of the Servant of God
   which have been sought out and collected.[48]

2. Discussion of the informative process conducted by
   the local Ordinary together with a decision concerning the formal decree allowing the introduction of
   the case.   The former includes the discussion of the
   validity of the informative process, the sanctity in
   general of the Servant of God (or of the martyrdom,
   in the case of a martyr), and the absence of obstacles to the cause.[49]

3. Discussion of the process *super non cultu* drawn up
   by the local Ordinary to determine whether unlawful
   cult has been offered to the Servant of God.[50]

In the exceptional case where there has been lawful veneration
of the candidate for beatification, the writings of the Servant of
God are considered, but the process *super non cultu* is omitted.
The *Congregatio plena* in ordinary session considers the Ordinary's

[45] Can. 2000.

[46] Cappello, *De Curia Romana*, I, 320.   For the officials required to be present
at such meetings, cf. S.R.C., decr. 25 nov. 1931—*AAS*, XXVII (1935), 310-311.

[47] The competence of the local Ordinary is determined according to Canon
2039. Canons 2042-2064 describe the three processes which are drawn up and
presented to the Congregation of Rites by the Ordinary.

[48] Can. 2070-2071; Oppenheim, *Introductio in Sacram Liturgiam*, II, 117-118.

[49] Can. 2082.

[50] Can. 2085.

informative process on the presence of lawful cult and then decides upon the decree of introduction of the case.[51]

When the cause of the Servant of God has been formally introduced and approved by the Roman Pontiff,[52] and the Congregation has decided whether to confirm the local Ordinary's sentence *de non cultu*,[53] a tribunal of at least five judges is delegated to draw up the apostolic process concerning the sanctity, miracles, etc., of the Servant of God.[54] The next step taken by the Congregation of Sacred Rites is at the completion of the apostolic process. It is the consideration of the validity of the process and is made by a *Congregatio peculiaris*. This board or commission consists of the Cardinal Prefect, the Cardinal *Ponens* of the case, three other Cardinals of the Congregation of Rites named by the Pope, and the following officials of the Congregation: the Secretary, the Protonotary Apostolic, the Promoter General, and the Subpromoter General of the Faith.[55] If the decision is favorable and the Roman Pontiff gives his approval,[56] the Congregation then proceeds to consider the matters contained in the apostolic process.

The heroic character of the virtues shown by the Servant of God or, alternatively, the martyrdom and its cause, are considered in three stages:[57]

1. *Congregatio antepraeparatoria,* at which the Cardinal

[51] Can. 2127-2128. It will be noted that these decisions, which had been assigned to the Rotal Auditors in 1878 and 1895 by Leo XIII, belonged to the *Congregatio peculiaris* set up by Pius X in 1908, until the provisions of the Code attributed them to the ordinary sessions of the *Congregatio plena.*

[52] Can. 2083.

[53] In the excepted cases, Canon 2129 determines that a delegated judge is to consider whether the lawful cult has been proved; it is his sentence that the *Congregatio plena* at this point decides whether to confirm or reject, according to Canons 2130-2131.

[54] Can. 2087-2088. The canons which follow these give detailed norms to be observed.

[55] Can. 2100. The constitution of this group differs somewhat from the one determined by Pius X in 1908, which included five Cardinals to be designated by the Congregation of Rites.

[56] Can. 2100, § 3.

[57] Can. 2102.

Ponens of the cause in question, the *Praelati Officiales,* and the Consultors are present.[58]

2. *Congregatio praeparatoria,* at which all the Cardinals of the Congregation of Rites are present, together with the *Praelati Officiales* and the Consultors.[59]

3. *Congregatio generalis,* held in the presence of the Supreme Pontiff, with all the Cardinals of the Congregation, the *Praelati Officiales,* and the Consultors assisting.[60] At this meeting the decision is made by the Pope, the others having only a consultative vote.[61]

After this series of *Congregationes,* a decree is published in the name of the Supreme Pontiff authentically declaring that the virtues or martyrdom have been established. The Servant of God may then be called "Venerable."[62]

Next a second series of three *Congregationes,* similar to the ones just described, is held to consider the miracles adduced on behalf of the Servant of God.[63] In the case of martyrs, however, if miracles are lacking, the Congregation of Rites decides whether to seek a dispensation from the Pope in order to omit this stage of the process.[64] Again, in the excepted case, where proof of lawful cult has been presented, once the decree has been published concerning the fact of immemorial cult and concerning the virtues or martyrdom, the Servant of God is considered equivalently beatified, if the Supreme Pontiff gives his confirmation to the cult.[65]

After the *Congregationes,* a decree of approbation of the miracles is issued. Then a new and final session is held in the presence of the Supreme Pontiff to determine whether the beatification may

---

[58] Can. 2105.

[59] Can. 2108.

[60] Can. 2112. Ojetti, *De Romana Curia,* p. 138.

[61] Can. 2114.

[62] Can. 2115.

[63] Canon 2117 determines the number of miracles which must be proved in the various instances.

[64] Can. 2116, § 2.

[65] Can. 2134.

be decreed.[66] It should be added that the approval of the Pope is required after each of the steps, not merely in connection with the formal *Congregationes,* but also to confirm the preliminary decisions of the Congregation of Rites in these processes.[67]

For canonization additional miracles must be adduced.[68] With the approval of the Supreme Pontiff, the Congregation of Sacred Rites issues a decree allowing the resumption of the cause and the drawing up of apostolic processes concerning the new miracles, as was done before for beatification.[69] After the validity of the new processes has been established, the threefold *Congregationes* are held to consider the new miracles, at the end of which the Roman Pontiff may decree the canonization.[70]

Subsequent to the Code, additional norms were provided by Pius XI in connection with his creation of the Historical Section of the Congregation of Rites. These concern the historical causes, namely, those in which there is lacking contemporary testimony to the facts, and in which there is no proof of depositions made at the proper time concerning the Servant of God.

In these circumstances, after the examination of the writings of the Servant of God and the usual informative process, the parts of the apostolic process are omitted concerning which no contemporary testimony is available. These may have to do with the life, virtues, martyrdom, or immemorial cult. In place of the omitted parts of the apostolic process, the matters are to be considered by the Historical Section according to the rules of scientific historical investigation, and the opinions and documents prepared by the Section are then to be used for the doctrinal consideration and decision by the first Section of the Congregation.[71]

[66] Can. 2124.

[67] Can. 2071; 2083, § 1; 2100, § 3; 2107; 2111; 2132.

[68] Two miracles are required for the canonization of those formally beatified, three in the case of those equivalently beatified. — Can. 2138.

[69] Can. 2139, § 1.

[70] Can. 2139, § 2; 2140.

[71] Pius XI, motu propr. *Già da qualche tempo,* 6 febr. 1930 — *AAS,* XXII (1930), 87-88. In 1939 norms were established for Ordinaries to follow in the preparation of historical causes for presentation to the Congregation, in S.R.C., *Normae Servandae,* 4 ian. 1939 — *AAS,* XXXI (1939), 174-175.

These are, in summary, the formal procedures of the Congregation of Sacred Rites. In part they are common to all the Roman Congregations, in part they are peculiar to this Congregation by reason of its special competence.[72] In their present form, they are the result of the efforts by Pius X to reorganize the Roman Curia, together with some changes introduced by the Code of Canon Law. This brief description of the Congregation's procedure may serve to define and clarify its structure and workings in those matters subjected to it by the Roman Pontiffs.

[72] Monin, *De Curia Romana*, p. 303.

CHAPTER VI

DECREES OF THE CONGREGATION

A. Kinds of Decrees

The term "Decree" as used here may refer to any of the acts
of the Congregation of Sacred Rites. In a general sense a decree
is what is established or determined after deliberation and examination of a given matter.[1] The use of the term in connection with the
Roman Congregations is by way of distinguishing their acts from
those of the Sovereign Pontiff, which may be Constitutions, Motu
Proprio, Apostolic Letters, and the like.[2] According to their form
or purpose, the decrees of the Congregation of Rites may be called
Declarations,[3] *Dubia*, Decisions,[4] Responses,[5] or Instructions;[6] they
may be Epistles,[7] Circular Letters,[8] *Decreta Generalia,* or simply
Decreta. It is in this broad sense, including the various kinds of
declaration or response, that the collected acts of the Congregation
are given the title *Decreta Authentica,* and it is in this sense that
the Congregation of Rites regularly refers to its acts, of whatever
kind, as decrees.[9]

The primary division of the decrees of the Congregation of
Sacred Rites may be made according to the twofold division of its
activity, sacred rites and the causes of the Servants of God. Acts
dealing with the latter have generally been published in connec-

---

[1] Van Hove, *Prolegomena,* p. 73.

[2] *Cicognani,* Canon Law, pp. 81-86.

[3] E.g., D. 1156; 4178; 4182; 4315.

[4] Oppenheim, *Institutiones in Sacram Liturgiam,* II, 109.

[5] E.g., D. 2916; 3023, ad 1.

[6] E.g., D. 4229; 4296; 4300; 4363.

[7] E.g., D. 4396.

[8] E.g., D. 3732; 3857; 3999; 4045; 4291.

[9] E.g., *Serventur Decreta,* S.R.C., *Messanen.,* 24 febr. 1680 — D. 1643, ad 10;
Standum Decretis, S.R.C., *Urgellen.,* 15 mart. 1888 — D. 3689, ad 2; *Iuxta
Decreta alias edita,* S.R.C., *Vicariatus Apostolici Senegambiae,* 28 nov. 1891 —
D. 3752, ad 1.

tion with individual beatification and canonization,[10] and the most important decrees in the individual processes are regularly inserted in the issues of the *Acta Apostolicae Sedis*. The general *Decreta*, on the other hand, are the decisions which concern sacred rites and ceremonies and which reveal the scope of the Congregation's competence. These logically include, when collected, a certain number of decrees giving general norms for the causes of beatification, etc.[11]

Decrees dealing with rites and related matters within the field of the Congregation may be classified in various ways, for example, according to their subject matter. This is done in the Index of the *Decreta Authentica,* where the decrees are listed alphabetically by subject. It is the arrangement also in some of the analytical collections of the decrees, in which an effort is made to establish broad categories of liturgical matters, together with divisions and subdivisions according to topic.[12]

The decrees are also to be distinguished according to their obligatory force. Thus they may be preceptive, issued by way of command with the force of law, or they may be directive, given as a norm of action approved for the observance of a specific law. Since a similar distinction is used with reference to the rubrics of the liturgical books, the decrees of the Congregation of Rites may be considered preceptive or directive, as they deal with preceptive or directive rubrics, respectively.[13]

More important than the above are the divisions made on the basis of the object and the extent of the decrees. By reason of their object or nature the decrees are concessionary or disciplinary. The concessionary decrees are those which grant privileges, favors,

---

[10] E.g., Bartolini, *Acta Sacrorum Solemnium quibus SS. D. N. Pius Papa IX XXVI Martyribus Iaponensibus ac Beato Michaeli de Sanctis Confessori Sanctorum Coelitum Honores Decrevit* (Romae, 1864).

[11] E.g., S.R.C., decr. gen. 22 dec. 1870 — D. 3233; S.R.C., *De Postulatoribus Litteris Conficiendis,* 15 ian. 1935 — *AAS,* XXVII (1935), 58.

[12] Gavantus, *Thesaurus Sacrorum Rituum* (Parisiis, 1647); Martinucci, *Manuale Ecclesiasticorum seu Sacrae Rituum Congregationis Decreta* (3. ed., Romae, 1853).

[13] Oppenheim, *Institutiones in Sacram Liturgiam,* III, 56.

and dispensations;[14] the disciplinary decrees are those which give decisions in the administrative order, instructions,[15] and interpretations.[16] Truly doctrinal decrees, which must be mentioned in a general discussion of the Roman Curia, do not properly emanate from the Congregation of Rites. Only the Holy Office is competent in doctrinal matters concerning faith and morals.[17]

Finally, the decrees of the Congregation of Rites may be distinguished by reason of the extent of their application into particular, general, and equivalently general. From a canonical point of view, this is the most significant division.

Particular decrees are those which are addressed to a particular person and are concerned with a particular matter or object. The person addressed may be a physical or moral person, frequently the latter, as when decrees are sent to dioceses or religious institutes. Decrees of this kind are indicated by the name of the person addressed, e.g., *Parmen., Mediolanen., Ordinis B. V. M. Mercede.*[18] Obviously, most concessionary decrees are particular in character.

General decrees, on the other hand, refer to the whole Church, both in their form and in their object. They are also called formally general decrees and are clearly distinguished by their titles: *Decretum, Decretum Generale, Dubium, Romana, Urbis et Orbis.* Sometimes the phrase, *ubique servari mandavit,* or the like indicates the general nature of a decree.[19]

Other decrees, more numerous in the past than the general decrees, are directed to particular persons, but deal with an object of general concern to the Church. These may deal, for example, with the interpretation or application of a general law of the

---

[14] Can. 253, § 2, mentions these in the enumeration of the matters belonging to the competence of the Congregation of Sacred Rites.

[15] Cf. *infra,* pp. 137-138.

[16] Coelho, *Corso di Liturgia Romana,* I, 80-81; O'Connell, *The Celebration of Mass* (3 vols., Milwaukee: Bruce, 1940-1941), I, 25-26.

[17] Can. 247, § 1.

[18] E.g., D. 1100; 229; 2774.

[19] An example of the latter is *Elboren.,* 17 iun. 1606: *Dictum Decretum locum habere non solum in Regnis Hispaniae et Lusitaniae, sed etiam in quibuscumaue aliis Regnis et locis per totum Christianum Orbem declaravit. —* D. 218.

liturgy or a general rubric. Although in form they remain particular decrees, because of their content they are called equivalently general.[20] The distinctions among decrees on the basis of their extension is of most importance in the consideration of their binding or obligatory force.

B. Obligation of the Decrees

The decrees of the Congregation of Sacred Rites are obligatory norms, binding in conscience those to whom they apply. As true laws, they have the force of law; their character as laws is clear from their inclusion in the liturgical law confirmed by the Code,[21] from their enumeration among the liturgical books governing the conduct of the holy liturgy,[22] and from the very language used in the text of the decrees.[23]

That the decrees of the Congregation have binding force is admitted by all.[24] Moreover, the Congregation itself has insisted upon the observance of its decrees, just as it has required the observance of the rubrics found in the liturgical books. In 1822, for example, it declared that the local Ordinary "is strictly bound to provide by suitable remedies that the Rubrics and the Decrees of the S.R.C. are properly observed; if any doubt should occur, recourse must be had to the same Sacred Congregation for a declaration."[25] In a similar way, with reference to specific rubrical mat-

---

[20] Callewaert, *Liturgicae Institutiones*, I, 133-134; Coelho, *Corso di Liturgia Romana*, I, 80-81; O'Connell, *The Celebration of Mass*, I, 26-27; Van der Stappen, *Sacra Liturgia* (5 vols., Mechliniae, 1898), I, 13.

[21] Can. 2; 6, 6°.

[22] S.R.C., decr. 17 maii 1911 — D. 4266; S.R.C., decr. 10 aug. 1946 — *AAS*, XXXVIII (1946), 371-372.

[23] E.g., *Atque ita rescripsit, declaravit ac servari mandavit* — D. 3574, 3575, 4254; *Atque ita servari praecepit* — D. 4282; *Hoc servandum praecepit S.R. Congregatio* — *AAS*, XXXIV (1942), 205.

[24] Monin, *De Curia Romana*, p. 216; Coelho, *Corso di Liturgia Romana*, I, 80; Prümmer, *Manuale Iuris Canonici*, pp. 138, 143; Bouix, *Tractatus de Jure Liturgico*, p. 152; Bargilliat, *Praelectiones Juris Canonici*, I, 371-372; Regatillo, *Institutiones Iuris Canonici*, I, 290.

[25] S.R.C., *Dubiorum*, 17 sept. 1822 — D. 2621. The decree concludes with these words: *Facta autem de praemissis SS.mo D. N. Pio VII Pont. Max. relatione per infrascriptum Secretarium, Sanctitas Sua cuncta benigne approbavit;*

ters the Congregation demands that the pertinent decrees be followed.[25] The obligatory force is the same as if the decrees had come immediately from the Sovereign Pontiff,[26] although they are not to be considered pontifical law unless they receive pontifical approbation *in forma specifica*.[27] Finally, the promulgation of the Code of Canon Law did not affect the obligatory force of the decrees, except in the instances where the liturgical law was expressly changed.[28]

The question may be raised, in what way and at what moment do the decrees of the Congregation begin to bind. This is determined by the Code for those decrees which form universal law: they are to be promulgated in the *Acta Apostolicae Sedis* and obtain their force upon the completion of three months from the day of the issue of the *Acta*.[29] It should be noted, however, that the decrees may be promulgated in other ways, as Canon 9 allows. Although the present practice of the Congregation is to publish its general decrees in the *Acta Apostolicae Sedis*,[30] a common manner of promulgation in the past was by insertion in the authentic collection of decrees.[31] Similarly, the Code allows an exception to the usual period of *vacatio* which may be more or less than three months.[32]

In the same connection, the Congregation of Sacred Rites has established a norm of authenticity for its decrees; this applies equally to particular and general decrees of whatever kind. "Re-

---

Decretumque desuper expedire et publici iuris fieri mandavit; locorum Ordinariis stricte praecipiens, ut omnimodam illius observantiam urgeant.

[25] E.g., *Serventur Decreta*, S.R.C., *Ventimilien.*, 18 iul. 1884 — D. 3614, ad 3; *Servetur Decretum in Bracharen. citatum*, S.R.C., *Lucionen.*, 29 dec. 1884 — D. 3624, ad 6; *Standum Decretis*, S.R.C., *Urgellen.*, 15 mart. 1888 — D. 3689, ad 2.

[26] S.R.C., *Ordinis Praedicatorum*, 23 maii 1846 — D. 2916.

[27] Cf. *supra*, pp. 51-52.

[28] Can. 2; 6, 6°.

[29] Can. 9.

[30] The transmission of copies of these decrees to the moderators of the *Acta* is to be done by the Secretary of the Congregation, according to the *Normae Peculiares* of 29 sept. 1908, cap. VI, n. 1° — *Fontes*, n. 6460.

[31] S.R.C., *Romana*, 8 apr. 1854 — D. 3023, ad 2.

[32] Can. 9.

scripts, responses to doubts, concessions, declarations of any kind, privileges, commentaries published in the name of the S.R.C. are of no force unless they are signed, according to law, by the Prefect together with the Secretary or Substitute; or, in case of necessity, at least by the Prefect or Secretary or Substitute." [84] This statement is a new formulation of an earlier requirement of the Congregation. [85]

The gravity of the obligation in conscience of a given decree belongs to moral theology to determine. According to the importance of the matter, the violation of the Congregation's decrees will be a grave or venial sin. [86] With reference to the degree of obligation, however, a distinction is made between preceptive and directive decrees. The first oblige strictly, for they are true laws to be observed according to their meaning. Directive decrees, on the other hand, afford a norm of lesser weight, to assist in the proper execution of the law itself.

The distinction between preceptive and directive decrees is controverted, at least under the aspect of preceptive and directive rubrics, and even the existence of directive (or non-preceptive) rubrics is questioned. [87] With reference to the decrees themselves, it may be said that those dealing with preceptive rubrics are preceptive, those dealing with directive rubrics are directive. [88] Yet it must be insisted that it is almost impossible to find rubrics in the liturgical books which are merely directive, that is, which give a direction or command while leavinig complete liberty of action. [89] In fact, the present law as found in the Code enforces and confirms all the rubrics which use mandatory language of any kind; this applies to the decrees of the Congregation as well. Thus the Code requires the celebration of the divine Office "according to

[84] S.R.C., *Monitum,* 28 ian. 1912 — *AAS,* IV (1912), 84; *Ephemerides Liturgicae,* XXXIII (1919), 282-283.

[85] S.R.C., decr. 11 aug. 1632 — *AIP,* I (1855), 1229-1230; S.R.C., *Romana,* 8 apr. 1854 — D. 3023, ad 1.

[86] Coelho, *Corso di Liturgia Romana,* I, 82; Noldin-Schmitt, *Summa Theologiae Moralis* (27 ed., 3 vols., Oeniponte, Lipsiae: Rauch, 1940-1941), I, 292-295.

[87] Menghini, *Elementa Iuris Liturgici,* pp. 118-119.

[88] Oppenheim, *Institutiones in Sacram Liturgiam,* III, 56.

[89] Oppenheim, *loc. cit.*

the proper and approved liturgical books,"[40] and the accurate observance of the rubrics by the celebrant of Mass;[41] it makes similar requirements for the administration of the sacraments[42] and sacramentals.[43]

There are, however, instances of decrees which permit a degree of liberty of action and thus are not strictly preceptive. Of this kind are the decrees which give a negative approval or toleration to practices not entirely in keeping with liturgical law,[44] as well as decrees in which a choice or a permission is given.[45] Those decrees which allow variant practices are more properly called facultative than directive, that is, they give a faculty or license to choose one or other course of action.[46] Facultative decrees are readily distinguished by the tenor of their language, from the use of phrases such as *tolerari potest, usum permitti posse, laudabilius, convenit.* If the Congregation specifically commands a single course of action, as is usually the case, the decree must be considered preceptive.

Another kind of declaration from the Congregation of Sacred Rites must also be mentioned, again from the point of view of obligatory force. This is the Instruction, the use of which in the Roman Curia was confirmed and defined by Benedict XV when he established the Pontifical Commission for the Interpretation of the Canons of the Code.[47] As mentioned before,[48] Instructions are not true laws but are rather explanations of and complements to the law itself. Benedict XV placed them in opposition to *nova Decreta Generalia* and explained that they have the purpose of

[40] Can. 135.
[41] Can. 818.
[42] Can. 733, § 1.
[43] Can. 1148, § 1.
[44] E.g., S.R.C., *Tuden.*, 23 maii 1846 — D. 2918, ad 11; S.R.C., *Cuneen.*, 2 iun. 1883 — D. 3576, ad 5.
[45] E.g., S.R.C., *De Zacathecas*, 31 mart. 1879 — D. 3489, ad 2; S.R.C., *Antibaren. et Scodren.*, 4 iul. 1879 — D. 3499, ad 1; S.R.C., *Auximana*, 9 maii 1885 — D. 3633.
[46] O'Connell, *The Celebration of Mass*, I, 18, 26; Oppenheim, *Institutiones in Sacram Liturgiam*, III, 56.
[47] Motu propr. *Cum iuris canonici*, 15 sept. 1917 — *AAS*, IX (1917), 483-484.
[48] Cf. *supra*, pp. 50-51.

bringing greater light and effectiveness to the laws with which they are concerned.[49]

Instructions strictly so-called seem to fall into the category of true directive decrees, that is, they give norms to be used but do not exact literal observance of their terms.[50] Because of their purpose and nature, Instructions cannot abrogate the law which they are designed to explain or execute, and they lose their force upon the cessation of the law in question.[51] Although they lack the force of law, Instructions are to be followed as ordinances proceeding from executive power,[52] but a lesser reason would excuse from their observance than one that would permit non-compliance with a law.

With reference to Instructions issued by the Congregation of Sacred Rites, it should, be added that the prescriptions of liturgical law may be repeated in them. These then have the full force of law.[53] The same is true when the language of an Instruction is clearly mandatory and preceptive. In practice this appears to be the case generally with Instructions of the Congregation of Sacred Rites. While this Congregation occasionally uses the term *Instructio* as a title for its declarations, these differ from the Instructions published by the other Congregations. They are not strict explanations of liturgical law or of the rubrics, but instead introduce changes of ceremonies.[54] Such Instructions have the obligatory force of law.

What has been said applies in general to the decrees of the Congregation of Rites. It may be summed up in this way: the decrees have the obligation of law unless the words of the decrees indicate otherwise. A more important matter is the consideration of those who are bound to obey the decrees. Here a division

[49] *Loc. cit.*

[50] Van Hove, *Prolegomena*, p. 75.

[51] Van Hove, *loc. cit.*

[52] Schmidt, "The Juridic Value of the Instructio," *The Jurist* (Washington, D.C., 1941-   ), I (1941), 314-315.

[53] Cicognani, *Canon Law*, pp. 87-89.

[54] S.R.C., Instructio, 12 ian. 1921 — D. 4363 (This Instruction has since been incorporated in the Roman Ritual, Tit. V, cap. 6); S.R.C., Instructio, 9 ian. 1929 — *AAS*, XXI (1929), 43.

must be made according to the extension of the decrees, as already described: general, particular, equivalently general.[55]

General decrees of the Congregation of Rites oblige all Catholics of the Latin Church; concerning such decrees there is no question.[56] It is no contradiction to find among the general decrees some which apply only to certain classes of those who are subject to the Church. Thus some decrees, though having universal obligatory force, may refer to prelates only or to canons only.

Particular decrees, that is, those which are particular both in form and in content, present no difficulty. They oblige only those to whom they are addressed. Since they have the nature of private replies or precepts, they are of strict obligation for the individuals addressed.[57] For them and for them alone particular decrees may be said to be *ius speciale.*[58]

Just as other persons are not bound to obey particular decrees not addressed to them, so they may not take advantage of permissions and favors contained in such decrees. There is an exception to this, in that those who receive an indult may benefit by a particular declaration concerning the same indult, even though the declaration was not directed to them. The Congregation of Rites determined this on the principle, *Ubi idem indultum, ibi eadem declaratio.*[59]

In spite of their restricted obligatory force, particular decrees have great value in the doctrinal interpretation of liturgical law. For this reason particular decrees, which in themselves do not require the promulgation of law, are often made public.[60] Those who comment upon rites and ceremonies use particular and gen-

---

[55] Cf. *supra*, pp. 133-134.

[56] Oppenheim, *Institutiones in Sacram Liturgiam*, III, 54; Bouix, *Tractatus de Curia Romana*, p. 376; Callewaert, *Liturgicae Institutiones*, I, 116.

[57] Cimitier, "La liturgie et le droit canonique," — Aigrain, *Liturgia* (Paris, 1930), p. 47; Callewaert, *Liturgicae Institutiones*, I, 115.

[58] Bargilliat, *Praelectiones Juris Canonici*, I, 372.

[59] S.R.C., *Andegaven.*, 4 dec. 1896 — D. 3933.

[60] A great number of decrees, although formally and materially particular, have been included in the authentic collections of decrees. The present practice of the Congregation of Rites is to insert only general decrees in the *Acta Apostolicae*

eral decrees indiscriminately to interpret the rubrics and liturgical law.[61] Moreover, the repetition of the same matter in successive particular decrees serves to indicate the *stylus Curiae* to be used as a norm in the absence of an express prescription of law.[62]

The final category of decrees, on the basis of extension, includes the equivalently general decrees, namely, those which have a particular form but which are general because of the matter treated. Such decrees always bind those to whom they are addressed, but distinctions must be made with regard to their universal obligatory force.

In 1905 the Congregation of Sacred Rites declared that a particular decree given earlier[63] was of universal obligation, "since the Decree refers to Rubrics affecting the entire Church."[64] In other words, such a decree (equivalently general) has the same obligatory force as a general decree, *tamquam Decretum Generale, seu Urbis et Orbis, ita ut ubique obliget . . . .*[65] This rule remains true of the decrees of the Congregation of Rites,[66] but it must be limited by the additional requirement of promulgation if the equivalently general decree is to have the force of law.[67]

Like formally general decrees, those which are equivalently general must be promulgated in order to create a universal obligation. Promulgation is not necessary, however, if the equivalently general decree only repeats an existing law, or if it is merely declaratory of a law concerning which there is no doubt.[68] As Canon 17, § 2, states, an interpretation of this kind is retroactively valid;

Sedis; if they were originally particular in form, they are usually given the title *Dubium* or *Dubia.* Particular decrees often appear in the *Ephemerides Liturgicae,* published under private auspices.

[61] O'Connell, *The Celebration of Mass,* I, 27, footnote n. 46.

[62] Can. 20.

[63] S.R.C., *Pisana,* 20 mart. 1903 — D. 4111.

[64] S.R.C., *Compostellana,* 15 apr. 1905: *Affirmative, quum Decretum Rubricas respiciat, universam Ecclesiam spectantes . . . .* — D. 4156, ad 2.

[65] *Loc. cit.*

[66] Cavalieri, *Opera Omnia Liturgica* (5 vols. in 1, Venetiis, 1778), cap. 3, § 3, n. 8; Michiels, *Normae Generales,* I, 488.

[67] Can. 9.

[68] Can. 17, § 2.

it binds in virtue of the law which it repeats or declares. In other cases promulgation is required: if the equivalently general decree establishes a new law, or if it gives an interpretation of law that restricts, extends or explains a doubtful law.[69]

From the point of view of subjects of the law, the decrees of the Congregation of Rites may be said to bind in conscience, as true laws, according to their extent. Particular decrees oblige only those to whom they are directed, general decrees and equivalently general decrees, in the strict sense, oblige all Catholics of the Latin Church who are concerned with their provisions.

C. Customs Contrary to the Decrees

No question need be raised concerning customs in liturgical law which are *praeter legem* or *secundum legem*. Such customs obtain legal force in accordance with the prescriptions of the Code;[70] these norms apply equally to liturgical law and to the law of the Code.[71] The formation of liturgical rites by custom is an important part of the history of the Catholic liturgy,[72] and the Congregation of Sacred Rites has recognized this in many individual instances, in spite of the modern uniformity of rites and ceremonies.[73]

According to the Code, customs *secundum legem* are the best interpreters of the law.[74] The Congregation of Rites has made use of customs of this kind in its decrees, for example, in connection with the assistance of the deacon at Benediction of the Blessed Sacrament,[75] and with reference to the genuflections made *coram*

[69] Regatillo, *Institutiones Iuris Canonici*, I, 78, 290; Cimitier, "La liturgie et le droit canonique," — Aigrain, *Liturgia*, p. 47; Oppenheim, *Institutiones in Sacram Liturgiam*, III, 55; Cicognani, *Canon Law*, pp. 604-605.

[70] Can. 25, 26, 28, 29.

[71] Moretti, *Caeremoniale*, I, 12; Van Hove, *De Legibus*, p. 13; Wernz, *Ius Decretalium*, III, 356.

[72] Oppenheim, *Institutiones in Sacram Liturgiam*, III, 105-108.

[73] E.g., *Ratione consuetudinis*, S.R.C., *Vilnen.*, 16 febr. 1906 — D. 4180, ad 1; *Seclusa legitima consuetudine*, S.R.C., *Dubia*, 2 maii 1924 — D. 4392, ad 1.

[74] Can. 29.

[75] S.R.C., *Parisien.*, 14 ian. 1898 — D. 3975, ad 4.

Sanctissimo.[76] In the same way the Congregation has very often indicated its approval of customs *praeter legem* or *praeter rubricas*. Examples of this are frequently found among the decrees: approval of the practice of removing holy water from the church during the Sacred Triduum where the custom exists,[77] the particular usage of carrying candles in processions during the Easter octave,[78] the local practice of chanting the final antiphon after the canonical hours at the altar of the Blessed Virgin,[79] the use of a small spoon for the water at the preparation of the chalice.[80] Thus many questions proposed to the Congregation have been answered with the phrase, *Servetur consuetudo,* and in the seventeenth century the Congregation insisted repeatedly that the *Caeremoniale Episcoporum* was not intended to destroy laudable customs.[81] It is in this spirit that the Code allows the observance of particular customs in the celebration of marriages.[82]

Although customs *praeter legem* are often recognized, the Congregation of Rites has not hesitated to condemn and prohibit those which it considers abuses.[83] This has the effect of removing the consent of the competent superior which is needed for lawful custom.[84] It is rather with customs contrary to law that the Congregation has usually been concerned. These it has often condemned, sometimes in the strongest terms,[85] and it is necessary to consider how customs contrary to the decrees may obtain the force of law.

[76] S.R.C., *Minoricen.*, 24 nov. 1899 — D. 4048, ad 5.

[77] S.R.C., *Marsorum*, 12 nov. 1831 — D. 2682, ad 54.

[78] S.R.C., *Pisana*, 12 nov. 1831 — D. 2684, ad 10.

[79] S.R.C., *Senen.*, 30 iun. 1883 — D. 3580, ad 3.

[80] S.R.C., *Baltimoren.*, 6 febr. 1858 — D. 3064, ad 4.

[81] S.R.C., *Salamantina*, 10 ian. 1604 — D. 154; S.R.C., *Salernitana*, 16 iul. 1605 — D. 184; S.R.C., *Viterbien.*, 7 iul. 1612 — D. 299.

[82] Can. 1100.

[83] S.R.C., *Nullius, seu Tullen.*, 24 nov. 1685 — D. 1757; S.R.C., *Mantuana*, 6 febr. 1875: *Praedictos usus non esse consuetudines, sed abusus omnino abolendos.* — D. 3337.

[84] Can. 25, 28.

[85] S.R.C., *Hispalen.*, 16 ian. 1677: *Consuetudines seu, ut melius dicamus, abusus omnes expositi, uti repugnantes Rubricis et Expositorum opinionibus, tolli omnino debent. Non sunt enim laudabiles, imo scandalosae, iis maxime qui amant observantiam bonorum rituum. Et ita declaravit, decrevit, atque praefata omnino tolli mandavit.* — D. 1588.

In the past it has been held by some that in liturgical law contrary customs could not arise.[86] Such a view applied to both the rubrics of the liturgical books and the decrees of the Congregation of Sacred Rites. It had a basis in the strong reprobation of contrary customs, for example, in connection with the celebration of Mass,[87] which culminated in the prescription of the Code that the celebrating priest observe accurately and devotedly the rubrics of the ritual books, *reprobata quavis contraria consuetudine.*[88] It had a basis, moreover, in the frequent condemnation by the Congregation of various particular contrary customs.[89]

Against this point of view it may be argued that, even before the publication of the Code with its distinct title on custom,[90] the Congregation of Rites recognized the possibility of contrary customs obtaining legal force. For example, it noted the requirement of prescription for lawful custom,[91] and accepted custom as the foundation of decisions given by it.[92] It indicated the value of custom and its force even by the use of the clause in its decrees: *quacumque consuetudine non obstante,* employed to overrule customs otherwise lawful.[93] Negatively, it should be added that there never was any law or decree absolutely prohibiting future customs contrary to liturgical law.[94]

[86] Cf. Van Hove, *Commentarium Lovaniense,* Vol. I, Tom. III, *De Consuetudine et de Temporis Supputatione* (Mechliniae, Romae: Dessain, 1933), p. 199; *Ephemerides Liturgicae,* XXXV (1921), 21.

[87] Pius V, litt. ap. *Quo primum tempore,* 14 iul. 1570 — *BRT,* VII, 841. By order of Urban VIII (1623-1644) the following notice was placed at the beginning of the Missal: *Mandat Sacra Congregatio in omnibus, et per omnia servari rubricas Missalis Romani, non obstante quocumque praetextu, et contraria consuetudine, quam abusum esse declarat.* Cf. S.R.C., *Romana,* 18 iun. 1689 — D. 1812.

[88] Can. 818.

[89] *Non obstante quacumque consuetudine etiam immemorabili,* S.R.C., *Catanen.,* 16 iul. 1663 — D. 1261; *Negative; et serventur Decreta hac supra re pluries edita,* S.R.C., decr. gen. 3 apr. 1821 — D. 2613, ad 4; *Consuetudinem . . . prorsus eliminandam,* S.R.C., *Senen.,* 30 iun. 1883 — D. 3580, ad 6.

[90] Can. 25-30.

[91] S.R.C., *Albinganen.,* 3 iun. 1662 — D. 1232.

[92] E.g., *Affirmative, posita consuetudine,* S.R.C., *Congregationis Missionariorum Oblatorum,* 15 iun. 1883 — D. 3578, ad 1.

[93] O'Connell, *The Celebration of Mass,* I, 31, footnote n. 29.

[94] *Ephemerides Liturgicae,* XXVIII (1913), 36.

The practice of the Congregation of Rites, even before the publication of the Code, confirms the view that contrary customs may arise. It frequently accepted such customs in particular cases, for example, the omission of the use of the *Sanctus* candle,[95] the position of the Subdeacon at the *Sanctus*,[96] or the use of cloth of gold vestments.[97] Thus it may be concluded that the practice of the Congregation gives no *stylus curiae* against all customs contrary to liturgical law,[98] and that sacred rites and ceremonies are governed by the general norms of customary law.[99]

This is confirmed by the Code of Canon Law, which does not exclude liturgical law from the operation of the norm stated for contrary customs.[100] As Van Hove pointed out, there is no reason for exempting the Congregation of Sacred Rites from the general principles established in Book I of the Code, or for extending the meaning of Canon 2 excessively.[101] Canons 25 to 27, and Canon 30, may thus be applied fully to the regulation of the liturgy and to the decrees of the Congregation of Sacred Rites.[102]

From this it follows that customs contrary to the decrees may obtain the force of law if they do not derogate from the divine law, if they are reasonable, and if they are lawfully prescribed for the period determined by the Code.[103] The law also declares that a custom which is expressly reprobated in law is not reasonable.[104] Such express reprobation excludes much liturgical law from the operation of contrary custom. In particular, the Code

[95] S.R.C., *Resolutionis Dubiorum*, 9 iun. 1899 — D. 4029, ad 2.

[96] *Servetur cuiuscumque Loci consuetudo*, S.R.C., *Marsorum*, 12 nov. 1831 — D. 2682, ad 30.

[97] S.R.C., *De Guadalaxara*, 28 apr. 1866 — D. 3145.

[98] Van Hove, *De Consuetudine*, p. 201.

[99] Wernz, *Ius Decretalium*, III, 357; *Ephemerides Liturgicae*, XXVII (1913), 187.

[100] Can. 27, § 1.

[101] Van Hove, *De consuetudine*, pp. 199-200. Canon 2 refers to the laws governing sacred worship, not to the *normae generales* when they happen to affect liturgical law.

[102] Michiels, *Normae Generales*, II, 188; Oppenheim, *Institutiones in Sacram Liturgiam*, III, 136; Moretti, *Caeremoniale*, I, 11-12.

[103] Can. 27, § 1.

[104] Can. 27, § 2.

itself reprobates certain customs concerning the vesture and insignia of canons,[105] the conferral of Orders,[106] and the rubrics governing the celebrant of Mass.[107] The latter rule refers to legislation found in the decrees of the Congregation which deal with the
celebrant of Mass, as well as to the rubrics.[108]

With regard to these contrary customs, it is the precise duty of
the Congregation of Sacred Rites to declare what must be condemned as an abuse or as unreasonable. Just as with non-liturgical customary law, the competent superior, in this case the Congregation, may require the correction of practices by withdrawing
legal consent.[109] Although the force of the canons of the Code
concerning custom is not in any way weakened, practically they
are to be applied more severely in connection with the matters
falling within the competence of the Congregation of Rites.[110] This
is evident from the frequent correction of unworthy customs and
the desire of the Congregation that doubtful matters be submitted
to it.[111] If it appears reluctant to permit broad liberty of action in
matters liturgical,[112] this stems from the very nature of the holy
liturgy and from the office of the Congregation to see to the observance of sacred rites and ceremonies.

D. Collections of Decrees

The many collections of the decrees of the Congregation of
Sacred Rites indicate its continual activity, its importance, and the
variety of ritual matters determined. All the published collections
are, by their nature and purpose, selective: they give only those
decrees which are of value to priests, students, and historians in

[105] Can. 409, § 2.

[106] Can. 978, § 3.

[107] Can. 818.

[108] Ferretti, "De Vi Consuetudinis quoad Singulos Libros Liturgicos Plenius
Investigata," *Ephemerides Liturgicae*, XXXII (1918), 141.

[109] Van Hove, *De Consuetudine*, p. 201.

[110] Michiels, *Normae Generales*, II, 188-189; Van Hove, *De Consuetudine*, p.
202; Ferretti, "art cit.," *Ephemerides Liturgicae*, XXXI (1917), 711-712.

[111] S.R.C., *Dubiorum*, 17 sept. 1822 — D. 2621, ad 1.

[112] Cf. S.R.C., *Triventina*, 3 aug. 1839 — D. 2792; S.R.C., *Angelopolitana*, 11
sept. 1847 — D. 2951, ad 13.

general. This does not mean, however, that the collections are ordinarily restricted to decrees which have the force of universal law, that is, general and equivalently general decrees. Many particular decrees are included, since even these have general value and interest if they show the *stylus curiae* with regard to favors and customs, or if they suggest norms which may be used in other cases. As mentioned before, the doctrinal use of particular decrees in commenting upon liturgical law is very common.[113]

Collections of the decrees under private auspices have been made since the first years of the Congregation of Rites. The earliest of these was the *Thesaurus* of Bartolomeo Gavanti (1569-1638).[114] He was a celebrated rubrician and commentator, as well as a consultor of the Congregation.[115] The collection of Gavanti, which was first published in 1627,[116] divided the decrees as they referred to the Missal or to the Breviary; the work was continued by the commentator Merati (1668-1744).[117]

Another collection often mentioned was made by Franciscus Pithonius, who died in 1729.[118] This was not restricted to decrees of the Congregation but included pontifical constitutions and other decrees referring to the sacred liturgy. Still another eighteenth century collection was made by Spiridius Talù and was declared authentic by the Congregation in 1762.[119]

These collections are either chronological or analytical in their arrangement of the decrees they include. Several of the latter

[113] Cf. *supra*, pp. 139-140.
[114] *Thesaurus Sacrorum Rituum.*
[115] Callewaert, *Liturgicae Institutiones*, II, 78.
[116] Bibliophilus, "De S. R. C. decretorum collectionibus," *Ephemerides Liturgicae*, XL (1930), 433.
[117] *Decreta Sacrae Rituum Congregationis in lucem primum edita a P. D. Bartholomaeo Gavanto . . . deinde a P. D. Cajetano Maria Merato . . . adaucta* (2. ed., Florentiae, 1743).
[118] *Constitutiones Pontificiae et Romanarum Congregationum ad Sacros Ritus Spectantes* (Venetiis, 1730) — Stickler, *Historia Iuris Canonici Latini*, Vol. I, *Historia Fontium* (Augustae Taurinorum: Apud Custodiam Librariam Pontif. Athenaei Salesiani, 1950), p. 334.
[119] Bibliophilus, "De S. R. C. decretorum collectionibus," *Ephemerides Liturgicae*, XL (1930), 435.

were published even in the nineteenth century.[120]   The analytical plan of course made such collections of great practical use.

Of much more importance, however, are the nineteenth century collections authorized by the Apostolic See.   The first of these was made by Luigi Gardellini (1757-1829), who was at the beginning of that century an Assessor of the Congregation of Rites and Sub-Promoter of the Faith.[121]   He included over four thousand decrees, arranged in chronological order from 1602 to the year of publication.   A second edition, published ten years later, brought the collection up to date.[122]   This time it included Gardellini's Commentary on the *Instructio Clementina*[123] and, as a supplement, 146 decrees from the earliest years of the Congregation, from 1588 to 1598.   The third (and final) edition of this collection was begun in 1856; later it was extended to the year 1887 and to decree no. 5993.[124]

The significance of Gardellini's collection came from the fact that each of the three editions was declared authentic by the Congregation of Sacred Rites.   The faculty to publish was granted, other editions were forbidden without permission, and the authority of the collection was to prevail in controversies.[125]   This authorization did not affect the extent of application of the individual decrees or change their binding force, but it determined

[120] Martinucci, *Manuale Ecclesiasticorum;*   Mühlbauer, *Decreta Authentica Congregationis et Instructio Clementina ex Actis ejusdem Collecta ab Aloisio Gardellini in Usum Cleri Commodiorem Ordine Alphabetico Concinnata* (3 vols. in 4, Monachii, 1863-1867; Supplement, 3 vols., 1876-1885). The latter, as its title indicates, was directly based on the authentic collection to be mentioned next.

[121] *Decreta Authentica Congregationis Sacrorum Rituum Nunc Primum ex Actis ejusdem S. C. Collecta* (5 vols., Romae, 1808-1816).

[122] *Decreta Authentica Congregationis Sacrorum Rituum* (7 vols., Romae, 1824-1826).

[123] The commentary was of private authority only.

[124] *Decreta Authentica Congregationis Sacrorum Rituum* (4 vols., Romae, 1856-1858; Vol. V, 1888).

[125] The decrees for the first and second editions are dated 1 ian. 1808 (Pius VII) and 14 sept. 1824 (Leo XII), respectively — Gardellini, *Decreta Authentica* (2. ed.), I, v-vi; for the third edition, 16 febr. 1856 — Gardellini, *Decreta Authentica* (3. ed.), I, v.

which decrees could be considered authentic. The value of insertion in the authentic collections as a means of promulgation was confirmed by the Congregation in 1854.[126]

Gardellini and those who continued his collections made use of decrees which were of importance or usefulness in the understanding of individual rites and ceremonies. Decrees referring to the organization of the Congregation itself were logically omitted, as were many decrees concerning the preparation of liturgical books and decrees of less general interest. The omissions were supplied in a private collection made in the middle of the nineteenth century.[127] This collection is primarily of historical interest and includes many decrees indicating the early development of the Congregation, covering the period from 1588 to 1700.[128]

In the last years of the nineteenth century a new collection became necessary, not only as a continuation of the earlier editions, but also as a codification of the replies given by the Congregation of Rites. With this purpose the *Commissio Liturgica*[129] prepared an entirely new collection, which appeared during the years 1898 to 1901. This was declared authentic by Pope Leo XIII, who abrogated any earlier decrees which were in disagreement with the new collection, excepting only indults and privileges of individual churches.[130] This did not alter the character of the decrees contained; particular decrees remained particular in extension and authority. But it did have the effect of eliminating conflict between individual decrees.

Of the five volumes of the new authentic collection which were published, three were devoted to the decrees themselves, the fourth contained the Commentary by Gardellini on the *Instructio Clementina* together with annotations on some of the decrees, and the fifth was a general index according to the subject matter of the decrees. The collection was later extended by the publication of additional volumes in 1912 and 1927. Together with these subse-

---

[126] S.R.C., *Romana*, 8 apr. 1854 — D. 3023, ad 2.
[127] *AIP*, VII (1864), 1-384; VIII (1865), 1137-1388.
[128] The first decree is dated 11 iun. 1588.
[129] Established by Leo XIII in 1891; cf. *supra*, pp. 37-38.
[130] S.R.C., decr. *Urbis et Orbis*, 16 febr. 1898 — *Decreta Authentica*, I, ix.

quent volumes of later decrees,[181] this collection remains authentic today, even after the Code of Canon Law,[182] and it is enumerated among the liturgical books of the Latin Church.[183]

The value and importance of the *Decreta Authentica* can hardly be over-estimated. More than four thousand decrees were included,[184] but very many of the decrees found in the earlier collections were omitted.[185] The manner in which this was done and the basis for the selection were described in the Preface to the first volume.[186] Decrees were omitted by the Commission which prepared the Collection if they were repetitious and so unnecessary, if they were contrary to later decisions, in conflict with the rubrics of the liturgical books, or obsolete because of new rubrics or changed circumstances. If the decrees considered similar matters, they were sometimes united as *Decreta Generalia, Dubia, Romana,* etc. Thus the decisions of the Congregation of Sacred Rites were brought up to date and codified for use and study.

E. Forms of the Responses

An understanding of the decrees of the Congregation of Sacred Rites requires a knowledge of the phrases commonly used in them, in reply to the questions or petitions. This Congregation uses the terms employed by the other Sacred Congregations, and certain others in addition, by reason of the nature of liturgical law.

[181] Vol. VI (Appendix I), S.R.C., decr. *Urbis et Orbis,* 24 apr. 1912; Vol. VII (Appendix II), S.R.C., decr. *Urbis et Orbis,* 26 ian. 1927. These do not abrogate conflicting decrees which might exist outside the collection.

[182] Can. 2.

[183] S.R.C., decr. 17 maii 1911 — D. 4266; S.R.C., decr. 10 aug. 1946 — *AAS,* XXXVIII (1946), 371-372. Over 1200 decrees of the S.R.C., which had been used in the preparation of the Code, were collected and published in the *Fontes,* n. 5156-6413. No further appendix to the *Decreta Authentica* has been issued since 1927, but there is a private collection of decrees taken from the *Acta Apostolicae Sedis* and elsewhere: *Collectio Decretorum ad Sacram Liturgiam Spectantium ab anno* 1927 *ad annum* 1946 (2. ed., Roma: Edizioni Liturgiche, 1947).

[184] Vols. I-III contain 4051 decrees, Vol. VI extends the collection to 4284, Vol. VII to 4404.

[185] The 5992 decrees of the last continuations of Gardellini's Collection were represented by 3681 decrees of the new *Decreta Authentica.*

[186] Pp. xiv-xv.

The following is a list of some of the formulas, with reference to decrees in which they appear:

1. *Affirmative.*

2. *Negative.*

3. *Provisum in primo* (or *secundo, praecedenti,* etc.)— The reply may be found in another response given in the same decree.[127]

4. *In decisis* or *In decretis*—A previous decree is re-affirmed.[128]

5. *Ad mentem*—The reply of the Congregation, affirmative or negative, is qualified by conditions or a clarification. The *mens* or intent of the Congregation may then be explained.[129]

6. *Dilata*—The matter is deferred to a later time, which may be indicated or left indefinite. In the published decrees of the Congregation of Rites, this reply normally appears when the *res dilata* is one of several doubts proposed together (and a solution is given in the course of the decree) or one to which a solution has been given ultimately.[140]

7. *Consulatur Sanctissimus*—The decision is reserved to the Roman Pontiff. In the published decrees, when this or any similar phrase is used, it is followed by an indication of the final disposition of the matter by the Pope.[141] The same is true of the next formula.

8. *Facto verbo cum Sanctissimo*—The decision exceeds the faculties of the Congregation and requires the approval *in forma communi* of the Roman Pontiff. This is also expressed in slightly different ways, e.g., *facta Sanctissimo relatione.*[142]

---

[127] E.g., D. 2429, ad 13; 2434, ad 2; 3015, ad 2-3, 6.
[128] E.g., D. 2298; 2332, ad 1-3; 2361.
[129] E.g., D. 2225; 2283, ad 7; 3416.
[140] E.g., D. 2219, ad 1; 2332, ad 4.
[141] E.g., D. 3246; 3906.
[142] E.g., D. 3415; 3939.

9. *Et amplius*—The case, to which a response (affirmative or negative) is given, should not be proposed again, since it is clear and evident. This formula is very frequently used in the published decrees of the Congregation of Rites.[143]

10. *Lectum*—The petition is not admitted and no response is given.[144]

11. *Non expedit or non expedire*—A denial of the petition as inopportune or inexpedient.[145]

12. *Nihil*—A refusal of a petition as incongruous or unworthy.[146]

13. *Utatur iure suo*—The petition is unnecessary.[147]

The formulas used in the decrees vary in their wording. There are many which are used regularly but present no difficulty. Other phrases are of lesser importance and some, such as *Gaudeat impretratis*,[148] *Dilata, Lectum,* are unlikely to appear often in the published decrees of the Congregation, since decrees of this kind are not of general interest.

Some formulas are peculiar to the *stylus* of the Congregation of Sacred Rites. There are several ways to indicate that the decree has a particular application only, for example, *in casu,*[149] *in casu de quo agitur,*[150] *attentis narratis* or *ex deductis,*[151] *pro gratia.*[152] Frequently the Congregation replies by a reference to the rubrics of a liturgical book: *Serventur Rubricae, servetur Pontificale Ro-*

---

[143] E.g., D. 2204 (in which the entire formula is expressed in this way: *Et amplius proponi vetuit*); 2361; 3412.

[144] E.g., D. 532; 1222; 1226.

[145] E.g., D. 600; 3616, ad 2.

[146] E.g., D. 532; 645; 2381 (*Nihil de nova audientia*).

[147] E.g., D. 3508: S.R.C., *Colonien.*, 8 maii 1700 — *AIP*, VIII (1865), 1388. Lists of these formulas are given by Cappello, *De Curia Romana*, I, 45; Coronata, *Institutiones Iuris Canonici*, I, 405-406; Regatillo, *Institutiones Iuris Canonici*, I, 291; Abbo-Hannan, *The Sacred Canons*, I, 302-303.

[148] I.e., no further favor will be granted to the petitioner.

[149] E.g., D. 2385; 3287; 3294.

[150] E.g., D. 3330; 3356.

[151] E.g., D. 571; 3251, ad 5.

[152] E.g., D. 3932, ad 2.

manum, servandum esse Caeremoniale,[153] or by a reference to previous decrees on the same subject: *Dentur Decreta, serventur Decreta prout iacent, iuxta Decretum.* In both of these cases the specific rubric or decree may or may not be indicated. Similarly, a reply may be given by a direction to follow the approved commentators on sacred rites: *Consulantur Rubricistae, etc.*[154]

A final mention should be made of the manner in which the Congregation of Sacred Rites (and the other Roman Congregations) phrases a reply to a double question. The answer is given in this way: "Affirmative to the first part, Negative to the second part," or vice-versa. This is best illustrated by means of an example:

> Whether the Procession of the Blessed Sacrament which immediately follows Vespers chanted with red or green vestments must be celebrated with the same vestments, or must vestments of white color be put on? Affirmative to the first part, negative to the second part.[155]

For the sake of clarity, questions proposed to the Congregation and the responses given frequently follow this pattern.

F. Archives of the Congregation

The practical need and value of carefully kept archives for the chief organs of ecclesiastical government is obvious. This was recognized by the Congregation of Sacred Rites from its first years. Its archives, which date from 1588, were first given a systematic arrangement by one of the early officials, Mucante, who was secretary from 1602 to 1617. He describes, in a preface to *Liber II* of the decrees compiled by him, something of the previous workings of the Congregation's secretariat and his own efforts to organize registers of the Congregation's acts.[156]

---

[153] E.g., D. 2179; 2246; 2319; 2363; 3236, ad 1-2; 3448, ad 12.

[154] E.g., D. 2683, ad 49. Van der Stappen, *Sacra Liturgia*, I, 15-16; Moretti, *Caeremoniale*, I, 10-11.

[155] S.R.C., *Westmonasterien.*, 27 maii 1911 — D. 4269, ad 13.

[156] *AIP*, VII (1864), 11-13.

From time to time it was necessary for the Congregation to take steps to preserve the documents submitted to it and copies of its own acts, as is indicated in some of the seventeenth century decrees. For example, in 1632 a special place in the Vatican Palace was assigned to the archives and one of the notaries chosen to care for it.[157] A few years later a decree was issued requiring that all the documents belonging to the Congregation which had become scattered throughout the city of Rome should be collected and placed in the archives at the Vatican.[158]

The registers of the Congregation, which, according to the plan of Mucante, included a *Registrum Servorum Dei* and a *Registrum liturgicum,* were interrupted during the years 1810 to 1814 after the Napoleonic occupation of the Papal States. At that time the archives of the Congregation of Rites from its institution were taken to Paris, together with the other Vatican Archives.[159] These were later restored to the Holy See, with the exception of certain documents having to do with the processes of the Servants of God, and replaced in the archives at the Vatican and at the office of the Congregation in the Palazzo della Cancelleria.[160] In 1936 most of the archival materials were moved to the new Palace of the Congregations in Piazza S. Callisto in Trastevere.[161]

The portions of the Congregation's archives which have been published have already been mentioned.[162] They are, of course, only excerpts from the material now located principally at the offices of the Congregation, in the Vatican, and in Paris. In the secret archives of the Vatican are kept the original *acta* having to do with canonizations and beatifications. These fill more than four thousand volumes.[163] In Paris, at the Bibliothèque Nationale,

---

[157] S.R.C., *Scriptuarum Sacrae Rit. Cong.,* 30 apr. 1632 — *AIP,* VII (1864) 241.

[158] S.R.C., *Notariatus,* 10 sept. 1642 — *AIP,* VII (1864), 289-290.

[159] Antonelli, "L'Archivio della S. Congregazione dei Riti," *Il Libro e le Biblioteche* (Romae: Pontificium Athenaeum Antonianum, 1950), p. 68.

[160] *Ibid.,* p. 71.

[161] *Loc. cit.*

[162] Cf. *supra,* pp. 145-149.

[163] Stickler, *Historia Iuris Canonici,* I, 335.

there are nearly eight thousand *positiones*, also from the processes of canonization and beatification.[164]

In the Congregation's own archives, there are the double registers begun in 1588 and continued to the present, *Registrum Sanctorum Dei* and *Registrum liturgicum*, as well as collections of approved liturgical books,[165] proper calendars of local churches and religious institutes, concessions of liturgical insignia made by the Congregation. There are also collections of the *positiones* in processes of the Servants of God since 1851, letters of petition in these cases and in connection with the naming of Doctors of the Church and patron saints, and printed *positiones* in the causes of beatification and canonization since 1814.[166]

In addition to these matters contained in the grand archives of the Congregation, there are collections in the offices of the Historical Section and in the Chancery of the Congregation. The former includes volumes of *positiones* prior to 1851, and other materials dealing with historical cases of the Servants of God, while the latter consists of documents referring to cases currently in process.[167] Although the archives are not open to the public, it is possible for scholars to obtain permission to consult documents which are not of a secret character.

The description of the archives of the Congregation of Sacred Rites completes the consideration of the Congregation's decrees. For the priest and the student of rubrical matters the published *Decreta Authentica* (and, since 1927, the decrees contained in the *Acta Apostolicae Sedis*) are of the greatest value. They are the expression of the Congregation's activity and, taken with the liturgical books approved by the Congregation and the proclamation of beatifications and canonizations, illustrate the manner in which it exercises authority over the law of the sacred liturgy, as an organ of the Apostolic See.

---

[164] Antonelli, "L'Archivio della S. Congregazione dei Riti," *Il Libro e le Biblioteche*, p. 72; *Analecta Bollandiana* (Parisiis, 1882   ), V (1886), 148-158.

[165] These include the Propers of dioceses and various moral persons.

[166] The earlier printed *positiones* are in Paris, as already mentioned.

[167] This description is taken from Antonelli's article cited above, in *Il Libro et le Biblioteche*, pp. 72-76. Cf. Stickler, *Historia Iuris Canonici*, I, 334-335.

CONCLUSIONS

1. The Congregation of Sacred Rites possesses true legislative power over the matters within its competence, with the restriction that legislation, as a grave and extraordinary matter, must be submitted to the Roman Pontiff for approval.

2. In the issuance of general decrees the Congregation is not bound by the provisions of the Motu Proprio *Cum iuris canonici*, except in matters of liturgical law which are included in the Code of Canon Law.

3. The Congregation of Sacred Rites has the full power to interpret authentically the liturgical law, with the exception of laws in the Code of Canon Law, which must be submitted to the Pontifical Commission for the Authentic Interpretation of the Canons of the Code.

4. General decrees of the Congregation of Sacred Rites and particular decrees which are equivalently general oblige all Catholics of the Latin Church; they require promulgation if they establish a new law or give an interpretation that restricts, extends, or explains a doubtful law.

5. The only true judicial power of the Congregation of Sacred Rites is in connection with the causes of the Servants of God, whether of the Latin or of the Oriental Churches.

6. In the definition of the competence of the Congregation of Sacred Rites, the phrase "sacred rites and ceremonies" refers to the entire liturgical law, taken strictly as comprising the rubrics and laws which govern Catholic worship.

7. Customs contrary to the decrees of the Congregation of Sacred Rites may obtain the force of law in accordance with the general norms of custom.

APPENDIX

The Name of the Congregation

The official name of the Congregation is *Congregatio Sacrorum Rituum,* "Congregation of Sacred Rites," according to the usage of the Constitution *Sapienti consilio* and the Code of Canon Law. By analogy with the names of the other Roman Congregations, to which *Sacra* is generally prefixed in Latin and in Italian, the Congregation is frequently called *Sacra Rituum Congregatio.* Both names appear in the decrees of the Congregation itself. In English it may be called "Congregation of Sacred Rites," which is its precise title, "Congregation of Rites," or "Sacred Congregation of Rites."

The Address of the Congregation

Petitions to the Congregation of Sacred Rites should be addressed, *Beatissime Pater,* as in the case of the other Congregations, but should be sent to the Prefect of the Congregation directly: All' Eminentissimo Signor Cardinale Prefetto della S. Congregazione dei Riti, Palazzo delle Congregazioni, Piazza S. Callisto, Roma.

The Congregation of Sacred Rites — 1954

The following are the members and officials of the Congregation, as listed in the *Annuario Pontificio* for 1954:

Cardinals

Gaetano Cicognani, *Prefect*

Eugenio Tisserant, Bishop of Ostia and Porto e Santa Rufina
Clemente Micara, Bishop of Velletri
Benedetto Aloisi Masella, Bishop of Palestrina
Adeodato Giovanni Piazza, Bishop of Sabina e Poggio Mirteto
Federico Tedeschini, Bishop of Frascati

Alessandro Verde	Celso Costantini
Pietro Segura y Sáenz	Maurizio Feltin
Alfredo Ildefonso Schuster	Giorgio Grente
Emanuele Gonçalves Cerejeira	Beniamino de Arriba y Castro
Edoardo Mooney	Fernando Quiroga y Palacios
Giuseppe M. Caro Rodriguez	Paolo Emilio Leger
Giacomo de Barros Camara	Crisanto Luque
Enrico Pla y Deniel	Giuseppe Wendel
Giuseppe Frings	Nicola Canali
Giovanni Gualberto Guevara	Giovanni Mercati
Antonio Caggiano	

Most Rev. Alfonso Carinci, Titular Archbishop of Selucia in
Isauria, *Secretary*

Msgr. Enrico Dante, *Substitute*

SECTION I

FOR THE CAUSES OF BEATIFICATION AND CANONIZATION

Msgr. Salvatore Natucci, *Promoter General of the Faith*
Msgr. Silvio Romani, *Assessor* and *Subpromoter General
of the Faith*
Sig. Guglielmo de Heredia, *Assistant (Aiutante di studio)*
Msgr. Gioacchino Sormanti, *Assistant*
Rev. Nicola Cardillo, *Assistant*
Msgr. Nicola Ferraro, *Assistant*
Sig. Giovanni Campa, *Scriptor*

Praelati Officiales

Most Rev. Andrea Jullien, *Dean of the S. R. Rota*
Most Rev. Pietro Canisio Van Lierde, Titular Bishop of Porfireone,
Sacristan of His Holiness
Msgr. Francesco Annibale Ferretti, *Protonotary Apostolic*
Msgr. Arturo Wynen, *Auditor* of the S. R. Rota
Msgr. Guglielmo Teodoro Heard, *Auditor* of the S. R. Rota
Very Rev. Michele Browne, O.P., *Master of the Sacred Palace*
Very Rev. Ferdinando Antonelli, O.F.M., *Relator General
of Section III*

Consultors

Most Rev. Luca Ermenegildo Pasetto, Latin Patriarch of
Alexandria

. . . . *Assessor* of the Holy Office

Most Rev. Pietro Pisani, Titular Archbishop of Constantia in
Scythia

Very Rev. Francesco Capponi, O. Min.

Very Rev. Luigi M. Manzini, of the Barnabites

Very Rev. Emiliano Bartolozzi, O.E.S.A.

Very Rev. Abb. Emiliano Lucchesi, C.V.U.O.S.B.

Very Rev. Luigi Castano, S.D.B.

Very Rev. Gaetano Stano, O.F.M.Conv.

Very Rev. Alberto Grammatico, O.C.

Very Rev. Fr. Clemente di Santa Maria in Punta, O.F.M.Cap.

Very Rev. Gabriele M. Roschini, O.S.M.

Very Rev. Lorenzo Binazzi, O.S.B.

Very Rev. Vittorio Genovesi, S.J.

SECTION II

FOR THE SACRED LITURGY

Consultors

The Masters of Pontifical Ceremonies

Msgr. Angelo Mercati

Msgr. Leone Gromier

Msgr. Felice Ravanat

Msgr. Igino Anglés Pamies

Msgr. Gioacchino Nabuco

Very Rev. Mario Righetti

Very Rev. Massimiliano Brandys, O.F.M.

Very Rev. Francesco Monay, O.F.M. Conv.

Very Rev. Luigi Paladini, C.M.

Very Rev. Antonino Silli, O.P.

Very Rev. Giovanni Michele Hanssens, S.J.

Very Rev. Giuseppe Pizzoni, C.M.

Very Rev. Pietro Siffrin, O.S.B.

Very Rev. Abb. Bernardo Capelle, O.S.B.

Very Rev. Giuseppe Andrea Jungmann, S.J.

Very Rev. Agostino Bea, S.J.

Section III

FOR THE HISTORICAL CAUSES OF THE SERVANTS OF GOD AND THE EMENDATION OF THE LITURGICAL BOOKS

Very Rev. Ferdinando Antonelli, O.F.M., *Relator General*
Very Rev. Giuseppe Löw, C.SS.R., *Vice-Relator*
Msgr. Giuseppe Rius y Serra, *Assistant*
Msgr. Amato Pietro Frutaz, *Assistant*
Rev. Giovanni Papa, *Assistant*

Consultors

Msgr. Felice Ravanat
Msgr. Angelo Mercati
Most Rev. Pio Paschini
Very Rev. Fredegando Callaey, O.F.M.Cap.
Very Rev. Mauro Inguanez, O.S.B.
Very Rev. Cuniberto Mohlberg, O.S.B.
Very Rev. Giuseppe M. Pou y Martî, O.F.M.
Very Rev. Carlo Silva-Tarouca, S.J.
Very Rev. Pietro Tacchi, S.J.
Very Rev. Gabriele Théry, O.P.
Very Rev. Abb. Anselmo Albareda, O.S.B.
Very Rev. Tommaso Käppeli, O.P.
Very Rev. Pietro Letùria, S.J.
S. E. Pio Franchi de' Cavalieri
Sig. Prof. Angelo Silvagni

OFFICIALS OF THE SECRETARIAT

Very Rev. Vittorio Genovesi, S.J., *Hymnographer*
Msgr. Silverio Mattei, *Assistant*
Rev. Traiano Crisan, *Assistant*
Msgr. Giuseppe Rius y Serra, *Archivist*
Msgr. Salvatore Indelicato, *Protocolist* and *Assistant Archivist*
Msgr. Armando Fattinnanzi, *Assistant Archivist*

OFFICIALS OF THE CHANCERY

Msgr. Orazio Cocchetti, *Notary* and *Chancellor*
Sig. Ovidio Meschini, *Assistant Chancellor*

BIBLIOGRAPHY
Sources

Acta Apostolicae Sedis, Commentarium Officiale, Romae, 1909-1929; Civitate Vaticana, 1929—

Acta et Decreta Sacrorum Conciliorum Recentiorum, Collectio Lacensis, 7 vols., Friburgi Brisgoviae, 1870-1892.

Acta Sanctae Sedis, 41 vols., Romae, 1865-1908.

Annuario Pontificio, Roma, *Notizie*, 1716-1861; *Annuario Pontificio*, 1862-1871; *La Gerarchia Cattolica*, 1872-1911; *Annuario Pontificio*, 1912—

Bartolini, Dominicus, *Acta Sacrorum Solemnium quibus SS. D. N. Pius IX XXVI Martyribus Iaponensibus ac Beato Michaeli de Sanctis Confessori Sanctorum Coelitum Honores Decrevit*, Romae, 1864.

Bouscaren, T. Lincoln, *The Canon Law Digest*, 2 vols. and Supplement through 1948, Milwaukee: Bruce, 1934-1949.

Breviarium Romanum ex Decreto Sacrosancti Concilii Tridentini Restitutum S. Pii V Pontificis Maximi Jussu Editum Aliorumque Pontificum Cura Recognitum Pii Papae X Auctoritate Reformatum.

Bullarum Diplomatum et Privilegiorum Romanorum Pontificum Taurinensis Editio, 24 vols. and Appendix, Augustae Taurinorum, 1857-1872.

Caeremoniale Episcoporum Clementis VIII, Innocentii X et Benedicti XIII Jussu Editum Benedicti XIV et Leonis XIII Auctoritate Recognitum.

Codex Iuris Canonici Pii X Pontificis Maximi Iussu Digestus, Benedicti XV Auctoritate Promulgatus.

Codicis Iuris Canonici Fontes, cura E.mi Petri Card. Gasparri ed., 9 vols., Romae: Typis Polyglottis Vaticanis, 1923-1939 (Vols. VII-IX, ed. cura E.mi Iustiniani Card Serédi).

Collectanea in Usum Secretariae Sacrae Congregationis Episcoporum et Regularium, Romae, 1863.

Collectanea S. Congregationis de Propaganda Fide, 2 vols., Romae, 1907.

Collectio Decretorum ad Sacram Liturgiam Spectantium ab anno 1927 ad annum 1946, 2. ed., Roma: Edizioni Liturgiche, 1947.

Corpus Iuris Canonici, ed. Lipsiensis secunda, post Aemilii Richteri curas instruxit Aemilius Friedberg, 2 vols., Lipsiae, 1879-1881.

Decreta Authentica Congregationis Sacrorum Rituum, 5 vols., Romae, 1898-1901; Vol. VI, 1912; Vol. VII, 1927.

Decreta Authentica Sacrae Congregationis Indulgentiis Sacrisque Reliquiis Praepositae ab anno 1668 ad annum 1882, Ratisbonae, 1883.

Decreta Sacrae Rituum Congregationis in lucem primum ed. a P. D. Bartholomaeo Gavanto . . . deinde a P. D. Cajetano Maria Merato . . . adaucta, 2. ed., Florentiae, 1743.

Decretales D. Gregorii Papae IX, Suae Integritati, una cum Glossis Restitutae, 2 vols., Romae, 1582.

Decretum Gratiani Emendatum et Observationibus Illustratum una cum Glossis, Gregorii XIII Pont. Max. Iussu Editum, 2 vols., Romae, 1582.

Denzinger, Henricus, *Enchiridion Symbolorum, Definitionum, et Declarationum de Rebus Fidei et Morum*, 26. ed. augmentata, Friburgi Brisgoviae: Herder, 1947.

Galante, Andreas, *Fontes Iuris Canonici Selecti*, Oeniponte, 1906.

Gardellini, Aloisius, *Decreta Authentica Congregationis Sacrorum Rituum Nunc Primum ex Actis ejusdem S. C. Collecta*, 5 vols., Romae, 1808-1816.

——————, *Decreta Authentica Congregationis Sacrorum Rituum*, 2. ed., 7 vols., Romae, 1824-1826; 3. ed., 4 vols., 1856-1858; Vol. V, 1888.

Hardouin, Jean, *Acta Conciliorum et Epistolae Decretales ac Constitutiones Summorum Pontificum*, 12 vols., Parisiis, 1714-1715.

Liber Sextus Decretalium D. Bonifacii Papae VIII, Suae Integritati una cum Clementinis et Extravagantibus, Earumque Glossis Restitutus, Romae, 1582.

Mansi, Ioannes, *Sacrorum Conciliorum Nova et Amplissima Collectio*, 53 vols. in 60, Parisiis, 1901-1927.

Martinucci, Pius, *Manuale Ecclesiasticorum seu Sacrae Rituum Congregationis Decreta*, 3. ed., Romae, 1853.

Memoriale Rituum pro Aliquibus Praestantioribus Sacris Functionibus Persolvendis in Minoribus Ecclesiis Benedicti XIII Pont. Max. Jussu Editum, Benedicti Papae XV Auctoritate Recognitum.

Missale Romanum, ex Decreto Sacrosancti Concilii Tridentini Restitutum, S. Pii V Pontificis Maximi Jussu Editum, Aliorum Cura Recognitum, a Pio X Reformatum et Benedicti XV Auctoritate Vulgatum.

Monumenta Germaniae Historica, Legum Tomus I, ed. Georgius Pertz, Hanoverae, 1835; *Epistolarum* Tomus I, Pars I, ed. Paulus Ewald, Berolini, 1891; Pars II, ed. Ludovicus Hartmann, Berolini, 1893; *Legum* Sectio III, *Concilia*, Tomus II, ed. Albertus Werminghoff, Hanoverae, 1904; *Epistolarum Selectarum* Tomus I, ed. Michael Tangl, Berolini, 1916.

Mühlbauer, Wolfgang, *Decreta Authentica Sacrorum Rituum Congregationis et Instructio Clementina ex Actis ejusdem Collecta ab Aloisio Gardellini in Usum Cleri Commodiorem Ordine Alphabetico Concinnata*, 3 vols. in 4, Monachii, 1863-1867; Supplement, 3 vols., 1876-1885.

Pii X Pontificis Maximi Acta, 5 vols., Romae, 1905-1914.

Pontificale Romanum Summorum Pontificum Jussu Editum, et a Benedicto XIV Pont. Max. Recognitum et Castigatum.

Rituale Romanum Pauli V Pont. Max. Jussu Editum Aliorumque Pontificum Cura Recognitum atque ad Normam Codicis Juris Canonici Accommodatum SS.mi D. N. Pii Papae XII Auctoritate Ordinatum et Auctum.

Schroeder, Henry J., *Canons and Decrees of the Council of Trent*, St. Louis: Herder, 1941.

——————, *Disciplinary Decrees of the General Councils*, St. Louis: Herder, 1937.

Sylloge Praecipuorum Documentorum Recentium Summorum Pontificum et S. Congregationis de Propaganda Fide, Romae: Typis Polyglottis Vaticanis, 1939.

Thiel, Andreas, *Epistolae Pontificum Romanorum Genuinae*, Vol. I, Brunsbergae, 1868.

Reference Works

Abbo, John A.—Hannan, Jerome D., *The Sacred Canons*, 2 vols., St. Louis, London: Herder, 1952.

Aigrain, René, *Liturgia*, Paris, 1930.

Andrieu, Michel, *Les Ordines Romani du Haut Moyen Age*, 3 vols., Louvain: Spicilegium Sacrum Lovaniense, 1931-1951.

Baart, Peter A., *The Roman Court*, 2. ed., New York, 1895.

Badii, Caesar, *Institutiones Iuris Canonici*, 3. ed., 2 vols., Florentiae, 1921-1922.

Bargilliat, M., *Praelectiones Juris Canonici*, 37. ed., 2 vols., Parisiis, 1923.

Batiffol, Pierre, *History of the Roman Breviary*, 3. ed., New York, 1912.

Baumstark, Anton, *Missale Romanum, Seine Entwicklung, ihre wichtigsten Urkunde and Probleme*, Eindhoven-Nijmegen, 1929.

Benedictus XIV, *Opera Omnia*, 12 vols., Romae, 1747.

Berutti, Christophorus, *Institutiones Iuris Canonici*, 5 vols., Taurini: Marietti, 1936-1943.

Beste, Udalricus, *Introductio in Codicem*, 3. ed., Collegeville, Minn.: St. John's Abbey Press, 1946.

Blat, Albertus, *Commentarium Textus Codicis Iuris Canonici*, 5 vols. in 6, Romae, 1919-1927.

Bona, Ioannes, *Rerum Liturgicarum Libri Duo*, Romae, 1671.

Bouix, Dominicus, *Tractatus de Curia Romana*, Parisiis, 1859.

——————————, *Tractatus de Jure Liturgico*, Parisiis, 1853.

Bouscaren, T. Lincoln — Ellis, Adam C., *Canon Law, A Text and Commentary*, Milwaukee: Bruce, 1946.

Brys, J., *Juris Canonici Compendium*, 10. ed., 2 vols., Brugis: Desclée, 1947-1949.

Callewaert, Camillus A., *Liturgicae Institutiones*, 2. ed., Vols. I-II, Brugis: Beyaert, 1925-1939.

Cance, Adrien, *Le Codé de Droit Canonique*, 7. ed., 3 vols., Paris: Gabalda, 1946.

Cappello, Felix M., *De Curia Romana iuxta Reformationem a Pio X Sapientissime Inductam*, 2 vols., Romae, 1911-1912.

——————, *Summa Iuris Canonici,* 3 vols., Vols. I-II, 4. ed.,
　　Romae: Aedes Universitatis Gregorianae, 1945.

——————, *Summa Iuris Publici Ecclesiastici,* 2. ed., Romae,
　　1928.

Cavalieri, Ioannes, *Opera Omnia Liturgica,* 5 vols. in 1, Venetiis,
　　1778.

Cavigioli, Giovanni, *Manuale di Diritto Canonico,* 3. ed., Torino:
　　Società Editrice Internazionale, 1946.

Chelodi, Ioannes, *Ius Canonicum de Personis,* 3. ed., curavit Pius
　　Ciprotti, Vicenza: Società Anonima Tipografica, 1942.

Cicognani, Amleto G., *Canon Law,* 2. ed., Reprint; Westminster,
　　Maryland: Newman, 1949.

Coelho, Antonio, *Corso di Liturgia Romana,* 5 vols., Torino, Roma:
　　Marietti, 1935-1940.

Cohellius, Jacobus, *Notitia Cardinalatus,* Romae, 1653.

Coronata, Matthaeus Conte a, *Institutiones Iuris Canonici,* 2. ed.,
　　5 vols., Taurini: Marietti, 1939-1947.

Corpus Scriptorum Ecclesiasticorum Latinorum, 70 vols., Vindo-
　　bonae, 1866—

Crnica, Antonius, *Commentarium Theoretico-practicum Codicis
　　Iuris Canonici,* Vol. I, Šibenik: Kačic, 1940.

Croegaert, Aug., *Les Rites et Prières du Saint Sacrifice de la Messe,*
　　2. ed., 3 vols., Malines: Dessain, 1948.

Dal Sasso, J., *Liturgiae Sacerdotalis Compendariae Institutiones,*
　　2. ed., Patavii: Domus Libraria Gregoriana, 1939.

De Luca, Joannes, *Theatrum Veritatis et Justitiae sive Decisivi
　　Discursus,* 16 vols. in 9, Coloniae, 1706.

De Meester, Alphonsus, *Juris Canonici et Juris Canonico-civilis
　　Compendium,* 3 vols. in 4, Brugis, 1921-1928.

De Puniet, Pierre, *The Roman Pontifical, A History and Com-
　　mentary,* New York: Longmans, 1932.

Dictionnaire d'Archéologie Chrétienne et de Liturgie, Paris: Le-
　　touzey et Ané, 1907—

Dictionnaire de Droit Canonique, Paris: Letouzey et Ané, 1924—

Dix, Gregory, *The Treatise on the Apostolic Tradition of Saint
　　Hippolytus of Rome,* London: Society for Promoting Chris-
　　tian Knowledge—New York: Macmillan, 1937.

Dooley, Eugene A., *Church Law on Sacred Relics,* The Catholic University of America Canon Law Studies, n. 70, Washington, D.C.: The Catholic University of America, 1931.

Duchesne, Louis, *Christian Worship: Its Origin and Evolution,* 5. ed., trans. M. L. McClure, London: Society for Promoting Christian Knowledge, 1920.

——————, *Le Liber Pontificalis,* 2 vols., Paris, 1886-1892.

Dziob, Michael W., *The Sacred Congregation for the Oriental Church,* The Catholic University of America Canon Law Studies, n. 214, Washington, D.C.: The Catholic University of America Press, 1945.

Eichmann, Eduard, *Lehrbuch des Kirchenrechts,* 2. ed., Paderborn, 1926.

Ferreres, Ioannes, *Institutiones Canonicae iuxta Codicem Novissimum,* 2. ed., 2 vols., Barcinone, 1920.

Fortescue, Adrian, *The Mass: A Study of the Roman Liturgy,* 2. ed., London: Longmans, 1913.

Florilegium Patristicum, ed. Bernhardus Geyer et Johannes Zellinger, Fasciculus VII, Pars I, *Monumenta Eucharistica et Liturgica Vetustissima,* ed. Johannes Quasten, Bonn: Hanstein, 1935.

Funk, Franciscus X., *Opera Patrum Apostolicorum,* 2 vols., Tübingen, 1881-1887.

Gavantus, Bartholomaeus, *Thesaurus Sacrorum Rituum,* Parisiis, 1647.

Geier, Fritz, *Die Durchführung der kirchlichen Reformen Josephs II,* Stuttgart, 1905.

Grimaldi, Felix, *Les Congrégations Romaines,* Siena, 1890.

Guéranger, Prosper, *Institutions Liturgiques,* 2. ed., 4 vols., Paris, Brussels, 1878-1885.

Haine, Antoine J. J. F., *De la Cour Romaine,* 2 vols. in 1, Louvain, 1859-1861.

——————, *Synopsis S. R. E. Cardinalium Congregationum,* Lovanii, 1857.

Hilling, Nicholas, *Procedure at the Roman Curia,* New York, 1907.

Hinschius, Paul, *Decretales Pseudo-Isidorianae et Capitula Angilramni,* Lipsiae, 1863.

Il Libro e le Biblioteche, Romae: Pontificium Athenaeum Antonianum, 1950.

Jaffé, Philippus, *Regesta Pontificum Romanorum ab Condita Ecclesia ad annum post Christum Natum MCXCVIII,* 2. ed., quam curaverunt S. Loewenfeld, F. Kaltenbrunner, P. Ewald, 2 vols., Lipsiae, 1885-1888.

Jombart, Emile, *Manuel de Droit Canon,* Paris: Beauchesne, 1949.

Jone, Heribert, *Commentarium in Codicem Iuris Canonici,* Vol. I, Paderborn: Schöningh, 1950.

Jungmann, Josef A., *Missarum Sollemnia, eine genetische Erklärung der römischen Messe,* 2. ed., 2 vols., Wien: Herder, 1949.

——————, *The Mass of the Roman Rite: Its Origins and Development (Missarum Sollemnia),* trans. Francis A. Brunner, 2 vols., New York: Benziger, 1950—

Kellner, K. A. Heinrich, *Heortology, A History of the Christian Festivals from their Origin to the Present Day,* St. Louis, 1908.

Kemp, Eric W., *Canonization and Authority in the Western Church,* Oxford: Oxford University Press, 1948.

Kennedy, Vincent L., *The Saints of the Canon of the Mass,* Studi di Antichità Cristiana, XIV, Vatican City: Pontificio Istituto di Archeologia Cristiana, 1938.

King, Archdale, *Notes on the Catholic Liturgies,* London, 1930.

Kirch, Conradus, *Enchiridion Fontium Historiae Ecclesiasticae Antiquae,* 6. ed., Barcelona: Herder, 1947.

Lebreton, Jules—Zeiller, Jacques, *The History of the Primitive Church,* trans. Ernest C. Messenger, 2 vols., New York: Macmillan, 1949.

Lega, Michael, *Praelectiones in Textum Iuris Canonici de Iudiciis Ecclesiasticis,* 4 vols., Romae, 1896-1901.

Leitner, Martinus, *De Curia Romana,* Ratisbonae, 1909.

Loomis, Louise R., *The Book of the Popes,* Records of Civilization: Sources and Studies, New York, 1916.

Lunadoro, Girolamo, *Relatione della Corte di Roma,* Venezia, 1664.

Maroto, Philippus, *Institutiones Iuris Canonici ad Normam Novi Codicis*, 2 vols., Vol. I, 3. ed., Romae, 1921.

Martin, Michael, *The Roman Curia*, New York, 1913.

Martin, Victor, *Les Congrégations Romaines*, Paris, 1930.

Menghini, Ioannes B., *Elementa Iuris Liturgici*, 2. ed., Romae, 1906.

Michiels, Gommarus, *Normae Generales Juris Canonici*, 2. ed., 2 vols., Parisiis: Desclée, 1949.

Migne, Jacques Paul, *Patrologiae Cursus Completus, Series Graeca*, 161 vols., Parisiis, 1857-1866.

——————, *Patrologiae Cursus Completus, Series Latina*, 221 vols., Parisiis, 1844-1855.

Monin, Arthur, *De Curia Romana*, Lovanii, 1912.

Moretti, Aloisius, *Caeremoniale iuxta Ritum Romanum seu De Sacris Functionibus*, 4 vols., Taurini: Marietti, 1936-1939.

Moroni, Gaetano, *Dizionario di Erudizione Storico-Ecclesiastica*, 109 vols., Venezia, 1840-1879.

Nabuco, Joachim, *Pontificalis Romani Expositio Juridico-Practica*, 3 vols., Petropolis, Brazil: Vozes, 1945.

Naz, Raoul, *ed.*, *Traité de Droit Canonique*, 4 vols., Paris: Letouzey et Ané, 1948-1949.

Noldin, Hieronymus—Schmitt, A., *Summa Theologiae Moralis*, 27. ed., 3 vols., Oeniponte, Lipsiae: Rauch, 1940-1941.

O'Connell, John B., *The Celebration of Mass*, 3 vols., Milwaukee: Bruce, 1940-1941.

Oesterle, Gerardus, *Praelectiones Iuris Canonici*, Vol. I, Romae, 1931.

Ojetti, Benedictus, *De Romana Curia, Commentarium in Constitutionem Apostolicam "Sapienti Consilio,"* Romae, 1910.

Ollivier, Sébastien, *La Sacrée Congrégation de la Consistoriale*, Montpellier, 1914.

Oppenheim, Philippus, *Institutiones Systematico-Historicae in Sacram Liturgiam*, Series I, 6 vols., Taurini, Romae: Marietti, 1938-1941; Vol. I, 2. ed., 1945.

Ottaviani, Alaphridus, *Institutiones Iuris Publici Ecclesiastici*, 3. ed., 2 vols., Romae: Typis Polyglottis Vaticanis, 1947-1948.

Parayre, R., *La S. Congrégation du Concile*, Paris, 1897.

Parente, Petrus, *Theologia Fundamentalis*, Collectio Theologica Romana, I, Romae, Taurini: Marietti, 1946.

Pastor, Ludwig, *The History of the Popes*, 40 vols., St. Louis: Herder, 1891-1953.

Phillips, Georg, *Kirchenrecht*, 7 vols., Ratisbon, 1845-1889.

Piolanti, Antonius, *De Sacramentis*, Collectio Theologica Romana, VI, 2 vols., Romae, Taurini: Marietti, 1944-1945.

Platus, Hieronymus, *De Cardinalis Dignitate et Officiis Tractatus*, 6. ed., Romae, 1836.

Poole, Reginald L., *Lectures on the History of the Papal Chancery*, Cambridge, 1915.

Potthast, Augustus, *Regesta Pontificum Romanorum inde ab anno post Christum Natum MCXCVIII ad annum MCCCIV*, 2 vols., Berolini, 1874-1875.

Prümmer, Dominicus M., *Manuale Iuris Canonici*, 5. ed., Friburgi Brisgoviae, 1927.

Quasten, Johannes, *Patrology*, Vol. I, *The Beginnings of Patristic Literature*, Westminster, Maryland: Newman—Utrecht, Brussels: Spectrum, 1951.

Raes, Alphonsus, *Introductio in Liturgiam Orientalem*, Vol. I, Romae: Pontificium Institutum Studiorum Orientalium, 1947.

Regatillo, Eduardus F., *Institutiones Iuris Canonici*, 4. ed., 2 vols., Santander: Sal Terrae, 1951.

Reiffenstuel, Anacletus, *Ius Canonicum Universum*, 5 vols. in 7, Parisiis, 1864-1870.

Righetti, Mario, *Manuale di Storia Liturgica*, Vol. I, *Introduzione Generale*, Milano: Editrice Ancora, 1945.

Romita, Fiorenzo, *Ius Musicae Liturgicae*, Taurini: Marietti, 1936.

Rousseau, Olivier, *The Progress of the Liturgy*, Westminster, Maryland: Newman, 1951.

Rozière, Eugène de, *Liber Diurnus ou Recueil des Formules usitées par la Chancellerie Pontificale du Ve au Xe Siècle*, Paris, 1869.

Salaville, Sévérien, *An Introduction to the Study of Eastern Liturgies*, London: Sands, 1938.

Schmalzgrüber, Franciscus, *Ius Ecclesiasticum Universum*, 5 vols. in 12, Romae, 1843-1845.

Schuster, Ildefonso, *The Sacramentary (Liber Sacramentorum)*, 5 vols., trans. A. Levilis-Marke, New York, 1924-1930.

Shotwell, James T.—Loomis, Louise R., *The See of Peter*, Records of Civilization: Sources and Studies, New York, 1927.

Simier, Jules, *La Curie Romaine*, Paris, 1909.

Sipos, Stephanus, *Enchiridion Iuris Canonici*, 3. ed., Pécs, 1936.

Sotillo, Lorenzo R., *Compendium Iuris Publici Ecclesiastici*, Santander: Sal Terrae, 1947.

Statistica della Gerarchia e dei Fedeli di Rito Orientale, Roma, 1932.

Stickler, Alfonso M., *Historia Iuris Canonici Latini*, Vol. I, *Historia Fontium*, Augustae Taurinorum: Apud Custodiam Librariam Pontif. Athenaei Salesiani, 1950.

Thibaut, Jean B., *La Liturgie Romaine*, Paris, 1924.

Toso, Albertus, *Ad Codicem Iuris Canonici Commentaria Minora*, 5 vols., Romae, 1921-1927.

Van der Stappen, J. F., *Sacra Liturgia*, 5 vols., Mechliniae, 1898.

Van Hove, Alphonse, *Commentarium Lovaniense in Codicem Iuris Canonici*, Vol. I, Tom. I, *Prolegomena*, 2. ed., Mechliniae, Romae: Dessain, 1945; Tom. II, *De Legibus Ecclesiasticis*, 1930; Tom. III, *De Consuetudine et de Temporis Supputatione*, 1933.

Vermeersch, A.—Creusen, J., *Epitome Iuris Canonici*, 3 vols., Vol. I, 7. ed., Mechliniae, Romae: Dessain, 1949.

Wernz, Franciscus X., *Ius Decretalium*, 6 vols., Romae, 1898-1914.

——————— — Vidal, Petrus, *Ius Canonicum ad Codicis Normam Exactum*, 7 vols. in 8, Romae: Apud Aedes Universitatis Gregorianae, 1923-1948; Vol. II, 3 ed., 1943.

Articles

Anonymous, "Des Congrégations Romaines et de leur Pratique," *Analecta Iuris Pontificii*, II (1857), 2230-2282; 2364-2424.

Antonelli, Ferdinando, "L'Archivio della S. Congregatione dei Riti," *Il Libro e le Biblioteche, Romae*: Pontificium Athenaeum Antonianum, 1950, pp. 63-76.

Bibliophilus, "De S. R. C. decretorum collectionibus," *Ephemerides Liturgicae*, XL (1930), 433-438.

Borella, Pietro, "S. Leone Magno et il 'Communicantes,'" *Ephemerides Liturgicae*, LX (1946), 93-101.

Capelle, D. B., "Le Main de S. Grégoire dans le Sacramentaire Grégorien," *Revue Bénédictine*, XLIX (1937), 13-28.

————, "Le pape Gélase et la messe romaine," *Revue d'Histoire Ecclésiastique*, XXXV (1939), 22-34.

Connolly, R. H., "Pope Innocent I *de nominibus recitandis*," *Journal of Theological Studies*, XX (1919), 215-226.

Ferretti, F., "De Vi Consuetudinis quoad Singulos Libros Liturgicos Plenius Investigata," *Ephemerides Liturgicae*, XXXI (1917), 678-682; 711-712; XXXII (1918), 36-40; 140-146.

Jedin, Hubert, "Das Konzil von Trient und die Reform der liturgischen Bücher," *Ephemerides Liturgicae*, LIX (1945), 5-38.

Kuttner, Stephan, "La Réserve Papale du Droit de Canonisation," *Revue Historique de Droit Français et Étranger*, 4. sér., XVII (1938), 172-228.

Menghini, Ioannes B., "De legibus liturgicis in peculiarem codicem redigendis," *Ephemerides Liturgicae*, XXXV (1921), 217-222.

Pastè, Romualdus, "Quid Liturgia?" *Ephemerides Liturgicae*, XLI (1927), 405-412.

Schmidt, John R., "The Juridic Value of the *Instructio*," *The Jurist*, I (1941), 289-311.

Periodicals

Analecta Bollandiana, Parisiis, 1882—

Analecta Iuris Pontificii, Romae, 1855-1868; Parisiis, 1869-1890; *Analecta Ecclesiastica*, 1893-1911.

Archiv für katholisches Kirchenrecht, Innsbruck, 1857-1861; Mainz, 1862—

Ephemerides Liturgicae, Romae, 1887—

Journal of Theological Studies, Oxford, 1899—

Jurist, The, Washington, D. C., 1941—

Revue Bénédictine, Maredsous, 1884—

Revue d'Histoire Ecclésiastique, Louvain, 1900—

Revue Historique de Droit Français et Étranger, Paris, 1855—

ABBREVIATIONS

AIP   —*Analecta Iuris Pontificii.*

AAS   —*Acta Apostolicae Sedis.*

ASS   —*Acta Sanctae Sedis.*

BRT   —*Bullarum Diplomatum et Privilegiorum Romanorum Pontificum Taurinensis Editio.*

D   —*Decreta Authentica Congregationis Sacrorum Rituum.*

Fontes   —*Codicis Iuris Canonici Fontes.*

JE   —Jaffé, *Regesta Pontificum Romanorum,* from 590 to 882.

JK   ————————, from the foundation of the Church to 590.

JL   ————————, from 882 to 1198.

MGH   —*Monumenta Germaniae Historica.*

MPL   —Migne, *Patrologiae Cursus Completus, Series Latina.*

Mediator Dei—Pius XII, ep. encycl. *Mediator Dei et hominum,* 30 nov. 1947—*AAS,* XXXIX (1947), 521-595.

S.C.C.   —Sacra Congregatio Concilii.

S.C.Consist. —Sacra Congregatio Consistorialis.

S.C.Rel.   —Sacra Congregatio Religiosorum.

S.C.Sac.   —Sacra Congregatio Sacramentorum.

S.R.C.   —Sacrorum Rituum Congregatio.

INDEX

Abbo-Hannan, 33, 71, 151
Abuses, correction of, 13, 67, 86, 142-143, 145
Address of S.R.C., 156
Administrative order, 59
Administrative power, *see* Executive power
Alexander III, 20
Alias nos, 25, 56
Allatae sunt, 11, 14
Amanuenses of S.R.C., 119-121
Ambrosian rite, 14, 76-77, 82
Andrieu, 20
Antiphonale Diurnum, 82
Antonelli, 153-154
Apostolatus officium, 65
Apostolic masters of ceremonies, 33, 38, 43, 118, 121
Apostolic processes, 126-127, 129
Apostolic See, power over worship, 9-14
  practice, 14-21
  reservation of powers, 14
  vacancy of, 62-66
Apostolicae Sedis, 29
Approbation of Roman Pontiff, 46-47, 104, 129, 155
  in forma communi, 51-52, 54
  in forma specifica, 52, 134
Archives of S.R.C., 152-154
Archivist of S.R.C., 119-120, 122
Arts, ecclesiastical, 73
Assessor of S.R.C., 119, 121
Assistants of S.R.C., 118-123
Auctorem fidei, 9
Auditors of Rota, 31, 118, 121, 127
Authentic interpretation, *see* Interpretation
Badii, 46, 64
Baptism, 4, 6, 13, 15, 18
Bargilliat, 45, 134, 139

Bartolini, 132
Batiffol, 19
Beatification, 128-129
  see Servants of God
Benedict XIV, 11, 14, 30, 118
Benedict XV, 43, 50-52, 56-58, 62, 108, 137
Benedictine rite, 77
Bibliothèque Nationale, 153-154
Bination, 80
Bishops and Regulars, Congregation of, 39-79
Bishops, Congregation of, 25
Bishops' rights over liturgy, 9-10, 12, 21
Blat, 55, 76
Blessings, 12, 73, 80, 84-85
Bona, 19
Boniface, St., 19
Books, concerning Servants of God, 88-89
Books, liturgical, vi, 4, 11, 13, 19, 20, 23-24, 28, 38-39, 67, 70, 78, 81-84, 86, 91, 125, 143
Borella, 16
Borromeo, 27
Bouix, 7, 10, 12-13, 30, 48, 63, 118, 134, 139
Breviary, 3, 23-24, 28, 82
Brys, 52, 61
Cabrol, 17
Caeremoniale Episcoporum, 28, 83, 142
Calendars, 70, 84
Callewaert, 1, 9, 12, 83-84, 100, 134, 139, 146
Cance, 64
Canon of Mass, 16-17
Canonization, 20, 130
  see Servants of God
Capelle, 17

Cappello, 6-7, 24-25, 30, 32, 34, 50-51, 61-63, 103, 105-107, 112, 117, 120, 151
Carmelite rite, 77
Carthusian rite, 77
Cavalieri, 140
Caviglioli, 121
Celestine I, 92
Ceremonies, *see* Rites and ceremonies
Ceremonial Congregation, 28, 32-35, 68, 76, 79, 98-99, 101-102
Chancellor of S.R.C., 118, 120, 122
Chant, liturgical, 9, 17, 38, 73
Chant, liturgical books of, 82
Charlemagne, 6, 19
Chelodi, 48, 52, 55
Christianae Reipublicae, 36, 90
Christus Dominus, 92
Church, power over worship, 5-8
Cicognani, 51-52, 76, 131, 138, 141
Cimitier, 139, 141
Cistercian rite, 77
Civil power, 6-9
Clement VI, 11
Clement VIII, 28
Clement IX, 35-36, 89
Clement XI, 32
Clement XIII, 65
Coactive power, 61
Code of Canon Law, 4, 43-44, 50, 56-57, 135, 156
Code of liturgical law, 4, 145-149
Coelho, 1, 16, 20, 133-134, 136
Coercive power, 61
Cohellius, 27, 33
Collections of decrees, 145-149
Commissio historico-liturgica, 37-39, 121
Commissio liturgica, 37-38, 148-149
Commission for ecclesiastical music, 38
Commission for interpretation, 50, 56, 59-60, 137, 155
Commission for Vatican editions of chant, 38-39

Commissions of Cardinals, 24
Commissions of S.R.C., 31, 36-37, 40-41, 43, 120-121
Competence, doubts of, 56
limitations of, 48-51, 72
meaning of, 67
of S.R.C., 67-91
Congregatio antepraeparatoria, 127
Congregatio generalis, 128
Congregatio peculiaris, 42, 127
Congregatio plena, 123-127
Congregatio praeparatoria, 128
Congregatio super correctione Euchologii Graecorum, 75
Congregatio super correctione librorum Ecclesiae Orientalis, 75
Congregationes, 129
Congregations, Roman, v, 24-26, 31-35, 39, 45, 62-66, 78, 91-102
Congressus, 123-125
Consistorial Congregation, 26, 56, 97, 101, 111
Consistory, 24
Constitution of S.R.C., 41-42, 117-122
Consultors of S.R.C., 30, 38, 43, 117-119, 122, 124-125, 128
Controversies, 58, 60, 62, 88
I Cor. 4, 1 — 8
I Cor. 11, 23 — 6
Coronata, 20, 34, 51-53, 59-60, 66, 71, 114, 151
Council, Congregation of, 25, 40, 55-56, 59, 71, 79, 96, 98-100, 105-113
Council, ecumenical, 10
Crnica, 54, 74
Cum in Ecclesia, 28
Cum iuris canonici, 50, 53, 56, 58, 137, 155
Cum novissime, 28
Cum nuper, 8
Cum sanctissimum, 28
Customs, *contra legem*, 142-145, 155
liturgical, 4, 10, 21, 141-145
praeter legem, 141-142
secundum legem, 141-142

Dal Sasso, 1
Decentius of Gubbio, 18
Decrees, 13, 54, 131-154
  concessionary, 132
  directive, 132, 136-138
  disciplinary, 132
  equivalently general, 133-134, 140-141, 155
  facultative, 137
  general, 50-52, 88, 131-133, 139, 155
  index of, 148
  kinds of, 131-134
  particular, 62, 133-134, 139-140, 149
  preceptive, 132, 136-137
  publication of, 120
  S.C.Prop. Fide, 101
Decreta Authentica, 37, 84-85, 102, 132, 139-140, 147-149, 154
De Luca, 29-30, 33, 117
De Meester, 51, 80
De Puniet, 19, 21
Development of S.R.C., 28-31
Discorus of Alexandria, 19
Discipline of sacraments, 79-80, 95-98
Discipline of sacred rites, 99-100
Dispensations, 62, 86-87, 94, 100
Dispensative power, 61
Divini cultus, 3, 9
Divino afflatu, 4
Divisions of S.R.C., 29-30, 43
Dix, 15
Doctrinal decisions, 7, 88, 91, 133
Doctrinal interpretation, *see* Interpretation
Dominican rite, 77
Dooley, 35-36, 89-90
Doubts, solution of, 68, 70, 84-85
Duchesne, 16, 19
Durandus, 21
Dziob, 75, 94-95
Editio iuxta Typicam, 81
Editio Typica, 81
Eichmann, 55

Emendato iam Kalendario, 28
Enforcement of liturgical law, 13, 61-62, 85-87
Establishment of S.R.C., 24-28
Eugene IV, 10, 15
Executive power, 49, 55, 58, 61-62, 138
Exercise of power over liturgy, 9, 14-22
Exorcisms, 73
Ex quo in Ecclesia, 28
Exultate Deo, 15
Faculties, 47, 80, 87, 102-103
  extraordinary, 64, 103-109
  liturgical, 104
  ordinary, 64-65, 109-115
  S.C.C., 98-99
  S.C.Prop. Fide, 100-101
  S.C.Sac., 96-97, 99, 101
Faith, matters of, 7, 77
Fast, Eucharistic, 92, 95, 100
Favors, concession of, 62, 70, 94, 100
Feast days, 6, 21, 23, 68, 84
Ferreres, 49, 76
Ferretti, 145
Florence, Council of, 10, 15
Formulas, 52, 149-152
Fortescue, 15-16
Gallican rite, 19
Gardellini, 147-149
Gattico, 32
Gavanti, 132, 146
Geier, 6
Gelasius I, 16-17
Gesualdo, 27-28
Già da qualche tempo, 44, 81, 129
Graduale, 82
Gregory I, 16-17
Gregory XIII, 25, 28, 34
Gregory XIV, 27
Grimaldi, 30, 33-34
Guéranger, 9
Hadrian I, 19
Haine, 32, 34
Hilling, 25, 32-34, 118, 123
Hippolytus, 15

Historical questions, 37-38, 121, 129
Historical Section of S.R.C., 44, 121,
   129, 154
Hippolytus, 15
History of S.R.C., 23-44
   after 1908, 42-44
   background, 23-24
   development, 28-32
   establishment, 24-28
Holy Office, 25, 41, 60, 62, 70, 77-78,
   88-89, 91-92, 94-96, 100, 133
Hymerius of Tarragona, 18
Hymnographer of S.R.C., 118, 120,
   122
Immensa aeterni Dei, 24-25, 33-34,
   45, 49, 56, 67-68, 79, 86
Immortale Dei, 8-9
In cotidianis precibus, 4
In ipsis Pontificatus, 35, 41, 89-90
Index, Congregation of, 25, 91
Indulgences, 35-36, 80
Indulgences and Relics, Congregation
   of, 35-36, 38-39, 41, 89-90
Indults, 139
Infallibility of Roman Pontiff, 61
Informative process, 126, 129
Innocent I, 18
Innocent III, 15, 20
Innocent VIII, 21
Innocent X, 8, 30
Inquisition, *see* Holy Office
Insignia, 87
Instructio Clementina, 82, 84, 147-
   148
Instructions, 50, 62, 131, 137-138
Inter omnigenas, 11
Inter pastoralis officii, 38
Interpretation, doctrinal, 139, 146
   general, 49, 55-58, 62, 98, 155
   merely declarative, 57
   particular, 55, 57
Invalidity of acts, 64
Jedin, 23
John, 3, 5 — 6
Jombart, 117
Jone, 50, 52, 55

Joseph II, 6
Judicial order, 59, 94-95, 125
Judicial power, 49, 58-61, 155
Jungmann, 16-17, 21
Jurisdiction, *see* Power
Jurisdiction, cumulative, 39, 79-80
Justin, 15
Kennedy, 17
King, 14, 19, 76
Kyriale, 82
Kuttner, 20
Laetentur caeli, 10, 15
Lalmant, 32, 34
Lateran Council IV, 15
Latin Church, 3, 23-24, 72, 75-76,
   92-95
Laureo, 27
Law, liturgical, *see* Liturgical law
Laws, general, 49-50, 62
Lay authority over liturgy, 6-11
Leclercq, 16
Lega, 32-34
Legislative power, 49-58, 155
Leo·I, 16, 19
Leo XII, 147
Leo XIII, 8-9, 14, 31, 35-38, 43, 54,
   83, 90, 102, 127, 148
Liber Diurnus, 17-18
Liber Pontificalis, 15-16
Licet ab initio, 25
Limitation of competence, 72, 75
Limitation of power of S.R.C., 78
Litanies, 13
Liturgical books, *see* Books, liturgical
Liturgical decline, 23
Liturgical law, v, 1-22, 38, 57-58, 155
Liturgical privileges, 17, 64, 87
Liturgical reform, vi, 6, 24, 38, 86
Liturgy, development of, 3
   sacred, v, 1-2, 5, 11, 73-74
   uniformity of, 4, 12, 21
Loomis, 16
Luke 22, 19 — 6
Lunadoro, 33
Maroto, 51
Martin, 32, 51, 80

Martinucci, 132, 147
Martyrology, 28, 83
Mass, 3, 6-7, 15-18, 73, 79, 95-98, 143
Masses, votive, 12, 20
Master of Sacred Palace, 118, 121
Matrimony, 96
Matthew 18, 18 — 10
Matthew 28, 18-20 — 6-7
Mediator Dei, 2-3, 5, 11, 14, 55, 74, 92
Meetings of S.R.C., ordinary, 124-126
Members of S.R.C., 117, 119, 121
Memoriale Rituum, 83
Menghini, 2, 5, 7-8, 10, 73, 136
Merati, 146
Michiels, 45, 51, 55, 57, 73, 140, 144-145
Missa pro populo, 80
Missal, 3, 12, 23-24, 28, 82
Monin, 5, 25, 31-32, 34, 37-38, 47-48, 59, 61, 72-73, 76-80, 87, 90, 95, 105-106, 124, 130, 134
Moretti, 83, 141, 144, 152
Moroni, 30, 33, 117
Mozarabic rite, 14, 76
Mucante, 117, 152-153
Mühlbauer, 147
Mystici Corporis Christi, 2
Nabuco, 83
Name of S.R.C., 156
Naz, 20, 62, 119
Noldin-Schmitt, 136
Non sine gravissimo, 11
Nostro Motu proprio, 38-39
Notary of S.R.C., 118, 120, 122
Nuncios, faculties of, 114
Object of power of S.R.C., 71-73
Obligation of decrees, 52, 132, 134-141
O'Connell, 133-134, 137, 140, 143
Octavarium Romanum, 82-84
Offices, divine, 3, 73, 84
of relics, 36   of saints, 67
Officials, appointment of, 119
major and minor, 118-119, 121
of S.R.C., 117-122

Ojetti, 31, 34, 37-38, 42, 118, 128
Oppenheim, 5, 7, 12, 17, 19, 48, 51, 73, 83-84, 92, 103, 105-107, 111-112, 115, 124, 131-132, 136-137, 139, 144
Orders, 72, 96
Ordinaries, 114
faculties, 114
power over liturgy, 10-14
Ordinations, 18
Ordines Romani, 20
Oriental Church, Congregation for, 57, 59, 91-95
Oriental Churches, 72, 75, 92-95, 155
Oriental rites, 14-15, 72, 75, 92-95
Orientalium, 14
Ottaviani, 6-8, 10, 46-47, 49, 58, 61
Paleo-Slavonic language, 76
Parente, 7, 61
Pastè, 1
Pastor, 23, 25, 27-30
Paul I, 19
Paul III, 25
Paul V, 28-29
Penitentiary, Sacred, 41
Pepin, 19
Permissions, granted by bishops, 12
Personnel of S.R.C., 117-122, 125, 156-159
I Peter, 5, 1-4 — 10
Phillips, 25, 30, 32, 117
Piolanti, 3
Pistoia, Synod of, 9
Pithonius, 146
Pius IV, 23, 25, 56
Pius V, 3, 23-25, 77, 84, 143
Pius VI, 9
Pius VII, 11, 134, 147
Pius IX, 11, 53, 75
Pius X, vi, 4, 26, 28, 31, 33, 36-40, 42-43, 45-46, 49, 53-56, 58-59, 63, 65, 69-72, 80-82, 84, 90-91, 98, 101-102, 105, 115, 118-119, 122-123, 127, 130
Pius XI, 3, 9, 43, 81, 93-94, 121, 122, 129

Pius XII, vi, 2-5, 11, 13-14, 55, 63-65, 74, 92
Platus, 32-33
Ponens, 124, 127-128
Pontificale, 28, 83
Potestas gratiosa, 61
Potestas iurisdictionis, 7
Potestas ministerii, 7
Potestas ordinis, 7, 11
Power, *see* Executive power, Judicial power, Legislative power
  basis of, 46-48
  delegated, 46, 62
  functions of, 49
  ordinary, 46-47, 62-65
  proper, 47
  supreme, 48
  vicarious, 47
Praelati Officiales, 118-119, 121-122, 128
Precedence, 68-69, 78-79, 85, 98
Prefect of S.R.C., 27, 36, 54, 117, 119-120, 123-124, 127, 135
Premonstratensian rite, 77
Prescription, 143-144
Privileges, 17, 64, 87
Procedure, administrative, 59-60
  causes of Servants of God, 60-61, 88, 125-130
  judicial, 59-60
  of S.R.C., 122-130
Process *super non cultu*, 126
Processions, 6, 12-13
Profuturus of Braga, 19
Promoter of faith, 118-119, 121, 127
Promulgandi, 53
Promulgation of law, 135, 140-141, 155
Propagation of Faith, Congregation for, 75, 93, 100-101
Propers of moral persons, 84-85
Prosper of Aquitaine, St., 92
Protocolist of S.R.C., 119-120, 122
Protonotary Apostolic, 118, 121, 127
Prümmer, 57, 134
Psalter, 3

Public law of church, 5
Quae in Ecclesiae, 36
Quanta semper cura, 43
Quasten, 15
Quo primum tempore, 3, 24, 77, 143
Quod a nobis, 3, 24, 77
Regatillo, 46-47, 52, 62, 71, 134, 141, 151
Regulars, Congregation for, 25
Reiffenstuel, 45, 87
Relation to other Congregations, 91-102
Relator General, 122
Relics, distribution of, 90
  sacred, 13, 18, 35-36, 41-42, 69, 89-91
Religious, Congregation for, 39-40, 59, 79, 98-100, 105-113
Reprobation of custom, 143-145
Reservation of powers, 14
Responses, 19, 102, 149-152
Restriction of power, 48-51, 72, 75, 78
Righetti, 14, 19
Rites and ceremonies, 2-3, 5, 26, 40, 67, 69, 73, 78, 86, 95, 125, 155
  profane, 32, 34, 68, 101-102
Rites, various, 14, 19, 72, 77, 82
Ritual, 28, 83, 138
Roman Curia, reform by Pius X, 39-42
Roman Pontiff, 9-14
Roman rite, 3, 6, 14, 16, 19, 76-77
Romanus Pontifex, 25
Romita, 17
Rota, Auditors, *see* Auditors of Rota
  Roman, 29-31, 39-40, 42, 58, 60, 78-79, 88
Rousseau, 9
Rozière, 17
Rubrics, 13, 86, 132, 134, 138, 155

Sacrae Congregationi, 38, 90
Sacramentals, 73, 80
Sacramentaries, 16-17, 19-20
Sacraments, 2-3, 6-8, 73, 79, 83, 95-98

Congregation of, 39-40, 52, 59, 70-71, 92, 95-98, 100, 105-114
Sacramentum Ordinis, 3
Sacred rites, *see* Rites and ceremonies
Sacristan of Holy Father, 118, 121
Saints, veneration of, 20, 23
Salaville, 15
Sancta Dei Ecclesia, 93-94
Sapienti consilio, 39-41, 43-45, 49, 54-56, 58-59, 65, 69-71, 80, 91, 101-102, 105, 122, 123, 125, 156
Schmalzgrüber, 29-30, 87
Schmidt, 138
Secrecy, oath of, 119
Secretary of S.R.C., 54, 117-121, 123, 127, 136
Sections of S.R.C., 43-44, 121, 125
Servants of God, 29-31, 41-44, 60-62, 68-69, 87-89, 94, 103-105, 125-132, 153-155
  processes of, v, 28, 60-61, 119, 125-130
  writings of, 126
Sfondrato, 27
Signatura, Apostolic, 39-40, 58
Simier, 25, 32, 34, 80, 90
Sipos, 51-52, 60, 66
Siricius I, 18
Sixtus V, 24-27, 33, 40, 45-46, 49, 56, 67-68, 74, 79, 86, 117
Solution of doubts, 62
Sotillo, 5
Stickler, 146, 153-154
Stipends, Mass, 96, 98
Stylus curiae, 140, 143, 146

Subpromoter of faith, 118-119, 121, 127
Substitute of S.R.C., 118-121, 123, 136
Super quibusdam, 11
Superstitious rites, 13, 78
Talù, 146
Toso, 57, 60, 79
Trent, Council of, 3, 8, 23-24, 56, 98
Uniformity of liturgy, 4, 12, 21
Universities, Congregation of, 26
Urban VIII, 143
Ut pestiferarum, 25
Vacancy of Holy See, 62-66
Vacante Sede Apostolica, 63
Vacantis Apostolicae Sedis, 63-65
Vacatio legis, 135
Valde solliciti, 4
Valiero, 27
Van der Stappen, 134, 152
Van Hove, 18, 32, 51, 54, 56-58, 76-77, 131, 138, 141, 143-145
Vatican Council, 10-11
Vatican Press, 82
Vermeersch-Creusen, 51
Vice-Relator, 122
Vienne, Council of, 21
Vigilance over rites, 69-70, 86, 100
Vigilius, 19
Wernz, 13, 24, 32-33, 61, 141, 144
Wernz-Vidal, 4, 50, 58-59, 63
Western Church, *see* Latin Church
Worship, internal, 2, 5
  private, v, 13
  public, v, 1-2, 5, 9
Zachary, 19

Canons of the Code

1—57, 72
2—5, 43, 53, 57, 73, 134-135, 144, 149
6—43, 53, 57, 134-135
7—45, 48
9—57, 135, 140
17—49, 55-57, 140
20—140
25—10, 141-144
26—141, 143-144
27—143-144
28—141-143
29—141, 143
30—143-144
66—63
73—63
74—87
75—87
135—137
183—63
197—46
208—63
241—63
243—44, 53, 56, 119
244—47-49, 52-53, 58, 60, 63, 125
247—25, 46, 60, 77, 88, 91-92, 95, 133
248—46
249—46, 52, 59, 73, 77, 92, 95-96
250—46, 59, 61, 98
251—46, 59, 61, 77, 100
252—46, 94, 100
253—43, 46, 54, 59, 61, 71-90, 93-94, 115, 133
254—46, 76, 101-102
255—46
256—46
257—46, 59, 61, 77, 91, 93, 95
259—59-60, 88
291—52
409—145
733—73, 137
755—13
759—13
818—137, 143, 145
821—96, 111
869—13, 96
909—110
978—145
1004—72
1148—137
1156—12
1193—110
1257—11, 13, 81
1261—13
1274—13
1275—13
1284—13
1292—12
1295—13
1304—12
1387—89
1390—81-82
1399—81
1552—59
1993—59-61
1999—88
2071—61, 88, 129
2083—61, 88, 127, 129
2087—127
2088—127
2100—61, 88, 127, 129
2102—127
2105—128
2107—88, 129
2108—128
2111—88, 129
2112—128
2114—128
2115—128
2116—128
2117—128
2124—129
2127—127
2128—127
2129—127
2130—127
2131—127
2132—88, 129
2134—128
2139—129
2140—129
2378—73

BIOGRAPHICAL NOTE

Frederick Richard McManus was born in Lynn, Massachusetts, on February 8, 1923. He attended Saint Joseph's School in that city and Boston College High School in Boston. From 1940 to 1942 he studied at the College of the Holy Cross, Worcester, and in the fall of 1942 he entered Saint John's Seminary in Brighton, Massachusetts. In 1947 he received the degree of Bachelor of Arts from Saint John's Seminary and, on May 1, 1947, he was ordained to the Priesthood at the Cathedral of the Holy Cross, Boston.

His first assignment after ordination was to Saint Catherine of Siena Church in Norwood, Massachusetts, where he remained until August, 1948, when he was appointed Master of Ceremonies of the Archdiocese of Boston. In the spring of 1950 he was appointed Secretary of the Metropolitan Tribunal of Boston, where he served until coming to the School of Canon Law of the Catholic University of America in October, 1951. He received the degree of Bachelor of Canon Law in 1952, and the Licentiate of Canon Law in 1953.

CANON LAW STUDIES

349. Bottoms, Rev. Archibald M., J.C.L., The discretionary authority of the ecclesiastical judge in matrimonial trials of the first instance.

350. Kekumano, Rev. Charles A., A.B., J.C.L., The secret archives of the diocesan curia.

351. McGrath, Rev. Robert Eamon, O.M.I., J.C.L., The local superior in non-exempt clerical congregations.

352. McManus, Rev. Frederick Richard, A.B., J.C.L., The Congregation of Sacred Rites.

353. Rodimer, Rev. Frank J., A.B., S.T.L., J.C.L., The canonical effects of infamy of fact.

354. Rouillard, Rev. Jacques, A.B., Ph.B., J.C.L., Une étude comparée du droit canonique et du droit civil paroissal de la Province de Québec dans l'administration des biens paroissaux.

355. Ryan, Rev. Thomas C., J.C.L., The juridical effects of the *sanatio in radice.*

356. Sullivan, Rev. Bernard Owens, J.C.L., Legislation and requirements for permissible cohabitation in invalid marriages.

357. Tatarczuk, Rev. Vincent Anthony, A.B., S.T.L., J.C.L., Infamy of law.

For a complete list of the available numbers of this series apply to the Catholic University of America Press, 620 Michigan Ave., N.E., Washington 17, D.C., for a general catalogue.

CPSIA information can be obtained
at www.ICGtesting.com
Printed in the USA
BVHW03*0022100318
509887BV00003B/118/P